Modern Prints And Drawings

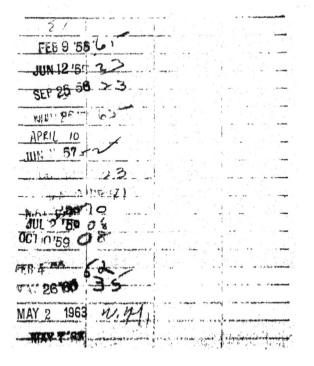

Modern Prints & Drawings

GOYA, FRANCISCO · *Colossus* · MEZZOTINT · 11½″ x 8⅛″ · Courtesy of Metropolitan Museum, New York

To illustrate Goya's mysterious, compelling power, his originality and mastery of the mezzotint medium I have chosen this his most enigmatic print in which through scale and emphatic contrasts of light and dark Goya creates an eerie mood It is a haunting, unforgettable, tantalizing conception

Modern Prints & Drawings

*A guide to a better understanding of
modern draughtsmanship*

SELECTED AND WITH AN EXPLANATORY TEXT BY

Paul J. Sachs

PROFESSOR OF FINE ARTS, EMERITUS, HARVARD UNIVERSITY
HONORARY CURATOR OF DRAWINGS, FOGG MUSEUM OF ART

Alfred · A · Knopf NEW YORK

L C CATALOG CARD NUMBER 54-6137

THIS IS A BORZOI BOOK,
PUBLISHED BY ALFRED A. KNOPF, INC

PUBLISHED SIMULTANEOUSLY IN CANADA BY
MC CLELLAND & STEWART LIMITED MANUFAC-
TURED IN THE UNITED STATES OF AMERICA

Preface

RECENTLY, when conferring a doctorate on Paul J Sachs, Yale University justified its thus honoring a Harvard man in these words *"Connoisseur, collector of works of art, teacher, counselor, you have inspired a generation of art gallery directors and curators with your generosity, wisdom and standards."* To these three virtues—generosity, wisdom and maintenance of standards—I should like to add three more which were essential to the authorship of this book· enthusiasm, modesty and youthfulmindedness

Having known the dynamic author for three decades it is a little embarrassing to recall that he is, officially, Professor Emeritus Both words in his present title are misleading: Paul J Sachs has neither the intellectual vanity nor the academic conservatism of the proverbial professor As for 'emeritus," I well remember one evening a few months ago sitting with him and two young colleagues around a table piled high with hundreds of photographs, many of which were to be reproduced in this book The discussion that began after dinner was strenuous. By midnight I glanced at our white-haired host who I knew had recently recovered from a serious illness He showed no sign of fatigue By 1 30 his three guests who averaged less than half his age staggered home exhausted, leaving him fuming. Such was his energy and excitement that he could have gone on until dawn Hokusai, the greatest artist of modern Japan, once described himself as "an old man mad about drawing " So, clinically speaking, is the author of this book, though, of course, his madness is produced not by the practice of drawing, but by the love of drawings

Paul J Sachs is as modest as he is enthusiastic One can even imagine him on his hundredth birthday exclaiming (to use the words of Hokusai again) "if only heaven would grant me five years more I might yet learn something about drawing ' On that evening I have just described, when he was submitting his own selection of prints and drawings to critics one or two generations his junior, he listened carefully to their opinions, sometimes accepting their advice, sometimes rejecting it, but always in a spirit of eager curiosity toward the unfamiliar and untraditional Nothing is harder for an art critic, or an artist, as he grows older than to respond sympathetically to new forms of art Very recently we have been embarrassed witnesses of rancorous outbursts on the part of several men old enough and great enough to have achieved some modicum of tolerance On the other hand, for the purposes of this book, the polite and passive acceptance of everything new on the part of the author would have been as fatal as irascible intolerance

What makes *Modern Prints and Drawings* valuable is not so much the admirable youthfulmindedness of the author as his capacity to bring to bear upon the drawings and prints of our own time his immense, cumulative, first-hand experience as a passionate knower and lover of the art of the past. Essentially loyal to his own time-tested and slowly matured taste, he has not included a single work which he does not himself find convincing after careful pondering. Sometimes we may not agree with him but we can heartily welcome what he has done.

ALFRED H BARR, JR

TABLE OF CONTENTS

Modern Prints & Drawings

TO META

Introduction

THIS is a picture book with brief comments about prints and drawings made in *modern times*. It is not a book in which I have felt called upon to find a niche, a pigeonhole, for every artist whose name appears in ambitious anthologies It is not a history Inevitably, for the sake of order and clarity there is a historic thread that connects the many artists illustrated in these pages, but this is not art history in the orthodox sense It is a personal selection of pictures I find important, some of which I have loved. I have also attempted to avoid the inclusion of mere novelties

We start with the ancestors of modern art, with the great moderns of the past, and come down to contemporaries at home and abroad As "docent" I have tried not to talk too much so that each artist may convey his own message in his own graphic language It has been my aim not to overstress "isms"—Impressionism, Post-Impressionism, Cubism, Expressionism, Surrealism, Futurism—so as not to deflect you from looking at the pictures Overemphasis on "isms," the habit of labeling and pigeonholing every artist, while a convenient device for the superficial, is a misleading and dangerous practice, in its oversimplification, in its implied insistence on one phase only of an artist's production. The practice tends to distract us from a full visual appreciation of the inherent merit, the individuality of a genius and ignores the conflicting counter-currents that usually underlie distinguished creation, the kind of creation that outlives the fashion of the moment and makes a work of art lasting and timeless. I have tried to say something relevant in the captions underneath each plate, chosen on the basis of quality, to illustrate the various movements

We all read current literature and listen to new music Let us *look* at new as well as old aspects of art Let us avoid the tiresome complaint that the times are out of joint We may be surprised to find that art in modern times is realistic as well as abstract, traditional as well as experimental, conservative as well as radical.

1

A talk with the late Mrs Elizabeth Sprague Coolidge and the novelist-playwright, Thornton Wilder, haunts my memory Mrs Coolidge, lover of classical compositions and patron of contemporary music, pointed out with disarming directness that in music a new

idiom of communication, a new "ism," has almost always been misunderstood, suspected, or disliked If a patron cannot commission works by a Beethoven or a Brahms, should he withhold his patronage because of failure on a first hearing to understand the creations of acknowledged men of genius like Schönberg or Stravinsky? The situation, she thought, must be the same in poetry and in the visual arts In the perspective of history, artists of the stature of James Joyce, T S. Eliot, Matisse, and Picasso may, perhaps, not take their places with the enthroned giants of the past. The judgment of time upon the ultimate place of our living artists is something we cannot know

PICASSO IGOR STRAVINSKY PENCIL 1920 PRIVATE COLLECTION

The conversation well started, Thornton Wilder gave us a foretaste of what he was to elaborate at Harvard Commencement exercises, 1951, in a notable address entitled *Thoughts for Our Times*. Only a man of vision could have spoken as he did that day He struck a note that will long echo in the minds and hearts of those who attempt to teach in spoken or in written words

His moving address opened with the sentence·—"I have been an intermittent teacher all my life and when I return to a university I find myself continually drawing comparisons, not comparisons between institutions, but comparisons between something far more striking and instructive—*comparison between attitudes*, tacit assumptions, the thought underworld of students .. who .. never knew that evenly running world to which one of our presidents gave the name of normalcy   . They find what they need from the currents of thought and literature that are about us all and it is how they are assimilated that is interesting to us The twentieth century is shifting its foundations and it is altering its emphasis with striking rapidity."

Like Wilder, I have taught the consecrated classics for almost forty years I have had to be attentive, also, to the masters of modern art If I had not been, my students would have waked me up to them. "There is a gulf between the generations, and it is up to us to be attentive to it   .. The modern student is all alive to the complexity of man in himself and others He is profoundly interested not only in good but in evil, and he assumes that life is morally difficult "

I have tried to keep the spirit of Wilder's words in the background of my thoughts because of the absence of generally accepted criteria in the field of contemporary art.

It has been exquisite torture to choose only about two hundred and ninety prints and drawings from among the number that might have been included. Those specialists who

2

chance to look at these pages will, I hope, agree that the main currents in the drawing and printmaking of modern times are illustrated by worthy examples. A host of influential artists had to be omitted in a period constantly changing in art as well as in science, in politics, and in industry "Change" is the keynote of all aspects of art from the time of David and Goya, the ancestors of modern art, down to the pioneers of our day·—Rouault, Matisse, Picasso, Henry Moore, Max Weber, Ben Shahn, and Calder. Walter Pach once said.— "Our problem in appreciating the greatness of modern art lies in following the unbroken line [the *tradition*] that leads from the older classics to those of the present day "

This book is also an introduction to studies by former students and their gifted associates who, building on their knowledge of the art of the past, have interpreted modern art by staging important exhibitions throughout the breadth of this land These they have described in monographs and catalogues, illustrated, as a rule, in black-and-white and with discriminating use of the all-too-prevalent color reproduction Museum curators of the younger generation have clarified the meaning of modern movements for those open-minded enough to look and listen.

A special tribute is due to the dynamic leadership of the group at the Museum of Modern Art, New York, whose generous policy has helped to make their important work so effective They have insisted on quality, on standards, and have given proof of their capacity to select the best of a genre. They have looked forward They have guided us in what Somerset Maugham once termed "the new state of the spirit," that is on the march

Many friends have responded to my requests for guidance My special thanks are due to W. G Russell Allen, trustee of museums in Boston, generous collector of prints and drawings of the past, as of the present, for the delight and benefit of the public. He has discussed with me the selection of many of the prints and drawings in this book.

My sense of obligation is very real to the staff of the Museum of Modern Art, New York: —particularly to James Thrall Soby, to Alfred H Barr, Jr., Monroe Wheeler, Dorothy Miller and William S. Lieberman; to Dorothy L. Lytle, Olive Bragazzi, Pearl Moeller, and Soichi Sunami With the collection of Mrs. John D. Rockefeller, Jr., as a foundation, Lieberman has, in a few years, built for the Museum of Modern Art the finest collection in the Western World of modern prints, giving us visual proof, to use Soby's words, that "ours has been a very great era in matters of artistic *exploration*."

I am indebted for help to Freeman Lewis, and for concrete guidance to Herbert M. Alexander of Pocket Books, Inc , also to Oscar Ogg, Amy Loveman, Van Henry Cartmell and Harry Dale of the Book-of-the-Month Club.

I express appreciation to those who have granted permission to reproduce their works of art either in the plates or in the text and to those who have allowed me to quote their words. Indebtedness for photographs appears, when necessary, in a courtesy line beneath the plates.

It is impossible to single out all those who have answered occasional questions To them I here express my sincere appreciation.

Thanks are due to James Johnson Sweeney, Director of the Solomon R. Guggenheim Museum, New York; to Rosamond Irvine of the Whitney Museum, New York; and to Olivia Paine, Lillian Greene and Alice Newlin of the Metropolitan Museum, New York

Thanks are due also to Edith Halpert of the Downtown Gallery, to Charles Alan of the Alan Gallery, to Rose Fried of the Rose Fried Gallery, to E Weyhe and Martha Dickinson of the Weyhe Gallery, to Curt Valentin and John Hohnsbeen of the Curt Valentin Gallery, to Pierre Matisse, to R. Kirk Askew, Jr., and George Dix of Durlacher Brothers, to Doll and Richards, to the late Erich Herrmann and the late Felix Wildenstein. They have been generous in their assistance

At the Museum of Fine Arts, Boston, thanks are due to Henry P Rossiter, Curator of Prints, and to Anna Hoyt and Eleanor Sayre, his assistants; at the Boston Public Library to Arthur W Heintzelman, Curator, and his assistants, Elizabeth Norman and Muriel F. Robinson, and to John N Burk, program annotator of the Boston Symphony Orchestra.

At the Fogg Museum of Art, Harvard University, I am grateful to John Coolidge, Director, and his secretary, Mary E. Field, to Frederick B Deknatel, to Charles Kuhn and to his secretary, Mary Wadsworth; to E. Louise Lucas, Librarian, and to her assistants, Helen Styles and Mary Ward, for painstaking bibliographical assistance, to Jakob Rosenberg, Curator of Prints, and his assistant, Ruth Magurn, to James Fowle, to Agnes Mongan, Curator of Drawings, and her assistant, Helen Willard; to Elisabeth Strassman, Registrar, to James K. Ufford, photographer, and his assistants, and to Milton Worthley, superintendent They have all been helpful in concrete ways.

In the Department of Printing and Graphic Arts, Harvard College Library, Philip Hofer and his assistants have been kindness itself as has John L. Sweeney. I wish to thank George W. Cottrell, Jr, for his kind help in providing the phonetic pronunciation of artists' names as they appear in the biographies

I also thank Professor Elting E. Morison of Massachusetts Institute of Technology for calling my attention to the Theodore Roosevelt letter In Providence Dr. Heinrich Schwarz of the Museum of Art, Rhode Island School of Design, has been of aid In the Baltimore Museum of Art Adelyn D. Breeskin, Director, and Gertrude Rosenthal, Curator, have given me valuable assistance. In the Chicago Art Institute my thanks go to Daniel C. Rich, Director, and Carl O. Schniewind, Curator of Prints, and his assistant, Harold Joachim, in the Cleveland Museum of Art to Henry Sayles Francis, Curator of Prints, in the National Gallery of Art, Washington, D. C, to Elizabeth Mongan, in the Philadelphia Museum to Carl Zigrosser; in New Haven to George H. Hamilton, Yale University; and to Henry Trubner, Los Angeles County Museum.

In England K T. Parker, Keeper, the Ashmolean Museum, Oxford, C. H Gibbs-Smith and James Laver, Victoria and Albert Museum, London, and John Overton of Penguin Books, Ltd, have been of help

In Paris I am grateful to my brother, Arthur Sachs, and his secretary, Mlle Monique Dufaure, to M. Jean Cassou, Curator of the Musée National d'Art Moderne, to M. Julien Cain, Director of the Bibliothèque Nationale; to M. André Blum, Curator of the Rothschild Collection, Louvre; and to Mme Jacqueline Bouchot-Saupique, Curator of Drawings of the Louvre, for their interest or help.

To former pupils and friends who have replied to occasional questions and whose names I may have inadvertently omitted I now express my gratitude

I am grateful to Mary E. Hagopian and Caroline Hollingsworth for their patience as secretaries. Mrs Robert Bogart and Mrs Anselm Beal have once again typed parts of the manuscript with great care

And, finally, I wish to express appreciation to Anne B Freedberg, my research assistant, for her work on the Biographies and her deep interest in the progress of this book.

PAUL J. SACHS

CAMBRIDGE, MASSACHUSETTS

PICASSO CLARIBEL CONE INK 1922 BALTIMORE MUSEUM OF ART

Chapter I

(A) DAVID AND THE GREAT MODERNS OF THE PAST

NO matter how daring or revolutionary a new style may appear to be, the tradition of European painting has affected its evolution even when the artist borrows motives from the art of primitive peoples, deals in pure abstraction, or plumbs the subconscious In spite of innovations, tradition played its role because the artists who became truly great spent every spare moment in museums They were also influenced by collectors, connoisseurs, and dealers Following the French Revolution, a new type of patron replaced the nobility and the church Modern artists, like the public, have been groping in an effort to understand social, political, and economic upheavals in this industrial, scientific age Communication between artist and public has been facilitated through illustrations in newspapers and popular magazines

Our journey of discovery starts with Goya, then moves to France—to David, Ingres, and the other

GOYA SELF-PORTRAIT ETCHING AND AQUATINT c 1797

"ancestors" of the modern movement It leads us to Cézanne, the last of the old masters and the first of the moderns The all-pervasive influence of Cézanne is still powerful forty-seven years after his death

Francisco Goya (1746-1828), the most distinguished and versatile Spanish artist since Velasquez, has a place of fundamental importance in modern graphic art He is the dynamic precursor of Romanticism, that contagious, emotional revolt in literature, music, and art against the kind of "authority" that David wielded in France In literature the typical Romantics were Victor Hugo, Wordsworth, and Byron, in music, Beethoven, Berlioz and Wagner Beethoven, indeed, had Napoleon in mind while composing his Eroica Symphony Goya influenced many artists, particularly Géricault, Delacroix, and Daumier He helped to shape Realist, Impressionist, and Expressionist viewpoints

Goya's art abounds in contradictions He has to his credit Eighteenth Century decorative paintings and designs for tapestry, portraits of Spanish aristocrats magnificent in color and characterization He was sensitive to the misery of his fellow men He lampooned with vitriolic line corruption at court, pretension in high places, the corroding effects of vice, the lack of moral standards among the clergy, and the degradation of poverty Not until he was fifty did Goya use the graphic media, particularly aquatint *The Caprices* savagely attacked superstition and corruption in high places Goya's style, though inspired by Rembrandt and Tiepolo, is completely his own If he had only done *Disasters of War* (Plate 5), a spontaneous burst of rage at Bonaparte's campaign against Charles IV, this would assure him of immortality He transformed terrifying nightmares into works of art that are permanent and imperishable, that transcend his period and his time

With the Revolution we link the name of *Jacques Louis David* (1748-1825), its pictorial interpreter. David, a dictator in art, was a student of Roman sculpture The work of the Eighteenth Century engraver Piranesi, the writings of Winckelmann, the excavations at Herculaneum and Pompeii fired the imagination of Europe David's famous cold, neoclassic picture, *The Oath of the Horatii* (p 260), designed to extol social, civic, and military virtues, was conceived as a political symbol in a moralizing classic tradition It was painted four years before the political revolution of 1789 The precisely drawn figures suggest sculpture. The picture served as a protest against Eighteenth Century decorative

he heard the cry of the earth His work is for the ages and, although not sufficiently valued in our day, is certain to exercise renewed influence in time to come

Camille Corot (1796-1875) was a sensitive observer of nature and painted in a light key His technique certainly influenced the Impressionists We do not illustrate his genius in black and white by one of his romantic, etched landscapes or by one of his early, impressive drawings of buildings, both classic and cubist in their definition of form We choose the serious, moving pencil portrait of Henri Leroy as a child (Plate 18) which is free of any calligraphic trick

Honore Daumier (1808-1879), master artist and caustic social critic (Plate 13), rebelled against academic restraints With his follower van Gogh, he was the versatile precursor of Expressionist draughtsmanship as we shall come to know it in Rouault, as well as among northern European artists Few of his contemporaries appreciated how rewarding was his study of the art of the past From Michelangelo he learned the construction of massive form, from Rembrandt, dramatic intensity through the pictorial and emotional use of light and shade Balzac said these true words about Daumier's drawing —"Here is a fellow who has Michelangelo under his skin "

In his long career Daumier knew both the influence of the classicist, Ingres, and the effect of Géricault, Delacroix, and the other Romantics He was practically a contemporary of the realist Courbet and of the lyrical singer Corot. Manet passed from the scene only a few years after Daumier's death The Impressionists, and the individualists—Degas and Cézanne—had already given the world some of their best work before Daumier, who was concerned with humanity and the subsurface of art, had lived his span

During his full life, in spite of the artistic currents that swirled about him, Daumier remained his own man He created with marked independence and consistency over three thousand lithographs for *Caricature* and the daily paper *Charivari** as well as a thousand woodcuts and still uncounted drawings and paintings No other draughtsman has ever left for the student of human nature so many penetrating observations of a passing epoch, no novelist has ever mirrored for posterity a more throbbing, varied world The medium of lithography proved a perfect vehicle for the nota-

*Most of which I have collected, in the last sixty years, in Paris

tion of his telling satire

Everything Daumier depicts is conceived as basic elemental, and absolute, everything is drawn in a grand style worthy of Rembrandt

Daumier may be compared in the field of graphic art to the novelist, Dickens They were both city men who observed and projected with rare insight the daily life, the varying emotions and activities of the townsman Daumier possessed the astonishing ability of Dickens to make his individuals representative of types Like Dickens, he pushed his comment to the point of ridicule and he too lampooned contemporary abuses in politics, commerce, and the legal profession His ability is unequaled in depicting through facial expression–stressed by the emphasis of gesture–the entire range of conflicting human emotions He rebelled against the academic restraints of the ordinary art school and sought his models in every part of Paris, drawing them from memory

MANET THE CHAIR LITHOGRAPH 1875

(B) MANET AND THE IMPRESSIONISTS

When I was a boy I visited in Paris the old connoisseur, collector, and dealer, Paul Durand-Ruel There I learned from whom the Impressionists received solid support at a time when they were faltering before the withering attack of their contemporaries The Durand-Ruel apartment was filled, room after room, with superb pictures by Manet, Monet, Sisley, Pissarro, and Degas. Renoir had even painted the panels of the doors The old

9

gentleman was seated in an armchair near a window and just over his head there hung the lovely picture by Degas, *Victoria at the Races,* now a treasure of the Museum of Fine Arts in Boston

At his home I gained insight to the change in French painting we call Impressionism influenced by Constable's vibrating landscapes with their division of color,* Turner's scientific naturalism in the handling of the fleeting effects of light; and Bonington's bright palette

Impressionism is the most easily understood of all the "isms" Manet (Plate 17), Monet (Plate 16), Renoir (Plate 21), and their group in France, Whistler, Sargent, Prendergast (Page 205), and their associates in America have taught us a way of looking at nature, to which we have become so accustomed that we do not even think about it They have all depicted with grace and usually in sunlight the aspects of a vanished world, carefree because they rendered only its surface

Claude Monet (1840-1926) The French Impressionists gained their designation from the title of a landscape by Monet, *Impression — Sunrise,* shown at a group exhibition in 1874 For a quarter of a century they shared their ideas, although their techniques differed Their underlying aim was to convey in their landscape painting how the aspect of nature alters with specific moments in time and the change of light They did not give their contemporaries a new concept of nature but rather a fresh way of seeing objects in light Since the essence of Impressionism is preoccupation with color and light, it is ordinarily difficult to find in the black and white range of prints or drawings the message they convey (Plates 15, 16)

Edouard Manet (1832-1883), keen observer (Plate 17), endowed with brilliant pictorial vision, was a member of the solid, prosperous, civil-servant class, a man of the world in the best tradition He was the articulate champion rather than the father of the Impressionist group.—a group that revolved about him at the Café Guerbois. In his propaganda on behalf of the Impressionists, Manet enjoyed the important backing of the influential writers, Baudelaire and Zola, who were the first to understand the significance of his art

After leaving the studio of the traditionalist Thomas Couture, Manet studied at the Louvre the design and the brush strokes of the great masters of Renaissance and Baroque painting He learned most from Giorgione, Velasquez, Goya, and Hals. The two-dimensional compositions and the bril-

*First shown in Paris at the Salon of 1824

liant patches of flat color in Japanese prints also exerted their influence Freed from academic idealism, he translated traditional subject matter and well-tried compositions into a modern formula that aroused virulent criticism, except among the younger painters whom he influenced For them and for their followers he opened a new world of exciting possibilities in design, color, and light.

Pierre Auguste Renoir (1841-1919) was a lover of flowers, of music, and of beautiful women (Plate 27) He recorded the happy aspects of life in sparkling color Despite a period in Gleyre's art school where he met some of the future Impressionists, he was essentially self-taught His self-imposed museum training as copyist at the Louvre accounts for his strong roots in the great European tradition of painting

Three aspects of Italian art helped form him — the brilliant color of Titian and the Venetians, the clarity of Raphael in painting and in drawing, the plastic values in Michelangelo's masterpieces He studied the pictures of Velasquez and Rubens His idols were the notable Eighteenth Century painters, Watteau, Boucher, and Fragonard He learned much from the works of both those bitter Nineteenth Century rivals—Ingres and Delacroix His interest in realism was deepened by the works of Courbet and Manet Though close to Cézanne, he also enjoyed the admiration of artists like Rodin

MANET CAFE INTERIOR INK 1869 FOGG MUSEUM

(Plate 23) and Toulouse-Lautrec (Plate 25)

Walter Pach, artist and sensitive contemporary critic, once said —"The faith in *tradition* is of special value today when few students copy the old masters—one of their chief means of learning from the past—and when there is a widespread notion that modern art is essentially different from the art of the past and may even suffer by contrast with it " To Renoir tradition was never an obstacle to originality "Raphael," said Renoir, "was a pupil of Perugino but that did not prevent him from becoming the divine Raphael "

Renoir shared the ridicule which critics and public alike heaped on luminous Impressionism This hostility we find difficult to understand in our day because of the complete acceptance of what was once reviled in its epoch because it was *modern*

Edgar Hilaire Germain Degas (De Gas) (1834-1917) was a convinced, determined individualist of keen intellect, yet a respecter of tradition He developed his skill by copying the paintings and drawings of such giants as Mantegna, Signorelli, Pontormo, Andrea del Sarto, and other Italians of the Renaissance as well as northern Sixteenth and Seventeenth Century artists like Durer, Holbein, Clouet, Poussin, and Rembrandt

Degas, a bachelor, prided himself on his exquisite taste Few of his own contemporaries, other than his friend the Parisian collector, Rouart, could match it He collected prints by Daumier, Gavarni, and Whistler; paintings by El Greco, Perroneau, and Tiepolo—and of course, the Nineteenth Century ancestors —Ingres, his god, Delacroix, and Corot, as well as examples by the Post-Impressionists —Cézanne, Gauguin, and van Gogh

Degas' unusual capacity is evident in his lithographs (Plate 24) and etchings as well as in his drawings He surpassed Ingres in sensitivity, in subtlety of draughtsmanship, in interpretation of character, and even in fidelity to the truth of the object Though Ingres himself was truly great, Degas is a master in capturing gesture, associated with particular exertions, particular professions

Japanese prints, first shown to him by the etcher Bracquemond and by Whistler, immediately excited him because of their brilliant color and their unorthodox arrangements of figures seen from above in daring postures and out of balance "He gave oriental distinction to occidental design "* The achievements in photography by the innovator, Nadar, fascinated Degas He observed that the camera saw unusual relationships of form and this supplemented, even if it did not equal, what the study of Japanese prints had taught him

As the outstanding, ever lucid individualist of his day, Degas fought the blighting control exercised by conservative academicians and teachers He furiously advocated freedom for the artist He

*Virginia Whitehill, Metropolitan Museum of Art

deplored the Impressionists' sacrifice of design and their loss of values in their excessive concern with shifting momentary effects of light His interest in light was the manageable light of interiors, not the uncontrollable outdoor light of the Impressionists "Do not speak the words 'open air' in my presence," he said with irritation He relied chiefly on line to suggest form However, late in life, with eyesight failing, he built form through color rather than through his unique abstraction of line The delicate color harmonies of his earlier periods, the brilliant pastel colors he used when vision failed were both rigidly controlled in the service of formal order He himself said —"I am a colorist with line '

Degas' greatness was recognized in America largely through the initiative of his protégée Mary Cassatt (Plate 26) It was she who persuaded her friend, Mrs Havemeyer, to acquire some of the finest examples of the master's work, bequeathed by her to the Metropolitan Museum of New York Since his death in 1917 the public has come to know other brilliant examples of his drawings and paintings in most of our museums Degas exerted an important effect on Gauguin, van Gogh, and Picasso who appreciated his superb draughtsmanship and his impeccable taste. Toulouse-Lautrec was fascinated by the originality of his inventions by the vitality and the unassailable dignity of his work, no matter what the subject

It was Degas' profound respect for the old masters that explains his passion for a certain rectitude in drawing which, as in the case of Toulouse-Lautrec, accounts for the fact that even vulgar models are transformed into exquisite images In the pages that follow let us try to be as tolerant, as catholic in taste, and as understanding as Degas was in his open-minded attitude toward and selection of works of art by Twentieth Century artists

MANET FAUN WOODCUT 1876

PLATE 1 (opposite left) INGRES DOM-
INIQUE *Two Nudes Studies for the Golden
Age* 1843-48 DRAWING PENCIL 15" x
11¼" Fogg Museum, Harvard University
(Grenville L. Winthrop Collection)

PLATE 2 (opposite right) SEURAT,
GEORGES *Copy of Ingres' Angelica* DRAW-
ING, PENCIL c 1878 9½" x 6" Jacques Lip-
chitz

These plates make clear at the start of our ad-
venture the danger or pigeonholing an artist as
the representative of a particular movement
The sensitive copy by Seurat of Ingres' *Angelica* offers visual proof of how lovingly Seurat,
the Post-Impressionist, studied Ingres, if we but
look at the calm, classic, made figures by Ingres
It is significant also, that today this Seurat
drawing is owned by Lipchitz, the sculptor

PLATE 5 · GOYA, FRANCISCO
This Is Worse · ETCHING AND AQUATINT
1810-20 · 6¼" x 7⅞" · Museum of Fine
Arts, Boston

This Is Worse is one of the most terrifying of Goya's realistic, gruesome etchings
from the *Disasters of War* It tells its own
horrible story as no words can. So impassioned a condemnation of war takes
on fearful meaning once again in our
troubled epoch Only Picasso has revealed with greater imaginative power,
though less literally, the utter horror, bru-
tality, and depravity of war in his prodigious, deeply disturbing *Guernica* (p 95)

PLATE 6 · GOYA, FRANCISCO · *Brave Bull* · LITHOGRAPH · 1825 · 12¼" x 16¼" · Museum of
Fine Arts, Boston

Brave Bull, from the *Four Bull* series, Bordeaux, 1825, illustrates Goya's capacity to record in powerful
draughtsmanship his observations of gestures and attitudes of men and animals in movement

14

PLATE 7 · GERICAULT, THEODORE · *The Hangman* · DRAWING, PENCIL AND WASH · C 1820
15¾" x 12⅜" · Musée des Beaux-Arts, Rouen

This drawing offers proof of the gulf that separates the leader of the Romantic Revolution from Ingres. In the harrowing scene of a contemporary event, a hanging in London, there are reminders of the line and wash of Rembrandt The drawing serves as a prelude to much that is to follow in France

PLATE 8 · DELACROIX, EUGENE   *An Arab Praying*   DRAWING, CRAYON AND CHARCOAL WITH
TOUCHES OF WATERCOLOR · C 1832 · 7⅞" x 10⅞" · Louvre, Paris

In countless sketches or finished drawings, as much as in his brilliant paintings, Delacroix reveals his passionate absorption in the exotic sights of North Africa, which he visited in 1832 as a member of a diplomatic mission to the Sultan of Morocco. Through flow of line alone, Delacroix endows this masterly drawing with the same strange luminous quality that characterizes his paintings.

PLATE 9 · GERICAULT, THEODORE   *Death of Hector*   DRAWING, PENCIL, PEN AND INK
11⅛" x 9½" · Fogg Museum, Harvard University (Grenville L Winthrop Collection)

There are reminders here of figures in the frescoes of Michelangelo Such powerful forms he also introduced into his famous picture, *The Raft of the Medusa*

17

PLATE 10 (opposite above) · GERICAULT, THEODORE · *Two Horses* · DRAWING, PENCIL · 1821 (Study for the *Adelphi Wharf* lithograph) · 7⅞" x 9⅜" · Louvre, Paris

PLATE 11 (opposite below) GERICAULT, THEODORE · *Entrance to Adelphi Wharf* LITHO-GRAPH · 1821 · 9⅞" x 12 ⁵⁄₁₆" · W G Russell Allen, Boston

Here there are echoes of the lessons Géricault learned in a study of horses on the Corso in Rome Horses were his lifelong preoccupation He continued to study them in England

Note the slow yet sure rhythmic forward movement of the great beasts in the drawing See how the master retains in the finished lithograph the vigor of execution so effective in the sketch

PLATE 12 · DELACROIX, EUGENE · *Tiger* · LITHOGRAPH · 1864 · 13¹⁵⁄₁₆" x 19¼" · Fogg Museum, Harvard University

Delacroix copied Goya's *Caprichos* He was also, like Goya, master of the medium of lithography invented by Senefelder, the German, only a generation earlier Note the skillful rendering of the penetrating eyes, the texture of the fur, the feline attitude of the beast Delacroix often visited the Jardin des Plantes in the company of the animal sculptor, Barye It was there that he observed tigers relaxing or made sketches of them in movement These he subsequently introduced into paintings inspired by Rubens and the Venetians.

19

PLATE 13 (opposite) · DAUMIER, HON-
ORE · *Rue Transnonain* · LITHOGRAPH · 1834
8¼" x 12½" · Philip Hofer, Cambridge

Solidity in this picture is derived from a study
of Michelangelo, dramatic intensity is achieved
through the pictorial device of charoscuro
learned from Rembrandt and Goya Daumier
renders emotion through his own dramatic use
of light and shade

PLATE 14 (left) · DAUMIER, HONORE
The Witnesses · LITHOGRAPH · 1872 · 10⅜"
x 9⅛" Metropolitan Museum, New York

Daumier used the medium of lithography each
week for many years in his incomparable productions for *Caricature* and *Charivari* This
print is as fine a cartoon as any done in his
prime The crowd of skeletons surges forward
toward the Council of War The skeletons are
alive See how they shout for vengeance as they
are about to storm the courtroom where Ba-
zaine is being tried

30.

PLATE 15 (opposite above)   PISSARRO, CAMILLE   *Pontoise* · DRAWING, PEN AND INK   1872-3
10⅞" x 17¾" · Wildenstein and Company, New York

This lovely drawing illustrates the sentence that Pissarro wrote to his son, Lucien 'One can make such beautiful things with so little''

PLATE 16 (opposite below)   MONET, CLAUDE · *Two Men Fishing* · DRAWING, CRAYON   c 1882
10" x 13½" · Fogg Museum, Harvard University

In these two exquisite drawings we have Impressionism without color Rarely among the handful of drawings by Monet has the effect of shimmering outdoor light on the surface of water been more tellingly rendered The pulsating quality of the light is due in part to the way in which the scratchboard takes the crayon

PLATE 17   MANET, EDOUARD   *The Races at Longchamps* · LITHOGRAPH · 1864   15⅜" x 20⅜"
Fogg Museum, Harvard University

Why is this scribble, done in fever heat, important enough to reproduce? Because an impression of a shifting scene has rarely, if ever, been better rendered in black and white; because the excitement of the race track is made so vivid that we want to shout and bet on the winner, because the significance of movement is stressed, and finally because there is present in the skillful rendering of the agitated scene a quality that is of importance in a work of art· complete consistency of treatment

23

PLATE 18 (left), COROT, CAMILLE *Portrait of Henri Leroy* · DRAWING, PENCIL · c 1835 · 10¾" x 9⅝" Fogg Museum, Harvard University

"Drawing," said Corot, "is the first thing to seek, then the volume." I illustrate his genius in black and white not by one of his romantic etched landscapes but by this serious, moving pencil portrait a drawing in which there is a complete absence of any calligraphic trick, a drawing which renders a *mood* miraculously The child reminds me of a youngster on the Rue de Bac, Paris, who each evening, years ago, solemnly stepped out of his parents' tobacco shop and with wide-open eyes and never a smile handed me my evening paper He seemed, like Henri, too serious, too delicate for his tender years. He lived on the very street where Corot's mother had a milliner's shop and where Corot was born

To appreciate this subtle drawing there is no need to consult X-ray, ultra-violet light, or any of the other modern, scientific aids often used to bolster insensitive vision In this instance, however, there is an amusing side to what was revealed by the ultra-violet light Then only could one read an inscription on the reverse of the blue mount which enframes the drawing The sentence not only identifies the little sitter but expresses the wish that the drawing remain in the family never to be sold

PLATE 19 (below left) MANET EDOUARD *Springtime (Portrait of Mlle Jeanne Demarcy)* · DRAWING, PEN AND BRUSH · c 1882 · 8¾" x 5⅛" Fogg Museum, Harvard University (Grenville L Winthrop Collection)

PLATE 20 (below right) · MANET, EDOUARD *Convalescent* · ETCHING AND DRYPOINT · 5⅛" x 4" · Museum of Fine Arts, Boston

"Tidy laying of lines was the last thing that Manet was thinking about, for either that or minute rendering of detail would inevitably have destroyed the broad luminosity for which he was striving Each of the crucial lines, however, is drawn with a freedom and assurance and, even more, with a rightness, which, had he not named the plate, would have prevented it from receiving any name other than that which it bears The pallor of the

sick woman, the weight of her body propped up in the pillows, and the tired gentleness of her dainty gesture could not have been more perfectly realized Everything which makes a Manet painting worth while is to be found in this little print, since for even his color he has succeeded in finding the precise black and white analogue"—William M Ivins, Jr

PLATE 21 RENOIR, AUGUSTE
Dance in the Country · DRAWING,
CRAYON · (Study for the painting,
1883, owned by Durand-Ruel)
9¼" x 4½" · César de Hauke, Paris

This appealing drawing, in which
rhythmic movement is captured with
great skill, was given by Renoir to
his friend, Portier Later on it entered
the collection of the distinguished
connoisseur, Dr G Viau, Paris. Paul
Lhote, a friend of Renoir, served as
the model for the man and Suzanne
Valadon for the woman

PLATE 22 · DEGAS, EDGAR · *The Song of the Dog* · LITHOGRAPH · c 1875 · 14¼″ x 9¾″ · W. G. Russell Allen, Boston

This is a satirical characterization of the singer of a popular song often heard at a night café on the Champs Elysées With judgment and with taste Degas tempered her obvious vulgarity. Her pose and gestures are what Degas found fascinating to record The downright rectitude of his drawing is revealed in such details as the profile, the mouth, and the rotund body. This is a masterly study for the brilliant gouache and pastel painting in the Art Institute of Chicago

PLATE 23 RODIN, AUGUSTE · *The Embrace* · DRAWING, PENCIL OUTLINE WITH BROWNISH AND
BLACK WATERCOLOR WASHES · 12¹⁵⁄₁₆″ x 9⁷⁄₁₆″ · Ashmolean Museum, Oxford

Rodin studied the rapidly changing attitudes of nude models as they moved about his studio on the Rue de
Varennes Audacious naturalistic drawings, closed in contour, were useful to the master in depicting
similar subjects in his sculpture

PLATE 24 · DEGAS, EDGAR · *After the Bath* LITHOGRAPH c 1890 · 14¾" x 11" Fogg Museum,
Harvard University

Under this lithograph, as under almost every etching and drawing that Degas ever made, his slogan seems
appropriate "I am born to draw " It is one of about sixty prints that Degas made in etching, aquatint, or
lithography Well placed within the rectangle of the paper it is as effective as a monochrome painting

29

PLATE 25 · TOULOUSE-LAUTREC, HENRI DE *Nude* COLOR LITHOGRAPH · *(Elles* series) · 1896
20¾" x 16" · Philip Hofer, Cambridge

PLATE 26 · CASSATT, MARY · *La Toilette* · COLOR AQUATINT DRYPOINT · 1891 · 14¹⁵⁄₁₆″ x 10½″
Metropolitan Museum, New York

Velasquez, Manet, and Courbet influenced Mary Cassatt, a representative by adoption of the Impressionist group in Paris She observed closely the integrity of Degas' draughtsmanship He taught her to avoid sentimentality Through Degas she came to know the design in Japanese prints, greatly admired by artists and collectors of the 90's This print, in color and line, reflects that influence: a typical amalgam of French Impressionism and of Japanese art seen through Western eyes

31

PLATE 27 (above)   RENOIR, AUGUSTE *Bathers* · DRAWING, RED CHALK · c 1884 · 49¼″ x 56¾″
Fogg Museum, Harvard University (Maurice Wertheim Collection)

The sculpturesque solidity of these two buxom nudes is rendered with gusto They are captivating in their exuberant, sensuous grace Joyous vitality such as this is seductive We follow with delight the curving linear rhythms which delineate the luscious roundness of the firm bodies, forming a well-organized decorative pattern In such a work Renoir bears comparison with drawings by Titian and Rubens

PLATE 28 (opposite) DEGAS EDGAR · *After the Bath* · DRAWING, CRAYON · 1890-92 · 31½″ x 39½″
Fogg Museum, Harvard University

The sensitive modeling, the rhythmic contour of this nude figure are hallmarks of the master Degas was always interested in observing and recording the movements of nude women in almost every conceivable pose There is no voluptuous or sensual note as we saw it in the Renoir *Bathers* above

32

PLATE 29   FORAIN, JEAN LOUIS · *Prodigal Son* · ETCHING AND DRYPOINT · 1909 · 19⅞₁₆" x 15⅝"
Museum of Modern Art, New York (Gift of Mrs John D Rockefeller, Jr)

Like Daumier, Forain had much to say about social institutions, the foibles of his fellow man, about war
and about courts of law Forain was a cartoonist but also a serious interpreter of Biblical themes, inspired
by Rembrandt Degas liked to have Forain drawings about him and Toulouse-Lautrec admitted that he
learned much of importance from the graphic work of Forain

34

Chapter 2
CEZANNE AND POST-IMPRESSIONISM*

POST-IMPRESSIONISM started about 1880 Because it is a merely chronological designation, it is a weak term for a movement of such great significance This rich and immensely varied body of new ideas, which moved from objective naturalism to a subjective art of self-expression, led to Cubism, Expressionism, abstract art, and to other movements that either dissect reality or abandon it for pure expression In the works of Cézanne, Seurat, Gauguin, van Gogh, Toulouse-Lautrec, and all their followers, light and color were as closely observed as by the Impressionists who came before them Color and light were made as descriptive and were deepened by an

CÉZANNE SELF-PORTRAIT LITHOGRAPH C 1899

interest in new spatial conceptions, solid form, abstract design, and more careful organization of the picture

The impact of *Paul Cézanne* (1839-1906) has been so great that today in thinking of sunlit, sunbaked France we see it through his eyes He has been called with the individualists Seurat, van Gogh, and Gauguin, a Post-Impressionist Call him what you like, it is important to remember that this innovator, considered a revolutionary in his twenties, did not rebel against the fundamental tradition of European painting Although opposed to the Ingres reactionaries, he followed practices that had their roots in Renaissance and Baroque painting That conceptual and traditional basis came to him by way of Delacroix and Manet, the Venetians, and from Caravaggio and Rubens. "To my mind," Cézanne said, "one does not substitute oneself for the past, one merely adds a new link to its chain "

Cézanne's favorite subjects were tranquil portraits, always serious, carefully composed still lifes, superb in their grandeur; balanced, impressive landscapes; and nude studies, usually of bathers, almost deliberately clumsy in rendering (Plates 190, 32)

Reverent in his attitude toward the art of the past and yet open-minded to new ideas, Cézanne allied himself with the Impressionist "rebels," attracted by their brighter palettes He met Manet, Sisley, Pissarro, and Renoir at the Café Guerbois, but after years of relatively close association, he exhibited with them only rarely after 1874 He too painted "in the open air," not slighting form as did his Impressionist colleagues, but adapting their discoveries He gave to his work a heightened sense of clarity and order which theirs lacked He used small emphatic brush strokes in place of the short, shimmering technique of the Impressionists, and this was but one of the steps Cézanne took in his long and determined search for a more personal formula He so arranged his brush strokes that they followed the dominant lines of the design Furthermore, he established in his painting a close harmony between color, rhythmically applied, and modeling, thus achieving more solid illusion of dimension and depth He progressed from the exact representation of nature or the mere interpretation of shifting impressions of light and atmosphere to absolute structure and intimations of abstraction. He insisted his objects be recognizable. Cézanne vigorously stated that he wished to "make of impressionism something solid and dur-

*When a group of collectors founded the Museum of Modern Art in 1929 the public did not fully appreciate the significance of the opening exhibition The works of the Post-Impressionists—Cézanne and Seurat, Gauguin and van Gogh—were gathered for this first show because they were especially revered by painters of the first quarter of the Twentieth Century. "These four," to use Barr's words, "founded new traditions and more important perhaps, rediscovered old ones. . All four had one element in common, *Impressionism as a point of departure* "

able like the art of the museums " The elements of abstraction implicit in his work were seized upon by Picasso, Braque, and a host of subsequent artists who, however, did not feel so compelled to represent as recognizable and familiar, the objects from which they abstracted new forms

After years in Paris, Cézanne withdrew from the world to his native city of Aix and remained a solitary worker the rest of his life Unknown to the public at large, considered queer by his neighbors, it was only during his last few years that his immense accomplishment was recognized and he was acclaimed by the younger generation of painters Ambroise Vollard (1867-1939), the most astute art dealer of the Twentieth Century, appreciated his greatness and held a one-man show of his work—but only eleven years before Cézanne's death!

Over thirty years ago it was Vollard who made me aware of the evolution in the art of the towering genius, Cézanne Subsequently J-V Pellerin and Charles Loeser, two distinguished connoisseurs, showed me their collections of Cézanne long before we at home had acquired worthy examples

Loeser was so convinced of the validity of his faith in Cézanne that in his will, signed in my presence in Florence on April 1, 1926, he made a unique bequest, to take effect on the death of his daughter Eight of his Cézanne paintings are left to the President of the United States and his successors in office for the adornment of the White House ' These paintings should be placed in one or more rooms of the White House in which there are no other paintings   The pictures   so placed   as to seem like apertures in the wall, windows displaying views of the outside   In the event that the President should refuse this bequest then the eight pictures   are to be used for the adornment of the United States Embassy in Paris "

Georges Pierre Seurat (1859-1891), a Parisian, whose early death was a bitter loss, modified the practice of Impressionism as did Cézanne Influenced by investigations into the properties of light by the physicists Chevreul, Helmholtz, and Rood, Seurat aimed to give a systematic, scientific basis to painting His orderly compositions were planned with vigorous care Some of the most beautiful and monumental pictures of the Nineteenth Century are the products of his mind and hand They are meticulously finished works, landmarks in modern art For these great pictures Seurat made preliminary studies (Plate 36) using a black-crayon method that approximated in black and white the pointillist technique of his oil paint-

SEURAT SUNDAY ON GRANDE JATTE ISLAND, OIL 1884-86 ART INSTITUTE OF CHICAGO, HELEN BIRCH BARTLETT MEMORIAL COLLECTION

ing The drawings are done always with the thought of simplicity, the elimination of unnecessary detail in order to achieve unity through the verity of form.

VAN GOGH DR GACHET ETCHING 1890

Vincent van Gogh (1853-1890), son of a Protestant pastor, was born in Holland and spent much of his disturbed and tragic life in France where he worked with frenzy and passion from 1886 to 1890 Largely self-taught, he was, like the French artist Rouault, a deeply religious and lonely man Coming from a family of art dealers, van Gogh labored ineffectually as a picture salesman He was torn between vocations, serving as lay preacher in England and going forth among Belgian miners as an evangelist But his true call was to painting, and here his genius lay

Van Gogh was one of the highly individual and great draughtsmen of the Nineteenth Century It is essential to point out that he drew before he painted Line (Plate 40) is one of the three basic components of van Gogh's art, quite as important as his brilliant color and his agitated brush strokes Indeed, in all of his oils, drawing is the spinal, vertebrate, and underlying backbone When he takes a loaded brush in hand, he actually draws with it. The paintings and drawings of van Gogh have been labeled Expressionist The creation of psychic tension through graphic means is one of the aims of an Expressionist. Van Gogh, the Post-

Impressionist, is an important and influential precursor of Expressionism

Years ago I was puzzled that I was able to acquire van Gogh drawings in Berlin but not in Paris For I had always associated the Dutchman, as other critics do today, with the French School But I did not then appreciate his aesthetic kinship to Northern Europe This may be the reason why Germans were interested in his work long before French collectors paid him much attention It is all the more significant that van Gogh had as great an influence in Germany and Norway as in France Compare his drawings (Plates 37-42) with those of Munch (Plate 113), Beckmann (Plate 139), Kirchner (Plate 138), Kokoschka (Plate 142), Nolde (Plate 134), and Otto Dix (Plate 151) See for yourself the strong evidence of emotional approach, the common denominator for all these artists

Van Gogh said —"I have risked my life for my work, because of it I have lost my reason "

GAUGUIN TITRE DE SOURIRE, WOODCUT c. 1900

Paul Gauguin (1843-1903), son of a Parisian newspaper editor and Creole mother, was for eleven years a successful stock broker and collec-

37

tor of Impressionist pictures In 1883 he gave up his business career, turned painter, and led the bohemian life of an artist, so dear to the hearts of romantics

Early in his career Gauguin developed a marked personal style His paintings of Breton peasants are characterized by rooted forms and decorative pattern, elements that endure in his later work Bold patches of bright red and yellow show the influence of Japanese color prints and van Gogh's brilliant palette Thus, Gauguin's pictures challenge Impressionism "For soft contours," says Barr, "they substitute rigid angularities, instead of hazy atmosphere they offer color surfaces, lacquer-hard."

In 1888 Gauguin voyaged to Tahiti to escape from the drabness, the febrile sophistication, and the inhibitions of his epoch He hoped for the release of his deeper instincts in contact with a more primitive society In Tahiti he gained better control of his color harmonies More plastic modeling replaces the flat surfaces of Japanese influence Elements of human interest are now powerfully evident The Tahitian phase of his work is strikingly revealed in his woodcuts and lithographs (Plates 44, 45) This is an almost explosive burst of new creativity, with greater emphasis on design than on bulk

After studying Gauguin, it becomes easier to understand the distinction, the independence of *Odilon Redon* (1840-1916) A solitary inward-seeker, he is revered as an explorer of the mystic This painter of brilliant flowers and butterflies has little in common, for instance, with the work of frenzied van Gogh Only the strange and little-known engraver, Bresdin (Plate 46), with whom he worked in 1862, influenced him His connection with other artists is difficult to discern, although he was known to have copied Delacroix in his youth The other-worldly, fantastic visions of Redon (Plates 47-51) are not related to Post-Impressionism but had some influence on Paul Klee If you must label Redon, bracket his name with those of Edgar Allan Poe, Baudelaire, and Flaubert whose work he illustrated, and with the Symbolist poets whose verses and plays he interpreted with the originality of an inspired mystic

TOULOUSE-LAUTREC THE SWAN LITHOGRAPH. 1899

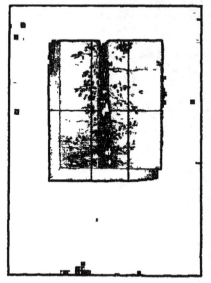

REDON THE DAY LITHOGRAPH 1899

About the cynical, aristocratic, sardonic cripple, *Henri de Toulouse-Lautrec* (1864-1901), direct descendant of the Counts of Toulouse, much has been written This delicate boy broke both his legs and was left a cripple at the age of fourteen Unable to ride, he drew his beloved horses all his life At eighteen he was apprenticed to Léon Bonnat, a fashionable if pedestrian painter who was, none the less, one of the greatest collectors and connoisseurs of drawing Strangely, Bonnat failed to appreciate the miraculous line of his student (Plates 52, 53) Lautrec was inspired by Velasquez, Goya, Brueghel, Brouwer, by Japanese prints which he collected avidly, by Forain, Manet, and, above all, by Degas, his lifelong idol * The influence of van Gogh and Gauguin is evident in those of his lithographs and posters in which bright color dominates the brilliant design

*Not long before her death Mlle Dihau told me a story about Lautrec She was a piano teacher immortalized by Degas, a friend of the circle of the Manets and the Rouarts, who made a precarious living by playing at night in the cabarets of Montmartre Until the end of her days, due to the generosity of the great French collectors David-Weill and Marcel Guérin, she was allowed to keep in her modest living room two famous pictures by Degas which they had bought for the Louvre, to be delivered, however, only after her death One of the pictures was the enchanting portrait of her at the piano, the other, a portrait of her brother, the bassoon player, the central figure in *The Musicians in the Orchestra* Early one Sunday morning there was a pounding at her door Lautrec forced himself into the room followed by revelers from Montmartre, men and women still in evening dress With apologies Lautrec brushed Mlle Dihau aside and, then pointing to the pictures by Degas hanging over their heads, he uttered these words — 'You are in the presence of great portraits by the master I worship Now you, devils, down on your knees "

At heart Lautrec stood aloof from the world he chose to portray, the world of Emile Zola, that intrigued him because of its essential power and urgency, its uncompromising reality, which vibrated savagely below the society of manners into which he was born In spite of its sordidness or more probably because of it, Lautrec took from the gutter the elements that made his a distinguished and exacting art (Plates 54-56)

As social critic, as analyst rather than storyteller, Lautrec depicted the seamy side of life in the 1890's Because his work charged headlong into Victorian prejudice, appreciation of its absolute integrity was long withheld Lautrec was, to my eyes at least, the last great draughtsman of the Nineteenth Century Prodigious worker, he executed nearly 400 prints and countless drawings between 1892 and 1900

With all his present popularity, more than a half-century after his death, there is still a tendency to evade penetration of his blatant subject matter and the discovery of the real achievements of a genius whose devotion to design contained the reverence of faith By making clear that great art may draw upon any subject matter, Lautrec ushered in one aspect of the Twentieth Century— the right of the artist to choose his material.

TOULOUSE-LAUTREC
VALSE DES LAPINS
LITHOGRAPH 1895

PLATE 30 (above left) · CEZANNE, PAUL *Milo of Croton after Puget* · DRAWING, PENCIL   c 1879
18⅞" x 12¼" · Baltimore Museum of Art (Cone Collection)

PLATE 31 (above right) · PUGET, PIERRE · *Milo of Croton* · STATUE Louvre, Paris

The spirited pencil drawing is based on a statue in the Louvre, one of three commissions that Pierre Puget (1620-94) received about 1670 from Colbert, his protector It is one of the best works by the only thoroughly Baroque, but overrated sculptor, among French masters Milo, an athlete of Croton, famous for his prowess in the stadium at Olympia, is represented by Puget at the moment when, as an old man, he tried to pull apart an oak tree and is about to be devoured by a lion because the cleft tree closed upon his left hand and left him helpless

It is interesting that Cézanne saw fit not to copy Puget in a literal sense He picked out the essentials of the plastic form

PLATE 32 (facing) · CEZANNE, PAUL *The Bathers* COLOR LITHOGRAPH · c 1898   16¼" x 20¼"
Fogg Museum, Harvard University

This is the most important print Cézanne has left us It is as typical a work as any of his characteristic formal paintings of figures in a landscape and is based on a large composition now in the Barnes Foundation, Merion, Pennsylvania

"If we had to account for the uniqueness of Cézanne's style in a phrase," says James M Carpenter, "we would attribute it largely to the fact that without altering to any great degree the traditional language of the art, he lays bare the constructive skeleton of painting "

What else strikes us in this print? First and foremost, the over-all calm, the restrained movement of the figures, the geometric design, the emphasis on the organization of the picture We are impressed by the volume and weight not only of Mont Sainte-Victoire in the background but also by the massive, slightly clumsy figures Cézanne realizes plastic form by the binding together of small strokes of changing color.

40

PLATE 33 · CEZANNE, PAUL · *Portrait of Victor Chocquet* · DRAWING, PENCIL · c 1880 · 5⅛" x 3⅝" · Adelyn D Breeskin, Baltimore

In its vitality this drawing differs from the usual solemn, static portraits by Cézanne In the best-known oil portrait of Chocquet he sits stiffly with crossed legs and seems awkwardly tall. Cézanne did not interpret Chocquet as Renoir did a hypersensitive, exquisite personality In our drawing, palpitating with life, our curiosity is aroused We feel that we must learn more about Chocquet, the first generous patron of Cézanne

PLATE 34 (opposite) · CEZANNE, PAUL *Cardplayer* · DRAWING, PENCIL WITH TOUCHES OF COLOR c 1891 · 19¹⁵⁄₁₆" x 14¼" · Museum of Art, Rhode Island School of Design, Providence

This serene pyramidal drawing, depicting intense concentration, is a study for Cézanne's ambitious painting of the *Cardplayers* (1890-92). Berenson and Mrs Panofsky, among others, have compared it to the *Supper at Emmaus,* by Caravaggio, so similar in composition Berenson says ".. the cinquecento artist concerns himself with chiaroscuro and outlines, and the last [?] of the great moderns with space and tactile values!"

The solidity of our figure, its monumental gravity, are impressive Color is introduced as if casually It helps to indicate volume With economy of means and perfect clarity Cézanne has told us all we need to know about this solemn, bulky, absorbed figure Here we have another instance of Cézanne's modified adherence to the great tradition of European painting

42

PLATE 35 · SEURAT, GEORGES PIERRE · *Portrait of Paul Signac* · DRAWING, CONTE CRAYON
c 1889-90 13¾" x 11" · Cachin-Signac Collection

This is one of Seurat's astonishing portrait drawings, a study of the influential painter, Signac What is it
that gives this drawing its special Seurat quality? It is the master's perfect solution of a problem in deep
black and luminous white, the rightness with which the head is placed on the paper As a rule in drawing
we look for the effective use of line to define form, as in the drawings of Toulouse-Lautrec. Here as in all
of Seurat's drawings we consider not lines but volumes produced with soft conté crayon

44

PLATE 36 · SEURAT, GEORGES PIERRE *Seated Woman* · DRAWING, CONTE CRAYON · c 1885
18⅞" x 12⅜" · Museum of Modern Art, New York (Gift of Mrs John D Rockefeller, Jr)

This calm, monumental figure, enveloped in atmosphere, a preparatory study for the epoch-making painting
of *La Grande Jatte*, takes on its full meaning when we observe how it is incorporated in the painting, where
each figure, though isolated and freestanding, is none the less an integral part of a great design composed
with utmost scientific care Both drawing and painting emphasize Seurat's contention that Impressionism
lacked form and structure *La Grande Jatte* hangs in the collection of the Art Institute of Chicago.

PLATE 37 · VAN GOGH, VINCENT · *Peasant Woman* · DRAWING, CRAYON   1885 · 15¾" x 13"
Vincent van Gogh, Laren

In this expressive figure there is a reflection of van Gogh's deeply troubled religious personality

The drawings and prints of Rembrandt influenced van Gogh early in life. As a painter he was attracted also by Millet's peasant types and went so far as to copy him in his own technique, creating variations on Millet themes

PLATE 38 · VAN GOGH, VINCENT · *At Eternity's Gate* LITHOGRAPH · 1882 · 19¾" x 13½" · Nelson A. Rockefeller, New York

No matter what the subject, all of van Gogh's work is saturated with emotion

PLATE 39 · VAN GOGH, VINCENT · *Postmaster Roulin* · DRAWING, PEN AND INK · 1888 · 23¼″ x
17½″ · Los Angeles County Museum, Los Angeles

Note in this emphatic drawing, a study for the brilliant painting in the Museum of Fine Arts, Boston, the
pattern of the sharp-angled lines, the strange eyes that individualize the sitter as do the awkward hands,
the energetic, convincing presentation of the whole solid figure Everything is set down with sympathetic
understanding Van Gogh presents his friend in a stiff, appealing, self-conscious pose and with an intense
gravity that characterizes this democratic personality as it does the Zouave Milliet (Plate 41)

48

PLATE 40 · VAN GOGH, VINCENT · *Grove of Cypresses* DRAWING, PENCIL AND INK WITH REED
PEN · 1889 · 24¹³⁄₁₆″ x 18⅝₆″ · Art Institute of Chicago (Gift of Robert Allerton)

Only the word *frenzied* properly describes the rhythm in this drawing Here there is the ever-present evidence of deep feeling and emotion in the rendering of flamelike, twisting cypresses Such intensity led to
madness.

49

PLATE 41 · VAN GOGH, VINCENT · *Zouave Officer Millet* · DRAWING, PEN AND BRUSH · 1888
12⅝" x 9⅝" · Justin K. Thannhauser, New York

50

PLATE 42   VAN GOGH, VINCENT   *The Fountain in the Hospital Garden* · DRAWING, PEN AND INK
1889 · 18⅞" x 17¹¹⁄₁₆" · Vincent van Gogh, Laren

The bright light of the south is reflected in this vigorous black-and-white drawing and in it, as in his agitated
paintings in colors of high intensity, van Gogh found toward the end of his tragic life his personal idiom as
an artist His draughtsmanship truly reflects the torment of his tortured soul He said in a letter from Arles·
"The emotions are sometimes so strong that one works without being aware of working   and the strokes
come with a sequence and coherence like words in a speech or letter "

PLATE 43 · GAUGUIN, PAUL · *Tahitian Woman* WATERCOLOR (POSSIBLY OVER WOODCUT BASE)
15¼″ x 9¼″ W G Russell Allen, Boston

We are aware at first glance at the woodcut (opposite page) of a break with the Nineteenth Century tradition We are attracted by the all-over rhythmic decorative quality of the print The style is new It is more abstract than anything that we have observed in Impressionist graphic art

William M Ivins, Jr , wrote. "His woodcuts   are planned as great mural paintings might be planned, their spaces are so important   . Broad spaces of black, solid heavy blacks of a kind so difficult to print on an ordinary press that it has rarely been essayed, are relieved by flashes of white, flame-like in their effect, and both are welded together by half-tints   Of all the woodcuts ever made none are more natural, none have more simply grown out of the medium and the tool, and none have had more of that curious richness of color which seems possible only in black and white "

Like the painting of 1892 of *Manao Tupapau*, the lithograph (opposite page) was inspired by the superstitious terror of Gauguin's native wife when the lamp in their hut went out and left her in darkness Gauguin concludes his analysis of the painting "I recapitulate the musical part—undulating, horizontal lines, harmonies of orange and blue woven together with yellows and violets their complementary colors and lighted by greenish sparkles The literary part The Spirit of a Living Girl united with the Spirit of the Dead Night and Day. This explanation of the genesis of my picture is written for the benefit of those who always insist on knowing the why and wherefore of everything. Otherwise it is simply no more than a study of the nude in Oceania "

PLATE 44 (above) · GAUGUIN, PAUL   *Woman at the River (Auti Te Pape)* · COLOR WOODCUT
1891-93 · 8⅛″ x 14″ · Museum of Modern Art, New York (Gift of Mrs John D Rockefeller, Jr)

PLATE 45 (below)   GAUGUIN, PAUL   *Watched by the Spirit of the Dead (Manao Tupapau)*
LITHOGRAPH · 1894 · 7⅟₁₆″ x 10¾″   Museum of Modern Art, New York (Gift of Mrs John
D Rockefeller, Jr)

PLATE 46 · BRESDIN, RODOLPHE · *The Good Samaritan* · LITHOGRAPH · 1861 · 22¼″ x 17⅝″
W. G. Russell Allen, Boston

Bresdin was an eccentric, solitary visionary, uninfluenced by his contemporaries but admired by Victor Hugo, Baudelaire, and Courbet He was known as Chien-Caillou, after Fenimore Cooper's Chingachgook The roots of his art are in Bosch, Brueghel, Dürer, and Callot, as well as Rembrandt, whom he idolized In this remarkable print, a luxuriant growth of trees and plants enfolds countless details—the product of his fantastic imagination. And yet a strange serenity, befitting the subject, is not lost in all the complexity of detail so meticulously rendered.

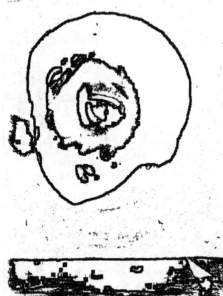

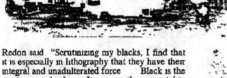

Redon said "Scrutinizing my blacks, I find that it is especially in lithography that they have their integral and unadulterated force   Black is the most essential color .   It conveys the very vitality of a being, his energy, his mind, something of his soul, the reflection of his sensitivity   These strange lithographs   appeal .   to minds that are silent and retain the rare resources of natural ingenuousness.   Saintly and silent material which resurrects and is a medium of refuge, I owe you gentle calm "

And the poet Mallarmé wrote in 1891. "In our silences you ruffle the plumage of reverie and night   . What is personal in you issues from your dreams Demonic lithographer, your invention is as profound as certain of your blacks' And you must know, Redon, I am jealous of your titles "

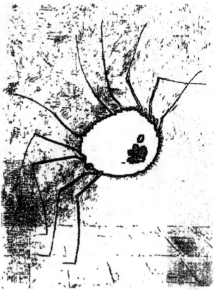

PLATE 49 · REDON, ODILON · *Don Quixote* · DRAWING, CONTE CRAYON · c 1880 · 11¾" x 8½" Fogg Museum, Harvard University

PLATE 50 · REDON, ODILON · *Reader of the Ramayana* · DRAWING, CHARCOAL · c 1885 · 19⅞″ x 14⅝″ Art Institute of Chicago (David Adler Collection)

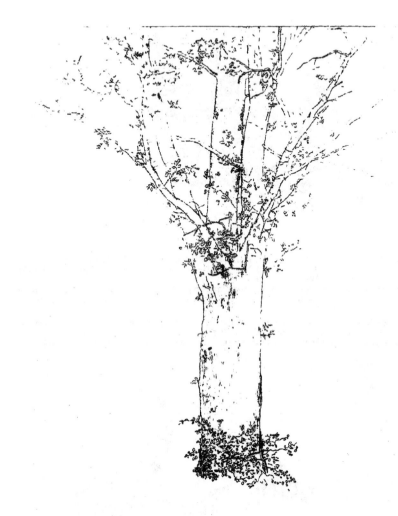

PLATE 51 · REDON, ODILON · *The Tree* · LITHOGRAPH · 1892 · 18¾″ x 12½″ · W G Russell Allen, Boston

Redon's use of contrasting black and whites in lithography was more stimulating to his contemporaries than the lyric content of this delicate, poetic print.

PLATE 52 (above) · TOULOUSE-LAUTREC, HENRI DE · *Study for the Black Countess* · DRAWING, CRAYON (From a sketch book, 1880-81) 6½" x 9¾" · Art Institute of Chicago (Robert A. Waller Memorial)

PLATE 53 (below) · TOULOUSE-LAUTREC, HENRI DE *Circus Rider* · DRAWING, COLORED CRAYON · 1899 · 12⅝" x 19¹¹⁄₁₆" · Fogg Museum, Harvard University (Grenville L. Winthrop Collection)

The accomplished drawing above, a miraculous quick memory "impression" worthy of a mature master, was made in Nice by Lautrec in his sixteenth year It offers brilliant proof of his powers of observation, his passion for drawing in boyhood, his lifelong love of horses, apparent also in the mature work below

PLATE 54 · TOULOUSE-LAUTREC, HENRI DE · *Yvette Guilbert* · LITHOGRAPH · 1894 · 13¼″ x 7″ · Fogg Museum, Harvard University

See how effectively Lautrec uses his telling blacks in these two pictures that face each other· the jet black of the stockings and the funereal gloves. Because this is more than realism these figures pulsate with life.

If you will but forget the subject matter in these and Plate 56 and rivet your attention on the miraculous craftsmanship, you will see that Lautrec, the distinguished draughtsman and colorist, is, like Degas, elegant and refined This accounts for the artistic dignity of his representations no matter how commonplace or even vulgar his models happen to be

PLATE 55 · TOULOUSE-LAUTREC, HENRI DE *Seated Clowness* · COLOR LITHOGRAPH · *(Elles*
series) · 1896 · 20¼" x 15⅜" · Philip Hofer, Cambridge

PLATE 56 · TOULOUSE-LAUTREC, HENRI DE · *Jane Avril Dancing* · DRAWING, OIL · 1893 · 39¾"
x 29" · Edward G. Robinson, Hollywood

"In 1893 Lautrec paid a graceful tribute to Jane Avril's interest in the fine arts by portraying her in a
coloured lithograph [see jacket] to be used as a cover of *L'Estampe Originale*, edited by Marty At the
left is the hand press, operated by Père Cotelle, on which Lautrec's lithographs were printed, at the right
stands Jane Avril attentively examining a proof "—Gerstle Mack

Chapter 3
THE SCHOOL OF PARIS, MATISSE AND THE FAUVES

W
E have seen how Impressionism and Post-Impressionism advanced modern art by immensely broadening the range of subject matter and then freeing the artist from literal and slavish depiction of the object

All the independent artists we have considered and the ideas that linked them now bring us to Vuillard, Bonnard, and Vallotton; to Matisse and

VUILLARD GIRL SEATED INK 1891 JOHN REWALD, N. Y

to Fauvism, the first movement that is definitely "modern " Close, lifelong friends, *Pierre Bonnard* (1867-1947) and *Jean Edouard Vuillard* (1868-1940) were untroubled men, lovers of Paris They designed posters and illustrated books of distinction They profited most by their visits to museums in each other's company They participated in discussion groups They debated whether they and their friends, Vallotton (Plate 165) and the sculptor Maillol (Plate 84), could translate the poetry of symbolism into the visual arts

The name "Nabis" (the Hebrew word for prophets is *Nebum*) was given to the group They were prophets of a style, opposed to the scientific procedure of Seurat and Signac The "Nabis" were backed by the brothers Natanson, publishers

of the liberal *Revue Blanche*, advocates of freedom of expression in the graphic arts as they were for the writing of Verlaine, Mallarmé, Apollinaire, Fénéon, and Gide

Vuillard caught the atmosphere of thrifty, middle-class French "interiors " Bonnard, a lyrical singer akin to Corot, captured the spirit of all he painted, never offering a mere literal statement

Gauguin furthered their interest in color before he left for Tahiti in 1891 Odilon Redon affected them by the technique of his lithographs though not at all by the mysticism of his unique prints and drawings

The importance of the art of Bonnard and Vuillard must not be undervalued because it was gay! They were neither solemn, nor assertive, nor radical innovators But for those who delight in pure painting and fine draughtsmanship, their work has ever been great because it is sound, honest, as it is captivating

Ambroise Vollard (1867-1939), though not a painter, was a figure of immense influence upon this epoch A dealer-patron (Plate 58) of remarkable astuteness, Vollard understood that even in the days of the illuminated manuscript, great illustrators were invariably great painters So, looking about him for artists to renew this tradition, he began with Bonnard and commissioned Redon (Plates 47, 48), Chagall (Plate 128), Rouault (Plate 72), and Picasso (Plate 96) to illustrate a series of superbly printed books These assure his immortality as much as his discovery of the artists for whom he helped win recognition

Vollard published two of Bonnard's illustrated books in 1900 Verlaine's *Parallèlement*, the artist's first striking success in the field, and in 1902 one of the finest books of the early years of the century, the *Daphnis and Chloe* by Longus

The name *Les Fauves* ("Wild Beasts") was applied derisively to a group of artists under the leadership of Matisse, Vlaminck and Derain, who exhibited at the Paris *Salons d'Automne* and Salons des Indépendants of 1904-07. These great masters, who had copied the art of the past, who were accomplished composers and draughtsmen in the traditional mode, shocked the public, as had Monet and his followers thirty-five years before The *Fauves*, in their use of strident, flat colors of high intensity and bold, black outlines and distorted forms, asserted their contempt for the often flabby construction of Impressionist painting For a brief time they became the leaders of the School of Paris which also included conservatives like

Bonnard and Vuillard and the sculptors Despiau (Plate 80) and Maillol (Plate 75) There was much in the technique and psychological content of the *Fauves* that shaped artists like Segonzac (Plate 81). Dufy (Plate 78) and Marquet (Plate 74) were both active *Fauves* The *Fauve* point of view helped pave the way for Expressionism in Northern Europe, along with the art of Gauguin and van Gogh In fact, the word "expressionism" was employed by the French critic Louis Vauxcelles Expressionists took nature as a point of departure, stressing their subjective, emotional reactions to it

Long before Matisse was famous, Leo Stein bought his pictures, Berenson fought for him, Edward Steichen brought his work to America, and Alfred Stieglitz exhibited it Matisse's greatest patrons were two fabulous Russian collectors of Twentieth Century art, Shchukin and Morosov Since then many American museums have acquired examples of Matisse for their permanent collections

Two events made the year 1951-1952 a Matisse year.—an impressive showing of his paintings at the Museum of Modern Art in New York and a notable book about the master's work * The Matisse exhibition opened in November 1951 and

later traveled to the great institutions in Cleveland, Chicago, and San Francisco

Why do I record such facts? Because I wish to emphasize at least once in these pages the importance of making such an exhibition so widely available. Our museums should be platforms for the presentation of still controversial figures like Matisse as well as artists of classic reputation The entire country needs museums that are open-minded and unafraid of the advanced

Walter Pach once said·—"No one knows today where authority resides in matters of contemporary art " How true!—when the influential critic, Bernard Berenson, recently dismissed abstract art with the destructive words "visual atheism ' The final word is ultimately voiced by many, not by one, and museums everywhere must make the materials available for judgment

Henri Matisse (b 1869), like so many of his contemporaries, began his training by copying the masters at the Louvre Pissarro, the most influential of the true Impressionists, put his stamp on his early landscapes. Cézanne, Gauguin, and Rodin affected him through works that came into his possession In Gustave Moreau's studio, in the early Nineties, Matisse met the group which was to be stigmatized ten years later as the "wild beasts " Ambroise Vollard gave him his first one-man show in 1904 That same summer the technique and the intensity of Signac's color exerted an influence on Matisse that became permanent From 1908 to 1911 Matisse conducted a school The American, Max Weber, was one of his students In 1908 Alfred Stieglitz gave him an exhibition at his exciting "291" Gallery in New York In 1913 paintings by Matisse were hung in the epoch-making Armory show In 1933 he completed his mural, *The Dance* This famous work decorates a wall in the Barnes Museum at Merion, Pennsylvania, shrine of a superb collection of Nineteenth and Twentieth Century French art, assembled by the passionate collector, the late Dr Albert C Barnes

Recently Matisse completed what he considers his masterpiece—the most ambitious project of his life—the Dominican Chapel at Vence The murals, the stained glass windows, the crucifix, the vestments, the altar cloth—everything is designed by his hand

Because his unusual management of color has

*Alfred Barr selected and Margaret Miller installed the exhibition with flawless effect Barr's scholarly *Matisse His Art and His Public* is the best book known to me on a living painter

commanded wide attention, his prints, his draw-ings, and masterful book illustrations (Plate 67) have been somewhat neglected Except for Picasso's etchings for Ovid, there are few illustra-tions produced in the Twentieth Century (or for that matter in any century) that can equal the superb Matisse portrait of the poet Baudelaire (Plate 66) There is little in the painting of Matisse to prepare us for the surprise of such sensitive delin-eation of character.

Georges Rouault (b 1871), an Expressionist, has been called the monk of modern art An ardent Catholic, he is an exceedingly complex figure, deeply influenced by the writers Huysmans* and Léon Bloy *+

Rouault was apprenticed to Hirsch in whose shop he studied Mediaeval glass. He received his early instruction in painting as the favorite pupil and friend of Gustave Moreau, an inspiring teacher

---

' Joris-Karl Huysmans (1848-1907), a French novelist of perverse tastes, a convert to Catholicism, a representative of the *Decadents* of his epoch, the author of *Marthe* (1876), *A Rebours* (1884), and other books

*+Léon Marie Bloy (1846-1917), Roman Catholic French writer, social reformer His attacks on society were vitri-olic Several of his autobiographical novels such as *The Woman Who Was Poor* and his letters have been translated

---

and a romantic mediaevalist Moreau used jewel-like colors and exacted recognition of their impor-tance He stimulated in Rouault a lifelong interest in Rembrandt and Daumier Rembrandt s prints fed Rouault's imagination as he came to know them in the home of his grandfather who was a col-lector Rouault acknowledges his debt to the graphic artist Forain (1852-1931) (Plate 29)

Rouault exhibited with the *Fauves* in 1905, although one would never imagine it by looking at his later work Rouault's connection with the group was a tenuous one He was never captured by any coterie

Few contemporary artists have been more sin-cere, more prolific than Rouault in his expressive aquatint etchings, in his lithographs, and in his wood engravings All are as bold in execution as his paintings The emphatic, black contour lines that frame his forms are wholly underived from aca-demic practice They reflect his passion for Twelfth and Thirteenth Century stained glass windows The emotional stress, the mood of pathos, no matter what the subject matter, have their roots in the prints of Rembrandt as well as in Mediaeval glass

Rouault, ascetic, unworldly, is the pious, reli-gious painter of the Twentieth Century (Plate 73), the penetrating portraitist (Plate 71), and, above all, the bitter commentator on present-day suffer-ing brought about by the cruelty of man, by war He points a warning finger at an unheeding world A tragic note is the theme and variation of his pro-found and visionary work. Although affected by Goya and Daumier, and the early works of van Gogh, this ardent Catholic stands apart His devout faith inspires all he touches, no matter how per-verse a number of his subjects may seem to the superficial observer In addition to his pictures of Christ, his portraits are human and varied James Thrall Soby has made penetrating comment upon these pictures Judges were for Rouault, as they had been for Daumier, "symbols of bourgeois corrup-tion " Mountebanks and clowns "weep for hu-manity", prostitutes, daringly painted, "stand monumental in accusation like figures of nightmare remorse " Rouault is a painter of sin and redemp-tion whose work "resembles a seat of moral judg-ment "

I have chosen for illustration several incompar-able prints·—the solemn portrait of Verlaine (Plate 71) and the most telling of the fifty-eight engrav-ings for *Miserere* (Plate 73) These bear witness to Rouault's genius in graphic art, immense and compelling as his painting

65

PLATE 57 · BONNARD, PIERRE · *Laundry Girl* · COLOR LITHOGRAPH · 1896 · 11½" x 7¾" · W G
Russell Allen, Boston

André Gide's remark about Bonnard's technical skill applies here "His very touch is mischievous, quite
independent of the subject " The *Laundry Girl*, carried out in flat areas of black and of subdued color, is
humorously touching and utterly French. The awkward figure trudges along a silent street, deserted but
for the pathetic little dog Only an artist ever on the alert for the pictorial in daily life could have made a
work of art in such simple and unembroidered terms

Bonnard and Vuillard are delightful, honest bourgeois artists untouched by the tensions and tragedies of
the Twentieth Century

PLATE 58 · BONNARD, PIERRE · *Portrait of Ambroise Vollard* · ETCHING · 1914(?) · 13¹³⁄₁₆″ x 9⅜″
Museum of Modern Art, New York

Those of us who knew Vollard remember well that his house was filled with cats that roamed everywhere
With few but telling strokes Bonnard presents the brilliant publisher and astute dealer in characteristic pose

PLATE 59 (above) · MATISSE, HENRI · *Nude Figure Study* · DRAWING, PEN, BRUSH, AND INK · Before 1910 · 10⅜″ x 8″ · Museum of Modern Art, New York (Gift of Capt. Edward Steichen)

This magnificent piece of draughtsmanship, done perhaps as early as 1906, has not, I believe, been reproduced elsewhere

Among the early lithographs by Matisse the one on the opposite page is among the finest. Form could hardly be more convincingly rendered with such economy of means

PLATE 60 (opposite) · MATISSE, HENRI · *Nude, Face Partly Showing* · LITHOGRAPH · 1914 · 19¾″ x 12″ · Museum of Modern Art, New York (Frank Crowninshield Fund)

68

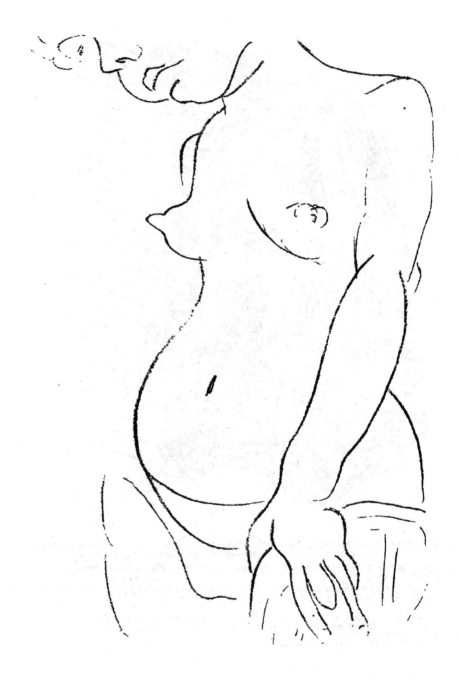

PLATE 61 · MATISSE, HENRI *Nude in an Armchair* · LITHOGRAPH · 1925 · 25″ x 18⅞″ · Walter
Pach, New York

After a lapse of eight years Matisse took up lithography once again and from 1922 to 1925 produced some
fifty distinguished prints of nudes The rich black lithographic accents help to give to this figure modeled
in chiaroscuro relief its sculptural roundness.

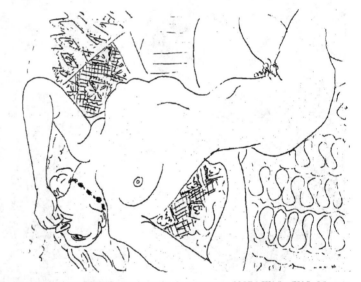

PLATE 62 (above) · MATISSE, HENRI · *Reclining Nude* · ETCHING · 1927 · 5¹³⁄₁₆″ x 7⅝″ · Museum of Modern Art, New York

PLATE 63 (below) · MATISSE, HENRI *Nude on Her Back with Necklace and Pillow* · DRAWING, PEN AND INK · 1935 · 17″ x 22″ · Owned by the artist

This drawing in its distinguished style is characteristic of the many pen drawings of extraordinary virtuosity of the years 1935-36 One is tempted to say that the beautiful foreshortened figure is rendered with ease as if floated on to the paper. The fact is that such nudes were drawn only after endless study by the master.

71

PLATE 64 · MATISSE, HENRI *Mlle Yvonne Landsberg* · DRAWING, PENCIL · 1914 · 20¼″ x 16¾″
Owned by the artist

This Lautrec-like image comes as a postscript to a lovely series of drawings and etchings of a young and rather pretty sitter whose mother had commissioned Matisse to do a portrait drawing The earlier portraits are more charming and doubtless better likenesses. But here Matisse let his hand move with great freedom, creating a drawing beautiful in its sweeping line and rhythm, even though grotesque as a characterization

PLATE 65 · MATISSE, HENRI · *The Plumed Hat* · DRAWING, PENCIL · 1919 · 20½" x 14" · John S. Newberry, Jr , Grosse Pointe Farms, Michigan

This is the best of a series of drawings made in preparation for the important painting in the Minneapolis Art Institute of the model Antoinette in her fantastic hat See how Matisse delineates the alert face and the delight with which he has described the plumes and ribbons in crisp arabesques. Margaret Scolari asked the master "where in creation he'd got that hat, so he laughed welcoming the question and said he'd made it himself He bought the straw foundation and the feathers and the black ribbon and put it together with pins on the model's head He said he had too much black ribbon so that he had to stuff it into the crown with dozens of pins "—Alfred H Barr, Jr.

PLATE 66 (opposite) · MATISSE, HENRI · *Portrait of Baudelaire* · ETCHING · 1930-32 · 12" x 9" · Museum of Modern Art, New York (Mrs John D. Rockefeller, Jr , Purchase Fund)

PLATE 67 (above) · MATISSE, HENRI · *Swan* · ETCHING · 1930-32 · 13" x 9¾" · Museum of Modern Art, New York (Mrs John D. Rockefeller, Jr , Purchase Fund)

In no other graphic works by Matisse will you find more remarkable simplification and elimination of all but the most essential elements than in the two pure line etchings that face each other on these pages They are illustrations for *Poésies de Stéphane Mallarmé* (1842-1898), the leader of the Symbolist school.

Charles Baudelaire (1821-1867), the great forerunner of Symbolism, the eccentric Romantic poet and critic who introduced the works of Edgar Allan Poe to France, is best known for his *Fleurs du Mal* (1857).

75

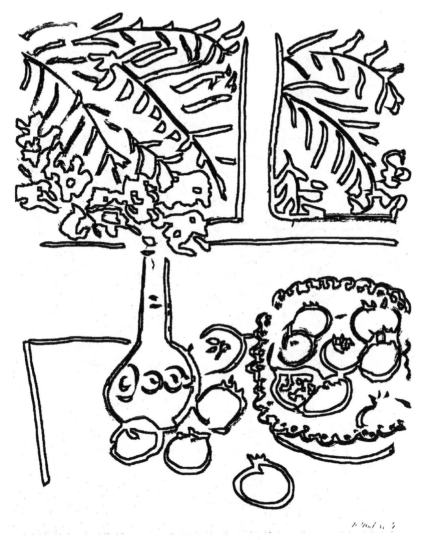

PLATE 68 · MATISSE, HENRI · *Still Life with Fruit and Flowers* · DRAWING, PEN, BRUSH AND INK
1947 · 30″ x 22″ · Detroit Institute of Arts (Gift of Robert Hudson Tannahill)

This large, powerful, decorative, luminous drawing—a vase with flowers on the table in the foreground, palms seen through the window, all broadly drawn with equal emphasis yet holding their places—reflects Matisse's interest, in old age, in the decorative arts of the Near East and in re-studying, in shorthand if you like, the problems of composing an interior with table, window, and palms out of doors. The colors and qualities of a painting are suggested with skill

PLATE 69 · MATISSE, HENRI *Anemone and Girl* · DRAWING, PEN AND INK · 1937 · Owned by the
artist
Here we have the linear arabesques, the calligraphy dear to the *Fauves*

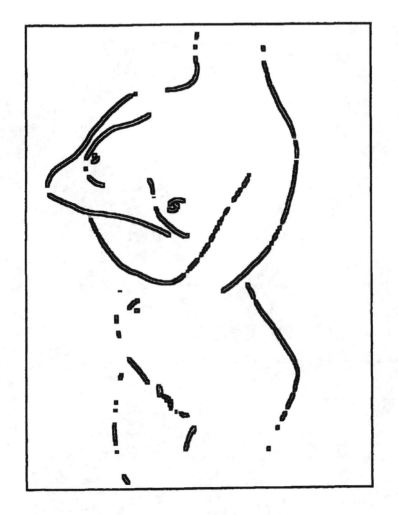

PLATE 70 · MATISSE, HENRI · *Nude Torso, Arms Folded* · MONOTYPE · 1914 (?) · 6¾″ x 5″
Museum of Modern Art, New York (Frank Crowninshield Fund)

Matisse took particular pleasure in his nine masterly, fluent, precise monotypes. technical achievements of a high order. In this example, the figure is swiftly drawn with startling economy of means

A monotype is a unique print To obtain a white line on a black surface the artist, with a sure hand, scratches a line on a plate coated with wet ink and then by printing he obtains the beautiful result here illustrated

78

PLATE 71 · ROUAULT, GEORGES · *Portrait of Paul Verlaine* · LITHOGRAPH · 1933 · 17¼" x 13"
Fogg Museum, Harvard University

This is one of the great portraits of the Twentieth Century It is a remarkable portrait of the sensual bohemian, the mystic, lyrical Symbolist, whose liaison with the poet Arthur Rimbaud was notorious

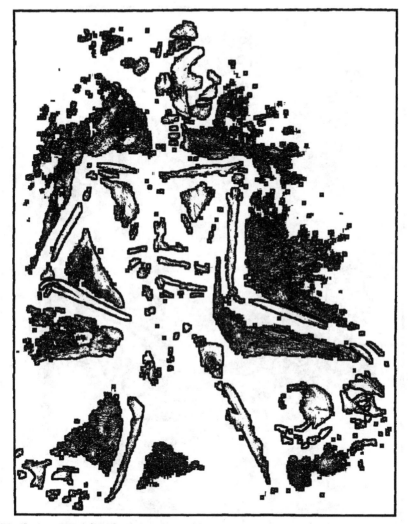

PLATE 72   ROUAULT, GEORGES · *"Man Is Wolf to Man"* · ETCHING AND AQUATINT OVER HELIO-
GRAVURE · (From *Miserere*)   1926 · 23" x 16½" · Fogg Museum, Harvard University

In Rouault's deeply religious work, bounded by dark heavy lines, the influence of Mediaeval stained glass is apparent. In this print we see also the influence of Goya.

We think, quite rightly, of Germany as the country where Expressionism achieved its finest flowering as a movement. In France, however, the work of Georges Rouault may be measured against that of any of his German contemporaries. Rouault tends to distort, to speak with intense emotion, to indulge in over-statement. Intimations of these same tendencies we have seen in the drawings of van Gogh

PLATE 73 · ROUAULT, GEORGES *Deposition* ETCHING AND AQUATINT OVER HELIOGRAVURE ("The righteous, like sandalwood, perfume the axe that falls on them," from *Miserere)* 1926 23″ x 16½″ · Fogg Museum, Harvard University

In this, a moving work, we see Rouault's relation to Rembrandt. In other works one notes the influence of Daumier

PLATE 74 (right) · MARQUET, ALBERT · *Nude with Long Hair* · DRAWING BRUSH AND INK · 1899 · 14¾″ x 8⅝″ Mme Albert Marquet

Marquet was always close to Matisse. In this drawing, enveloped in atmosphere and done with such economy, he is no slavish imitator of nature. A kind of oriental, unembroidered shorthand characterizes this figure. This method he also used in his many atmospheric landscape sketches. He is as "relaxed" in his drawing as in his painting, more at ease than most of the *Fauves*. We see here a kinship with Manet.

PLATE 75 (opposite) MAILLOL, ARISTIDE. *Reclining Nude* · DRAWING, SANGUINE, TRACES OF CHARCOAL. · c 1932 · 21¼″ x 30¹¹⁄₁₆″ · Art Institute of Chicago (Gift of Mr and Mrs. William N Eisendrath)

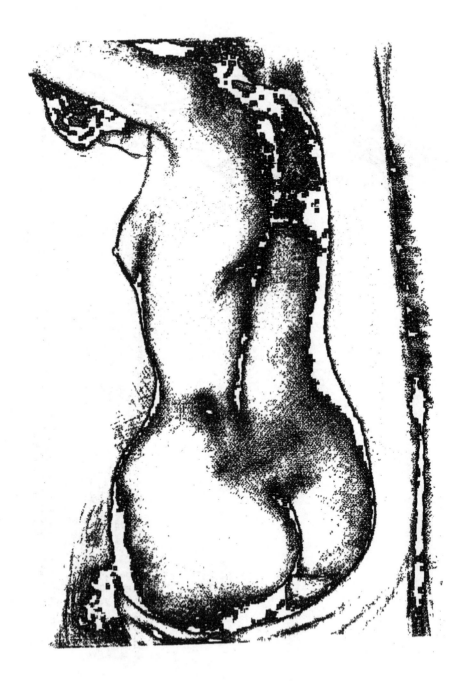

PLATE 76 (above) · ROUSSEAU, HENRI *War* LITHOGRAPH c. 1895 · 8¾" x 13" · Museum of
Modern Art, New York

PLATE 77 (below) ROUSSEAU, HENRI · *War, or the Horseman of Discord* · PAINTING, OIL ON
CANVAS 1894 · 44⅜" x 75¾" · Louvre, Paris

This is one of the few authentic *primitive* works of our sophisticated society It is also the only print that
the *douanier* has left us, a lithograph made in 1895 after the painting of the previous year The idea is
fully developed in the painting in which we see a woman mounted on an apocalyptic black horse riding
over skeletons It was Rémy de Gourmont who gave the artist the commission to do a lithograph of the
same subject which appeared in *L'Imagier.*

84

PLATE 78 · DUFY, RAOUL · *Fishing* · WOODCUT · 1912 · 12¹¹⁄₁₆″ x 15¹⁵⁄₁₆″ · Museum of Modern Art, New York (Gift of Victor S Riesenfeld)

Dufy is best known for his gaily colored paintings Too few appreciate his emphatic woodcuts such as *Fishing* They are effective because of his skillful use of pure white on a jet black ground

PLATE 79 · DERAIN, ANDRE · *Nude* LITHOGRAPH 19¼" x 15" · Fogg Museum, Harvard University

In this beautiful lithograph we see Derain's interest in Renaissance models There is little in this picture to suggest his participation in the early days of the *Fauve* movement It is frankly and joyously devoted, like Renoir's *Bathers* (Plate 27), to sensuous delight in the charm of woman It represents that long con-servative French tradition to which in his heart, and by reason of his birth, Derain was always faithful

PLATE 80 · DESPIAU, CHARLES   *Seated Nude* · DRAWING, RED CRAYON · 11¾″ x 7¾″ · Museum
of Modern Art, New York (Gift of Mrs Saidie A May)

Despiau had for thirty years, prior to his death, been acclaimed as one of the foremost sculptors of our
time due to the serene, grave elegance of his portrait busts

PLATE 81 · SEGONZAC, ANDRE DUNOYER DE · *Portrait of Colette* · ETCHING 1930 (Courtesy
Museum of Modern Art, New York)

Segonzac, in this arresting etching of great freedom, has given us the likeness of Sidonie-Gabrielle Colette
at fifty-seven She is a brilliant novelist and semi-autobiographical essayist, widely known at eighty simply
as Colette Acclaimed in France as an outstanding author, some of her work is available in translation

PLATE 82 · SEGONZAC, ANDRE DUNOYER DE · *Illustration for "Bubu de Montparnasse"*
ETCHING · 1929 · (Courtesy Museum of Modern Art, New York)

We have here, in black and white, a survival of Impressionism in the Twentieth Century

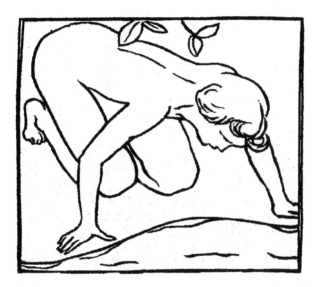

PLATE 83 (above) · MAILLOL, ARISTIDE *Shepherd Corydon* · woodcut (Page from the *Eclogues* of Vergil) · c 1913 · 3¹⁵⁄₁₆" x 4⅛" · Museum of Modern Art, New York (Henry Church Fund)

PLATE 84 (opposite) · MAILLOL, ARISTIDE · *Pipe Player* woodcut c 1913 · 3¹¹⁄₁₆" x 4" · Museum of Modern Art, New York (Henry Church Fund)

With perfect taste, Maillol created the graceful woodcuts for this, one of the choicest books of the Twentieth Century

As in his sculpture, so in his book illustrations, the serenity is Greek. Maillol's German patron, Count Kessler, took him to Greece in 1908. There he met Hofmannstahl, who suggested to him that he illustrate the *Eclogues* of Vergil, of which this is the title page (English edition published by Emery Walker, Ltd , for the Cranach Press, London, 1927 The page margins are even wider in the original) La Fontaine was also one of Maillol's favorite poets

THE ECLOGUES OF VERGIL

IN THE ORIGINAL LATIN WITH AN
ENGLISH PROSE TRANSLATION BY
J. H. MASON: & WITH ILLUSTRATIONS

DRAWN AND CUT ON THE WOOD
BY ARISTIDE MAILLOL

PLATE 85 · LA FRESNAYE, ROGER DE · *Studies of a Clarinetist* · DRAWING, PENCIL · c 1918
10¼" x 8" · Museum of Modern Art, New York

This drawing suggests only mildly that La Fresnaye is allied to the Cubists It does scant justice to one of
the leading artists of the century His true stature is revealed only in his paintings

92

PICASSO *LES DEMOISELLES D'AVIGNON* 1907 OIL MUSEM OF MODERN ART, N Y

Chapter 4
CUBISM, SURREALISM, OTHER MOVEMENTS

IN COMING to Cubism we must make the effort to read the artist's own graphic language—a substantially new one. The public experienced great difficulty when it first saw Cubism (Plate 91) and was enraged because Picasso and Braque had invented a new pictorial mode which seemed impossible to understand

The words of Max Jacob (Plates 93, 104) serve as a touchstone:—"a work of art stands by itself and not by virtue of the comparisons that can be made with reality."

Picasso's famous 1907 picture *Les Demoiselles d'Avignon* launched a new movement in modern art "Cubism . started by reducing forms to their simplest geometrical essence and ended by taking nature apart and reassembling it in flat patterns of logically ordered beauty "* Many influences had prepared the soil for Cubism —chiefly, intimations

*John I H Baur, *Revolution and Tradition in Modern American Art* Cambridge, Mass , Harvard University Press, 1950, p. 48.

of abstraction in the art of Cézanne and the intense excitement evoked by West African masks and Negro sculpture, rediscovered by artists in curio shops, rather than in museums, where they had been solemnly gathering dust for decades

PICASSO THE NUDE MODEL ETCHING 1927

Pablo Ruiz Picasso (b. 1881), a Spaniard by birth, settled permanently in Paris in 1904 He is, I am convinced, the most influential, the most original, the most inventive, the greatest of living artists in either his graphic style or his daring experimentation * Picasso's classic mode is illustrated sharply in Plate 100 in contrast with Plate 94, a furious, terrifying outburst against the horrors of modern war It is fortunate for our purpose that in his most revealing prints and drawings Picasso is as great a master as in his brilliant canvases I allot to Picasso more illustrations than to any other artist so that his commanding stature can be revealed

*I have collected Picasso's prints and drawings and studied his prodigious and unpredictable output for thirty-five years My acquisitions have ranged from early, conservative portraits of his writer friends made at the turn of the century to one of the savage drawings (Plate 94) connected with the famous *Guernica,* his most publicized work.

through his own work, in the descriptive language of his own invention

On reaching Paris Picasso studied the old masters at the Louvre He was fascinated by the creations in flat color and line of van Gogh, Gauguin, and Toulouse-Lautrec However, by 1904 a personal style emerged A radical follower of Cézanne and a rival of Matisse, he is the bold originator of many startling innovations.

In a large print of 1904, perhaps his best known etching, *The Frugal Repast* (Plate 86), Picasso gives us in black and white the melancholy, somewhat sentimental mood of his Blue Period (1901-1904) paintings. There followed, as the result of astonishing concentration and industry, whole groups of paintings of immense accomplishment and marked influence —the sad sweetness of his Rose and Circus Periods (Plate 87), the first Classic Period, a brief El Greco Period Then when Picasso was only twenty-six his complete absorption in Cubism became evident The very name of Picasso brings to mind baffling Cubist inventions which he developed in association with Braque (Plate 91) There followed in 1913 a new technique called "collage", the pasting of scraps of paper, bits of string, pieces of cloth, and a host of fanciful objects capable of attachment to a picture surface A period of realistic, graphic portraiture ensued At the same time he continued to invent Some of the work of this period could hardly be called beautiful, for power and intensity are his primary aim *The Bathers* (1918) (Plate 100), however, is a lovely example of Picasso's draughtsmanship It establishes beyond question or debate that Picasso is master of pure line when he chooses to use it I acquired this drawing in Paris shortly after it was finished during World War I It seemed to me in 1918, as it has over the years, timeless, imperishable, intensely personal, but above all, in the great tradition of European draughtsmanship.

Year after year there is no slackening in Picasso's pace His varied designs for the Russian Ballet are often accompanied by telling line portraits of personalities like Diaghilev and Stravinsky At the same time Picasso reveals his interest in Greek and Roman mythology and also produces some of his late Cubist paintings such as *The Three Musicians* There is always something new like the disturbing, emotional *Three Dancers* which appeared shortly after the 1924 manifesto of Surrealism The picture is "convulsive" and "disquieting," which were precisely the two words of highest praise then current among the Surrealists In 1931, four years after

Picasso painted his unforgettable, terrifying *Seated Woman,* we are again overwhelmed by his endless creative capacity, in a series of exquisite etchings, commissioned by Ambroise Vollard, that prince of publishers Examples of these and related prints are reproduced in Plates 95 and 96

The Picasso portrait of Vollard (Plate 97) belongs here because this enigmatic dealer of remarkable vision backed Picasso as early as 1901!

It seems fitting in a necessarily limited selection of his work to end our consideration of Picasso with a drawing, Plate 94, on the theme of his large painting of *Guernica,* a monochrome which is itself an enormous drawing in black and white

Guernica, completed in 1937, is the outstanding as it is the most startling wall decoration of our century This disquieting masterpiece is on view in the Museum of Modern Art, New York It might well be called "a triumph of death" It will serve to keep immortal the name of the ruthlessly bombed town of Guernica Not even Goya (Plate 5) has left for posterity so terrible an indictment of war, of depravity, and of bestiality

Georges Braque (b 1882) started life as an artisan, apprenticed to a house painter He has remained a master craftsman, never losing interest in the surface texture of wood even when later in life he created the pictures we prize today, reticent, sensitive, of exquisite harmony. Leaving Le Havre at eighteen for Paris, he made copies at the Louvre In 1905 he exhibited brilliant landscapes with Matisse and the *Fauves,* whom he left about 1907 For the next seven years, in association with Picasso, he concentrated on the development of

Cubism He subjected himself to a rigid discipline which involved sober, logical, geometrical simplification and abstraction with virtually no reference to recognizable forms (Plate 91)

Artists are rarely helpful when they speak to us in words rather than in their own graphic language and yet we have a touchstone to Braque's philosophy and practice in his statement —' We must not imitate when we wish to create   I like the rule, the discipline which controls and corrects Nobility arises from reticence of emotion "

Fernand Léger (b 1881), an architectural draughtsman, was inspired by Cézanne's simplified landscapes and figures which could be reduced to their "basic" shapes of blocks, cylinders, and cubes At thirty Léger no longer followed Picasso and Braque closely but developed a personal geometric formula in which color plays an important role Léger's work has sometimes been described as "abstract cubism" sometimes as "a purist's aesthetic of the polished machine." He loved machines, he loved brilliant color, which he combined with a cool logic A typical work is *The Vase* (back cover). He has said that he paints from "the machine" as others do still lifes or nudes

Jacques Villon (b 1875) is typically French What do I mean by that? Villon is French in his love of order, in his insistence on honest craftsmanship, in the gravity of his work (Plate 106) which links him with the tradition of the classic past.

Young American artists are annoyed when their work is criticized for lack of what the French call *"matière "* Villon is typically French in his *matière* —the substantial physical and material surface of

95

his canvases which solidly acquired craft makes both distinguished and literally lasting and durable

Villon went considerably farther toward abstraction about 1920-22 than had the founders of Cubism, Picasso, Braque Villon's dominant interest after 1930 was painting, where the linear framework is as apparent as in his accomplished prints (Plate 107) This structure stabilizes the object through an orderly use of line set down with precision; through color he creates lyrical counterpoint

The Armory show, 1913, gave us our first knowledge of Villon as a painter. More recently the impact of Villon's work is strongly affecting Americans in the graphic field

Surrealism*

Surréalisme, translated from the French, means "beyond realism." It claims for its own the realism of the inner spirit, of the stream of consciousness, of the psyche, as opposed to surface reality. The word was first given currency by André Breton's Surrealist manifesto of 1924 This puzzling phe-

*Those who seek further guidance will find it in a richly illustrated volume of the Museum of Modern Art, New York, entitled *Fantastic Art, Dada, Surrealism.*

96

nomenon is one of the revolutions which started with Cubism, it came into dominance following World War I

Surrealist artists often aimed at the visualization through automatic rhythmic drawing of what psychoanalysts refer to as unconscious experience Leonardo da Vinci had already in the Fifteenth Century suggested the possibilities of self-revelation through automatic drawing

Pictures related to Surrealism or Dada are here chosen for their aesthetic value, just as one might consider a picture by Leonardo or Durer, not merely for its fantastic elements but primarily as a work of art

A gifted artist like the Spaniard, *Salvador Dali* (b 1905) records the weird, sick images of his dream world (Plate 108) in a meticulous technique worthy of the great Flemish masters "I am the first," he says, "to be surprised and often terrified by the images I see appear on my canvases I register without choice and with all possible exactitude the dictates of my subconscious, my dreams—the manifestations of that obscure world discovered by Freud, one of the most important discoveries of an epoch, reaching to the most profound and vital roots of the human spirit "

Joan Miró (b. 1893) is, like Dali, a Surrealist. In 1928, I found myself dismayed at the Valentine Gallery in New York, where this puzzling Spaniard had his first American showing (Plate 109). There were a few things, but only a few, that fascinated me in this exhibition of Miró's irrational, imaginative pictures, painted in a mode to which I had no key. Suddenly, however, I realized that there was something in this work that I could understand I had recently returned from Catalonia in Spain, where I had been under the guidance of Plandiura, merchant and princely collector, whose treasures were in those days kept in an upper floor of his counting house, fragrant with the odor of coffee and spices Thinking of this trip, I recognized in Miró the kind of exciting color Plandiura had shown me in Spain Surely. I thought, Miró knew and reflected in his work a nostalgic yearning for the brilliance of Spanish illuminated manuscripts as well as the bright colors in the frescoes of Twelfth Century Romanesque churches near Barcelona Then, at last, Miró's gaiety; the whimsical linear craftsmanship delighted me

This experience seems to me the essence of *learning to see* At first I did not understand, but by stubbornly trying the closed door, it opened to me and revealed a new vista of experience—still to be explored, certainly, but all alight Those who make the same effort can also learn access to fresh experience if they are unafraid of the new and strange, and determined to try

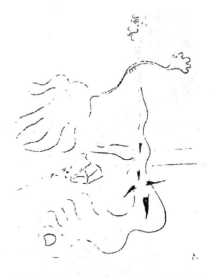

MIRO STATUE CONTE CRAYON 1926 MUSEUM OF MODERN ART, N Y

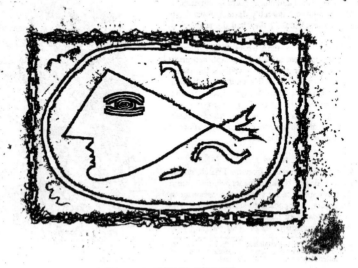

BRAQUE MILAREPA ETCHING AND AQUATINT 1950

PLATE 86 · PICASSO, PABLO · *The Frugal Repast* ETCHING ON ZINC · 1904 · 18⅛″ x 14⅞″ · Art Institute of Chicago (Alfred Stieglitz Collection)

PLATE 87 · PICASSO, PABLO · *La Toilette de la Mère* · ETCHING ON ZINC · 1905 · 9¼" x 7" · Jakob Rosenberg, Cambridge

This engaging picture reflects Picasso's tender, sympathetic vein It represents an incident in the life of a wandering family of *saltimbanques* and belongs to the Circus Period paintings

Plate 86 is, perhaps, the best known, as it is the most popular, of Picasso's approximately 750 etchings, aquatints, drypoints, engravings, and lithographs produced throughout his prolific career as a painter He gives us in black and white the pathetic, somewhat sentimental mood of the 1901-04 Blue Period paintings Note the elongation of the motionless, emaciated bodies, the long arms; the hands with skeleton-like fingers, the arresting gestures; the sad, somber, haunting eyes mannerisms these, based probably on inspiration drawn from the Spanish individualist, El Greco (1541-1614)

PLATE 88 (above) · PICASSO, PABLO · *Portrait of Leo Stein* · GOUACHE 1905 · 10¼" x 7⅛"
    Baltimore Museum of Art (Cone Collection)

PLATE 89 (opposite) · PICASSO, PABLO · *Head of a Woman* · DRAWING, CRAYON AND GOUACHE
    1909(?) · 24⁵⁄₁₆" x 18¾" · Art Institute of Chicago (Charles L. Hutchinson Memorial)

Thus far we have looked at examples of the sentimental, sensitively romantic prints of 1904-05. The connection between African Negro art (only recently exhibited as *art* in our museums) and a Cubist head like this is not difficult to see. It is the same connection that we find in the epoch-making *Les Demoiselles d'Avignon* (p. 93). Ever since adventurous artists began to explore the expressive power and craftsmanship of African Negro sculpture and masks, as of other primitive and exotic forms of art, such works have exerted a marked influence on Picasso, on Modigliani, on Max Weber, and on other modern artists.

Through the use of emphatic areas of light and dark this head is deliberately disintegrated, dislocated, simplified, and deformed with conviction. It helps us to understand some of Picasso's sculptured heads

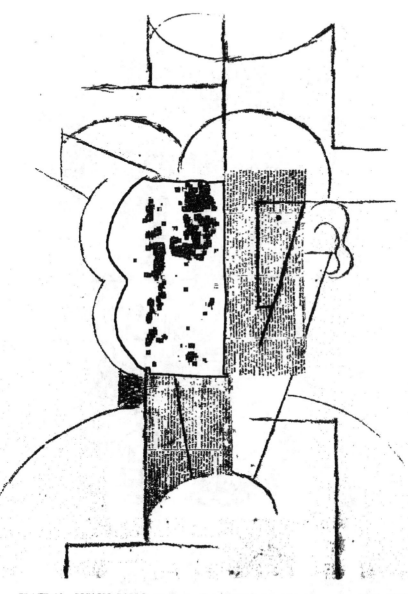

PLATE 90   PICASSO, PABLO · *Man with a Hat* · PASTED PAPER, CHARCOAL AND INK   1912 · 24½″
x 18⅝″ Museum of Modern Art, New York

PLATE 91 · BRAQUE, GEORGES · *"Bass"* · ETCHING · 1912 · 18" x 13" · Fogg Museum, Harvard University

Defenders of Cubism and abstract art have often quoted (though it may not be Cubist gospel) the following passage, from Plato's *Philebus,* in which Socrates praises the intrinsic beauty of geometrical forms.

"What I am saying is not indeed directly obvious I must therefore try to make it clear I will try to speak of the beauty of shapes, and I do not mean, as most people think, the shapes of living figures, or their imitations in paintings, but I mean straight lines and curves and the shapes made from them, flat or solid, by the lathe, ruler and square, if you see what I mean These are not beautiful for any particular reason or purpose, as other things are, but are always by their very nature beautiful, and give pleasure of their own quite free from the itch of desire; and colors of this kind are beautiful, too, and give a similar pleasure "

PLATE 92 · PICASSO, PABLO · *Portrait of Mlle Léonie in a Chaise Longue* · ETCHING · 1910 7¾" x 5½" · Fogg Museum, Harvard University

This is an example of the type of *analytical cubism*—in the nature of laboratory experiment—which Picasso and Braque developed between 1909-12. We do not attempt to explain what is after all not science but a question of sensibility This is a good place to recall Picasso's words "Through art we express our conception of what nature is not "

PLATE 93 · PICASSO, PABLO · *Portrait of Max Jacob* · DRAWING, PENCIL. 1918 · 13" x 9¾" · Mme Dora Maar

Nothing could better illustrate the versatility of Picasso than the two pictures that face each other The portrait of Max Jacob, in the best tradition of old-master draughtsmanship and somewhat influenced by Ingres, is a likeness of his intimate friend in the expanding literary circle which included Paul Valéry and André Breton This is not a study or a preparation but a finished work of art made as an end in itself

In this portrait we have proof, more eloquent than words, that in spite of the austere discipline to which he deliberately subjected himself in the newly invented field of Cubism, Picasso's delight in producing realistic drawings of superlative distinction had not and, indeed, has never waned.

PLATE 94 · PICASSO, PABLO · *Study, After Guernica* · DRAWING, PEN, INK, AND WATERCOLOR
1937 · 15⅛″ x 10″ · Fogg Museum, Harvard University

This powerful study is connected with, but subsequent to, the famous *Guernica* mural (p 95) Picasso
has used the principle of simultaneity He has combined in one representation several aspects of the
terrifying head He has looked at the head from different angles instead of making several different drawings He has, in other words, created a composite image He suggests with emphasis, through omission
and through distortion, the anguish and horror suffered by the civilian victims of the bombing attack on
the town of Guernica No realistic approach to the subject could convey a comparable sense of tension
and horror.

"It is interesting to recall that Aeschylus tells us that 'grief bites ' "—Graham Sutherland

PLATE 95 · PICASSO, PABLO · *The Love of Jupiter and Semele*   ETCHING · 1930 · 8⅞" x 6⅞"
Museum of Modern Art, New York (Gift of James Thrall Soby)

This is one of thirty serene, enchanting illustrations of mild but calculated distortion, used to decorate a page from Ovid's *Metamorphosis* (published by Albert Skira in 1931) It is one of the most exquisite books of the Twentieth Century Each page is notable for the perfect harmony between illustration and type The beauty of the illustration is enhanced through the happy placing of the picture within the rectangle.

PLATE 96 PICASSO, PABLO · *Monkey* · AQUATINT 1936 · 10⅞" x 8⅝" · Department of Printing and Graphic Arts, Harvard College Library

Like all the other astonishingly naturalistic aquatints for the *Histoire Naturelle* by Buffon, the *Monkey* is perfect in technique. Once again it illustrates Picasso's ever new and surprising pictorial inventions. Rarely has the fundamental character of birds, insects, domestic animals, and beasts been pictured as faultlessly, as tellingly, as in this book commissioned by Ambroise Vollard.

PLATE 97 · PICASSO, PABLO *Portrait of Vollard* · AQUATINT · 1936 · 13¾″ x 9¹¹⁄₁₆″ · Museum of Modern Art, New York (Acquired through the Lillie P Bliss Bequest)

It is interesting to compare this powerful, penetrating portrait with the one by Bonnard (Plate 58)

PLATE 98 (opposite) · PICASSO, PA-
BLO · *Minotauromachy* · ETCHING · 1935
19¼" x 27⅜" · Museum of Modern Art,
New York

PLATE 99 (right) · PICASSO, PABLO
Satyr and Sleeping Woman · AQUATINT
AND ETCHING · 1936 · 12¾₁₆" x 16⅝₁₆"
Museum of Modern Art, New York

"In 1933 Skira and Tériade launched the
magazine *Minotaure*. In an age which
largely ignores traditional legend, the
mythological [Cretan] monster of its title
seized the imagination of many artists, in
particular Picasso   The figure [mino-
taur] had previously appeared in his art
but this is the first sustained treatment of
it. . . . By the end of 1934 the themes of
minotaur and bull ring had become inex-
tricably woven in Picasso's mind Both
are present in his most ambitious print,
the great *Minotauromachy* of 1935 The
minotaur, a powerful and ominous crea-
ture, tries to extinguish the light of a
candle held by a little flower girl The
monster advances upon the unconscious
female matador She holds a sword but it
is the minotaur who seems to direct its
thrust The small, terrified horse is dis-
emboweled It staggers under the weight
of its prostrate rider. At one side a
bearded man climbs a ladder, and from a
window, two seated women with a brace
of doves are silent witnesses to the scene
Although the meaning of the allegory remains obscure, *Minotauromachy* is Picasso's most important print, a disquieting and unforgettable image It contains,
as well, many elements represented in the
large *Guernica* mural [p. 95] of 1937."
—William S Lieberman

PLATE 100 · PICASSO, PABLO · *Bathers* · DRAWING, PENCIL · 1918 · 9⅛" x 12¼" · Fogg Museum, Harvard University

This is a brilliant example of Picasso's draughtsmanship in the great classic tradition It is a complex composition of skillfully interwoven, mildly distorted, non-sensual nudes. Details are subordinated in the interest of design In its purity we see the influence of Greek vase painting That influence Picasso absorbed directly in the Department of Greek Vases at the Louvre and not second-hand from Ingres Picasso was not the first to be thus influenced That same classic influence left its mark on the few surviving nudes of Antonio Pollaiuolo (1433-1498), the most powerful and gifted of the Florentine naturalists of the Fifteenth Century

Only a master draughtsman could have achieved in one continuous line such structure and movement as Picasso achieves Like the prints of this period this exquisite drawing reflects his digression from Cubism to flowing forms

112

PLATE 101 · PICASSO, PABLO · *Pastorale* · ETCHING, PRINTED IN GREEN · c 1945 · 10¹¹⁄₁₆″ x 13¹⁵⁄₁₆″
Museum of Modern Art, New York (Acquired through the Lillie P Bliss Bequest)

Picasso is a master printmaker Nothing could better illustrate his versatility as draughtsman, his endless powers of invention, than the contrast between this gay *Pastorale*, the classic *Bathers* opposite, and the superb aquatint of the *Satyr and Sleeping Woman* (Plate 99)

113

PLATE 102 · PICASSO, PABLO *Minotaur Carrying a Dying Horse* GOUACHE AND INDIA INK 1936
19¾" x 25¾" · Owned by the artist

114

PLATE 103   PICASSO, PABLO   *Women and Dying Minotaur* · GOUACHE AND INDIA INK   1936
19¾" x 25¾" · Owned by the artist

This drawing is a study for a curtain for *Le Quatorze Juillet,* a revolutionary play by Romain Rolland The
play was dedicated "to the people of Paris" and produced by the French government in 1936 Seven composers contributed the music, Koechlin, Roussel, Honegger, Ibert, Auric, Lazarus, and Milhaud

PLATE 104 · GRIS, JUAN *Portrait of Max Jacob* · DRAWING, PENCIL · 1919 · 14¼" x 10¼" · James Thrall Soby, New York

Contrast Gris' masterly drawing of Max Jacob with the same subject by Picasso (Plate 93) Then contrast the two drawings that face each other on these pages The pure line drawing above is a crystal-clear likeness, a masterpiece of the Twentieth Century With economy of means Gris used fluent curving lines to define form. The picture on the right with its clear distinction of planes shows how, in a different idiom but with equal clarity, Gris used the lessons of Cubism Sharp edges define the rectangular forms with assurance and precision The drawing explains Max Jacob's words "A work of art stands by itself and not by virtue of the comparisons that can be made with reality"

116

PLATE 105 · GRIS, JUAN · *Self-Portrait* · DRAWING, CHARCOAL AND GOUACHE · 13½″ x 10½″
Justin K Thannhauser, New York

PLATE 106 (above) · VILLON, JACQUES · *Portrait of Baudelaire* · ETCHING · 1920 · 16⅝″ x 11″
Museum of Modern Art, New York (Gift of Victor S Riesenfeld)

This is one of two versions of the head of Baudelaire based on the sculpture (1911) by the artist's brother,
Raymond Duchamp-Villon (1876-1918) We see the master's sensitive feeling for planes in translating a
piece of sculpture into a black-and-white picture; the influence also of Cubism

PLATE 107 (opposite) · VILLON, JACQUES *Down and Out (Bibi La Purée)* · COLOR AQUATINT
AND ETCHING · 1900 · 14½″ x 10⅜″ · Museum of Modern Art, New York

This print shows what is evident in his paintings (but is more clearly revealed here) · that the linear framework adds distinction to Villon's pictures.

PLATE 108 (above) · DALI, SALVADOR · *Cavalier of Death* · DRAWING, PEN AND INK · 1934 or
1936 · 33½" x 22⅜" · Miss Ann Clark Resor, Greenwich, Connecticut

The Surrealist drawing of the *Cavalier of Death* may seem fantastic, baffling, but with great technical skill
Dali has given us a convincing transcript of his inner vision

PLATE 109 (opposite) · MIRO, JOAN · *Self-Portrait* · DRAWING, PENCIL ON CANVAS · 1938 · 57½" x
38¼" · James Thrall Soby, New York

Since brilliant color plays so important a role in Miró's humorous Surrealist creations, we have chosen a
work in which color is not needed to underline its meaning. This is Miró's most ambitious drawing in large
format. It is of its kind a superlative drawing and an astonishing image. How can we explain it? In 1938
Miró felt the urge for self-analysis in order to clarify his aims and in this portrait "we have the perfect
symbolic realization," says Sweeney, "of Miró in his true character of naive, fantastic, mischievous poet
and meticulous craftsman "

The powerful calligraphy, the craftsmanship, we can all appreciate in this disturbing, haunting image.

120

PLATE 110 · SELIGMANN, KURT · *Caterpillar* · DRAWING, VARNISH, CRAYON, AND WASH · 1952
27½" x 22" · Fogg Museum, Harvard University

This drawing by the Surrealist Seligmann is a "fantasy" based on his observation of a caterpillar in his garden It represents an interest in "forms" akin to Sutherland's (Plate 172) This type of drawing represents a radical departure from Seligmann's earlier practice

122

PLATE 111 · TANGUY, YVES · *Untitled* · DRAWING, PENCIL · 1949 · (Courtesy Pierre Matisse, New York)

The color harmony of Tanguy's fantastic, Surrealist painting, as also the beauty of his accomplished sensitive line, leads us into a silent labyrinth, a dream world in which we do not miss specific subject matter This is an imaginative abstract drawing of great originality, pulsating with a life of its own as it reproduces itself endlessly across the page

123

PLATE 112 LIPCHITZ, JACQUES · *Mother and Child (Bull's Head)* · DRAWING, WATERCOLOR,
GOUACHE, AND LITHOGRAPHIC CRAYON · 1939 · 21½″ x 14½″ · Private collection, New
York

This double image combines an imploring woman, symbol of pathos, and a bull's head, symbol of power
It is a preparation for the moving, massive sculpture completed in 1945 and now in the Museum of Modern
Art, New York.

124

Chapter 5

EXPRESSIONISM AND ABSTRACT ART IN NORTHERN EUROPE

BARLACH ILLUSTRATION FOR SCHILLER'S "AN DIE FREUDE"
WOODCUT 1927

THE underlying purpose of Expressionism is to stress subjective, *emotional* reactions to the visual world rather than make a pictorial transcript of the world of appearances.

The word was used by Matisse who said — "What I am after above all is expression."

Gauguin, van Gogh, Rouault, as well as Matisse, made contribution to Expressionism through their decorative flat patterns, unorthodox in color, their simplified drawing, their vibrating technique; their emotionalism Indeed, their preoccupation was chiefly with rendering emotion and feeling, which they believed best achieved through color of high intensity—essential canon of the *Fauve* movement in France.

Expressionist art suits the Northern temperament However, Germans have always been more distinguished in black and white than in color, though Grunewald (c 1465-1528), the true ancestor of German Expressionism, was one of the few gifted colorists that Germany produced The best of North European Expressionist art in the Twentieth Century is to be found in woodcuts and drawings inspired by the crude but effective graphic work of the early Fifteenth Century, by the noble prints of Durer and Hans Baldung Grien, and by the drawings of Grunewald

In contrast with the loose association of the Fauves in France, the German Expressionists formed an organization in 1905 to further their common interests. This group of young artists survived for ten years and was known as *Die Brucke—* The Bridge *Die Brucke* was much influenced by *Edvard Munch* (1863-1944), prolific Norwegian painter, contemporary of Bonnard and Vuillard. Munch's position is central in the development of modern print making, anticipating as he did by almost ten years the work of his German Expressionist colleagues It was in Germany, his home from 1892-1908, that Munch was most appreciated.

For Munch subject matter was of prime importance, so it is not surprising that this visionary was a penetrating portraitist In his woodcuts he was inspired by the work of Gauguin and Vallotton which he came to kndw in Paris. Munch is at his best in his 700-odd prints, through which he made his most valuable contribution to the art of the Twentieth Century No other painter excelled him in his masterful versatility in all graphic media. He was struck by Gauguin's simplified patterns, by van Gogh s intensity The dour mood of Ibsen and the playwright's penetrating influence are revealed in the dramatic *Death Chamber* (Plate 114), a vivid recollection of the death of his own sister.

MUNCH PORTRAIT OF STRINDBERG LITHOGRAPH. 1896

Love fear, suffering and death — these were Munch's obsessions

Munch was closer than his predecessors in France to what became the German type of Expressionism, concentrating as he did upon emotional content, on the "truly Northern feeling for the anxieties of life "[*]

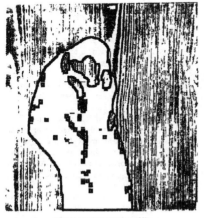

MUNCH THE KISS WOODCUT 1902

The impact of Munch's work was widely disseminated in Germany through woodcuts like *The Kiss*

James Ensor (1860-1948) is of greater stature in the art of Belgium than any painter since Rubens He belongs to the generation that counted among its notables Munch, Seurat, van Gogh, and Toulouse-Lautrec His work anticipated the fantasies of Klee and Chagall. Ensor gave an unappreciative public his most significant work before 1900 [**] The *Entry of Christ into Brussels* (1888) was called sacrilegious and was not officially exhibited for forty years.

Ensor was a versatile master of demonic fantasy and sardonic humor who delighted from early childhood in the grotesque carnival masks that filled his mother's souvenir shop in Ostend, on the Belgian seacoast His world of masks was another herald of the Expressionist movement Ensor was heir in his paintings to the rich color of Rubens and

[*]Jakob Rosenberg, "German Expressionist Printmakers," *Magazine of Art*, vol 38, no. 8, p 302
[**]Libby Tannenbaum (*James Ensor*, Museum of Modern Art, 1951) made clear to my generation, who had neglected him, the significance of Ensor

126

in his etchings (Plate 117) to the graphic skill of Rembrandt

This artist, strange and individualistic in his maturity, was a gifted traditional painter in his early period *The Cathedral* (Plate 119), the best known of Ensor's etchings, was done in 1886 Compare this print with another portrait of a building by Meryon (p 240), with whom Ensor had much in common Meryon, like Ensor in this particular print, was dear to the heart of the typical Nineteenth Century collector who reveled in cityscape scenes

Although he affirms tradition in his early work, Ensor became like Cézanne a Twentieth Century path-breaker, starting in 1883 His progress toward Surrealism and Expressionism, anticipating Klee and Chagall, fed upon Bosch (1450?-1516) and Brueghel (c 1520-1569), and the fantastic art of

KIRCHNER SWISS COWHERD WOODCUT. 1917

the Frenchman, Jacques Callot (1592-1635)

Ernst Ludwig Kirchner (1880-1938), with Schmidt-Rottluff (Plate 133), Erich Heckel (Plate 136), and Emil Nolde (Plate 134), formed *Die Brucke*, a group comparable to the *Fauves*, their contemporaries in Paris Kirchner was the first of the German group to value the emotional content of the work of van Gogh (Plate 38) and Edvard Munch (Plate 114) as well as the artistic value of primitive African sculpture

Kirchner, a consumptive, withdrew to Switzerland from a world that did not understand him His paintings and prints of landscape reveal his love of nature In writing about Walt Whitman's *Leaves of Grass*, Kirchner said —' The scent of the earth, of life, clings to him He is free! He possesses the true spirit of the artist who can give and love without desiring "

Kirchner turned out many remarkable portraits like that of the dealer. *Ludwig Schames* (Plate 138), a woodcut of 1917 While perhaps not for the aesthete (and few German Expressionists ever are) Kirchner none the less is unforgettable in his rugged power, vitality, original design, and nervous, restless, broken touches In Switzerland Kirchner continued to work until 1938 when he took his own life

Emil Nolde (b 1867) was much older than the other members of *Die Brücke* His powerful woodcut of *The Prophet* (Plate 134) is a Twentieth Century variation on an age-old theme

The strange world of *Max Beckmann* (1884-1950) seemed "shocking" over forty years ago when I saw it for the first time in a Secessionist exhibition in Berlin His later, richly matured productions (important as those of any of his generation in Germany) have never ceased to astonish

BECKMANN HEAD OF AN OLD LADY DRYPOINT 1916

With growing consistency and power, he gave body to the imaginative visions that overwhelmed a mind distraught with persecution and the tragedies of war His unusual color combinations heightened the effect of his unorthodox painting

Whether it be a print (and he made over 300), a drawing, or a painting, you will never grasp the meaning or the power of his profound conviction if you look for anything gracious in his restless, symbolic conceptions (Plate 139) This towering, German-born artist toward the end of his productive life came to teach at Washington University, St Louis, and there exerted a wide influence as he had in earlier years in Germany He came to us not as an unknown Berlin Secessionist, a subjective Expressionist, for as early as 1929 he had been a prize winner at the Carnegie International Exhibition in Pittsburgh

Beckmann's black and white portraits (Plate 135), like his paintings, document his personal vision, his deep disillusionment He who creates seems ill at ease in the company of gracious French or Italian works. For years I have tried to hang his prints in my living room with French masters Always the Beckmanns have had to be taken down and sent on their way to a museum wall or portfolio There, properly isolated, they come into their own The reason is that their pictorial protest is too grim, too full of feeling for daily contemplation That, I think, is true of most German or, rather, Expressionist work

Beckmann calls to mind the sterner aspects of Picasso and Rouault, but even more, the intensity of Munch However, the fundamental, underlying influence is far more remote It is Mediaeval German art translated into modern idiom

Ernst Barlach (1870-1938), like Beckmann, was deeply influenced by Fifteenth and Sixteenth Century German art He was an independent Expressionist poet, draughtsman, and sculptor whose short trips abroad extended his horizon but did little to modify his style In Paris he came to admire the peasant types immortalized by Millet (p 8). Barlach stated that his brief stay in Russia did not influence his practice His massive black and whites, like his sculpture, are intense in their depiction of pain or joy His vigorously drawn, heavy figures are like sculpture in their solidity (Plate 131) The brutal thrust of his work is unrestrained, arms are usually outstretched, muscles taut in vehement gesture (p 125) Charles Kuhn[a] says of Barlach's world that it "is a smoldering ruin left

[a] Director, Busch-Reisinger Museum, Harvard University

127

by a ruthless system", that Barlach portrays "the suffering and hardships of Germany with a sense of impending doom."

Wilhelm Lehmbruck (1881-1919), a German sculptor and draughtsman, reveals in his beautiful, plastic etched nudes (Plate 144) Expressionist qualities of grace that are never met with in Barlach's uncompromising work Yet, with astonishing economy of means, he somehow evokes deep inner feeling Compare Lehmbruck's etching with Rodin (Plate 23) and see how the French sculptor in his drawing falls short of Lehmbruck in his strange, rhythmic abstraction

Paul Klee (1879-1940), master of humorous, unexpected improvisations made lively through the use of playful lines, was born in Switzerland the son of a French mother and a Bavarian musician In his youth Paul played the violin in his father's orchestra As a maker of prints and drawings he revealed the gift of a caricaturist who fed his youthful imagination on the aquatints of Goya, the engravings of Blake, and the paintings and lithographs of the visionary Redon, in literature, on Baudelaire Schonberg was his friend On moving to Munich in 1900, he came to know through exhibitions in the German city, the works of Cézanne, Matisse, and van Gogh Visiting Paris in 1912 and until World War I, he enjoyed the friendship of Picasso and the French writer, Guillaume Apollinaire More important was his collaboration under Vandensky, Marc and their Blue Rider group in Munich itself

After the war, he met Walter Gropius, whose direct influence on modern design in architecture has been all-pervasive. Gropius conceived the brilliant idea of inviting the painter Klee, together with Kandinsky (Plate 148) the Russian, and Feininger (Plate 196), an American long resident in Germany, to join the faculty of the famous Bauhaus in Weimar. Gropius thus exerted an indirect but potent influence on modern graphic art Klee worked and taught there until 1928.

Klee's pictures (Plates 120, 122-126), better than any words, show why he is so highly regarded as the best of the fantastic artists of our century He is an imaginative genius who in his graphic work reveals a strange amalgam of something childlike, artless, and unspoiled together with the complete sophistication of a worldly wise, ever-whimsical adult His bizarre, dream-like, poetic drawings, all light in touch, reveal a singer in line whose unique performances are also akin to the music that penetrated the very soul of the total man—music as though rendered on silent strings

128

CHAGALL MUSICIAN INK 1938

Marc Chagall (b 1887), a notable etcher of our time, is as original a print maker as Rouault and often as sensitive as Klee. He is a whimsical painter whose original dreams are rooted in memories of his Russian Jewish background, whose affections have always remained close to his native town of Vitebsk He is a stage designer who uses strong color reminiscent of Russian folk art.

The masterpieces of the Louvre excited Chagall on first reaching Paris in 1910 The Nineteenth Century painters from David to Cézanne, the revelations at the *Salon des Indépendants* and the shops of dealers—all this wealth of material, most of it foreign to his emotional nature, worked upon him But unperturbed, he continued to depict his childlike vision of the world he had lost. In Paris he was discovered by the poet Cendrars, friend of Léger, Max Jacob and Guillaume Apollinaire, defenders of Cubism Chagall accepted the discipline inherent in Cubism without changing his subject matter, which led him to focus on the picture plane and a firmer utilization of space

World War I forced him to return to Russia in 1914 He remained eight years While there, among other projects, he decorated the State Jewish Theater. On his return to Berlin in 1922 his first group of prints—*Mein Leben* (Plate 127)—an autobiographical series, was published by Paul Cassirer In 1923, in Paris, he started to illustrate an edition of Gogol's novel *Dead Souls,* for Vollard, with 96 etchings Then in 1926 and again in 1931, at Vollard's urging, he embarked on two congenial tasks —the first offered him scope to develop his lifelong interest in animals—the illustration of the Seventeenth Century classic, *The Fables of La Fontaine* (Plates 128-130), the second an elaborate undertaking—the illustration of the Bible, for which he had completed 105 prints when Vollard died in 1940

On coming to America in 1941, two events proved of significance —an acquaintance with the work of S W Hayter (Plate 210), innovator of engraving techniques, and in 1942 the invitation of Léonide Massine to put on a new ballet—*Aleko*—in Mexico City Chagall invented the gay costumes and scenery, followed two years later by perhaps his finest achievement in stage design, the sparkling sets for Stravinsky's *Firebird*

In spite of affinities with the Surrealists and the German Expressionists, who tried without success to claim him as their own, Chagall has remained a dynamic independent

Abstract Art

With open minds let us continue to permit the artists, whether their work be abstract or not, to address us through their own graphic means

If we take stock of the ground we have covered, it will be clear that among the Impressionists there were intimations of abstraction. By this I mean the manner in which, although the emphasis was on color and light, they tended to abstract new forms from familiar objects This was no more than an intimation. The next and clearer step was apparent in Cézanne's actual emphasis on form (Plate 32) which carried him to the boundaries of geometry with his reiteration in statement and in practice of the sphere, the cylinder, and the cone Building on the work and the words of Cézanne, the next step was taken by Picasso and Braque who gave us something close to abstraction (Plate 92) in their analysis of form, which led in turn to the subse-

quent geometrical abstractions of the Twentieth Century.

We need not agree that the abstract painters are "the heirs to all the culture of the ages,' but we cannot deny that they are lively and articulate

Granted that the movement is often confusing, it is a fact that in all centers of artistic activity, in America as well as in Europe, abstraction has made a strong appeal to creative minds and in the last decade it has almost come to dominate American art In the American section of this book we shall see that abstraction has engaged the attention of such outstanding men as Weber (Plate 189a, b), and Marin (Plates 191, 192), Demuth, Sheeler and Feininger (Plates 194-197); Hartley and Stuart Davis (p 207) and sculptors like Calder (Plate 201)

As lay observers can we then afford to look upon so vital a movement as no more than a private fantasy and dismiss it as does Berenson? Or had we better keep in mind this opening paragraph in Una E Johnson's *New Expressions in Fine Print Making*—"Genuinely creative art, reflective of the twentieth century, is often complex and sometimes obscure It is neither appreciated nor enjoyed by every observer in the same, or even similar measure It requires of the observer not only thoughtful consideration, but a sense of the tempo and mood of his time. It is not an art of anecdote, nor can it be duplicated by a child of six, as is often naïvely suggested."

It was in 1910 that the first purely abstract picture was produced in Northern Europe by *Wassily Kandinsky* (1866-1944), author and Russianborn painter, widely traveled and long resident in Germany In 1910, after painting his first abstraction, he tried to expound in *The Art of Spiritual Harmony* a new theory dedicated to abstract design of color and line to express emotion and mood Words do not help very much to explain Kandinsky —not even his own! His lithograph (Plate 148) conveys a visual message in a vocabulary untranslatable into prose, just as the system of musical notation conveys sound

We shall see when we come to the American section, Kandinsky's widespread influence in America as in Europe, an influence which was furthered at the time of the Armory show of 1913

PLATE 113 (right) · MUNCH, EDVARD · *The Cry* · LITHO-GRAPH · 1895 · 13¾" x 9⅞" · National Gallery of Art, Rosen-wald Collection

In this tense, disquieting print note the sinuous, flowing lines not unlike those of Toulouse-Lautrec, a line that is characteristic in *Art Nouveau* decorative designs of the 1890's and in German Expressionist art

PLATE 114 (opposite) · MUNCH, EDVARD · *Death Cham-ber* · LITHOGRAPH · 1896 · 15½" x 21½" · Fogg Museum, Har-vard University

This important, impressive print is the masterpiece among the many works that Munch has left us This is *timeless* storytelling of a high order burned into our memory through the effective spotting of areas of ebony black on untouched white paper and through the elimination of everything except the essential and the significant A brooding melancholy pervades the print We are gripped by it as by an Ibsen play We feel that we are participants in the hour of tragedy and share the tension Indeed, most of Munch's early work conveys this sense of disaster or of impend-ing disaster There is about it a mood of Northern Scandinavan melancholy This is a milestone in European Expressionism

PLATE 115 (opposite) · MUNCH, EDVARD · *Sick Girl* (*Convalescent*) COLOR LITHOGRAPH · 1896 · 16⅝" x 22¼" Museum of Art, Rhode Island School of Design, Providence

This touching picture instantly arouses sympathy. Munch is successful in conveying the mood of the *Sick Girl*, through the masterly drawing of the trembling lips, the far-away look in the tired eye.

PLATE 116 (right) · MUNCH, EDVARD · *The Young Model* LITHOGRAPH · 1894 · 16⅝" x 10¾" · Museum of Modern Art, New York

This lithograph is related to the painting *Puberty* (1894) in the National Gallery, Oslo, and to the 1902 etching of the *Night* Frederick Deknatel points out that Felicien Rops (1833-1898) had long been known to Munch and that this print recalls *Le Dernier Amour de Don Juan*

PLATE 117 (above) · ENSOR, JAMES · *The Scavenger* · ETCHING, HANDCOLORED BY THE ARTIST
1896 · 4¾" x 3¼" · Private Collection, New York

PLATE 118 (opposite) · ENSOR, JAMES · *Self-Portrait with Demons* · COLOR LITHOGRAPH · 1898
21" x 14¹¹⁄₁₆" · Museum of Modern Art, New York

This 1898 color lithograph, a version of Ensor's picture *Demons Tormenting Me,* was made under the auspices of the magazine, *La Plume,* as a poster for an exhibition of his works in Paris It suggests the *Art Nouveau* type of French poster, a style that Ensor used with enthusiasm in his drawings several years later

PLATE 119 · ENSOR, JAMES · *Cathedral* · ETCHING ON ZINC · 1886 · 9¾₆″ x 7⁷⁄₁₆″ · Museum of Modern Art, New York

Because the building is so well represented, this print was dear to the hearts of Nineteenth Century collectors, as were all of Meryon's prints (p. 240). Today we are fascinated by something further in this forthright picture It is the way the beautifully rendered Cathedral dominates a vast seething mass of humanity "this towering possibility of salvation rising above the greedy mass"

PLATE 120 (above) · KLEE, PAUL · *Virgin in the Tree* · ETCHING · 1903 · 9⁷⁄₁₀″ x 11¾″ · Fogg
Museum, Harvard University

PLATE 121 (below) · PISANELLO, ANTONIO · *Allegory of Luxury* · DRAWING, PEN AND BISTRE
c 1435 · 5⅛″ x 6″ · Albertina, Vienna

In Klee's case, once again, we see how tradition plays a role even though quite rightly we think of Klee
as one of the most original artists of modern times Ruth Magurn of the Fogg Museum was the first to
point out that this Klee print is but a variation, a free copy, of the famous *Allegory* by Pisanello (c
1395-1455) in Vienna. The contour of the two figures is similar Klee is admired as the most appealing
of all fantastic artists because of his whimsicality, as we shall see in the pictures that follow.
Although he has used color with sensitiveness, he is primarily a graphic artist and a master of line He had
a considerable influence on the Surrealists Max Ernst and Miró

137

PLATE 122 · KLEE, PAUL · *Portrait of Flechtheim* · DRAWING, PEN AND INK · 1928 · 11⅜" x 9¼"
E. Weyhe, New York

Eyes responsive only to realistic art are on first acquaintance puzzled by the originality of Klee, master of unreality. However, few observers fail to fall under the spell of a witty drawing such as this even before they are told that Alfred Flechtheim, the art dealer, who had a passion for prize fighting and boxing, is here shown punching the bags

PLATE 123 · KLEE, PAUL · *Old Man Figuring* · ETCHING · 1929 · 11¾" x 9⅜" · Museum of Modern Art, New York

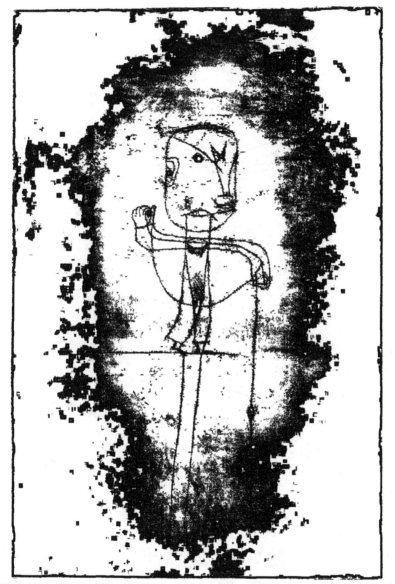

PLATE 124 · KLEE, PAUL · *The Angler* · DRAWING, INK AND WATERCOLOR · 1921   19¼″ x 12½″
John S Newberry, Jr , Grosse Pointe Farms, Michigan

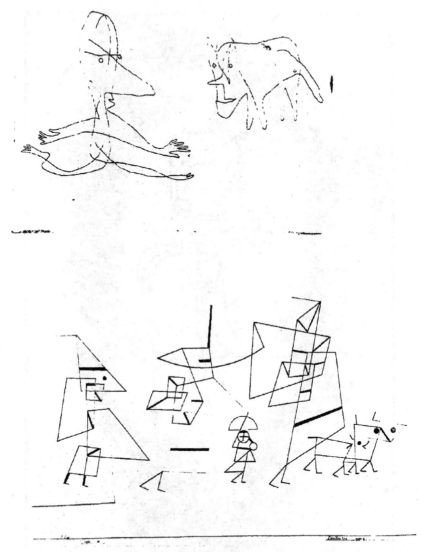

PLATE 125 (above) · KLEE, PAUL · *Why Does He Run?* · ETCHING · 1932 · 11¹³⁄₁₆″ x 19⅜″
Museum of Modern Art, New York

PLATE 126 (below) · KLEE, PAUL · *Family Promenade* · DRAWING, PEN AND INK WITH WATERCOLOR
1930 · 15¾″ x 22⅝″ · Klee Foundation, Berne, Switzerland

141

PLATE 127 · CHAGALL, MARC · *The Grandfathers* · DRYPOINT · *(Mein Leben* series) · 1923
10⅞" x 8⅐" · Museum of Modern Art, New York (A Conger Goodyear Fund)

PLATE 128 · CHAGALL, MARC *The Cat Metamorphosed Into a Woman* · ETCHING AND DRYPOINT
1927-31 · 11⅝″ x 9½″ · Museum of Modern Art, New York

The delightful prints (Plates 128, 129, 130) were done by Chagall to illustrate the *Fables of La Fontaine*, commissioned by Ambroise Vollard, published by Tériade, Paris, 1952 They are richly luminous illustrations, poetic in their own right There is no suggestion in these pages of Chagall's Russian-Jewish heritage which is seen at its best in his fantastic, irrational paintings, brilliant in color, or in his prints like that in Plate 127 Chagall is, like Klee and di Chirico, a precursor of Surrealism, particularly in his painting

PLATE 129 · CHAGALL, MARC · *Fox and Stork* · ETCHING AND DRYPOINT · 1927-31 · 11⅝″ x 9³⁄₁₀″
Museum of Modern Art, New York

PLATE 130 · CHAGALL, MARC · *Lark and Farmer* · ETCHING AND DRYPOINT · 1927-31 · 11⅜"
x 9⁹⁄₁₆" Museum of Modern Art, New York

PLATE 131   BARLACH, ERNST · *Peasant Woman* LITHOGRAPH   1912 · 10″ x 12⅜″ · Museum
of Modern Art, New York

This is a characteristic lithograph from *Der Tote Tag*, a portfolio of twenty-seven lithographs illustrating
a drama by Barlach which was published in Berlin in 1912 by Paul Cassirer Barlach here emphasizes
the heaviness of the figure The emotional quality that we find in his sculpture often appears in his prints
His work is distinguished in its realistic, powerful simplicity He chooses simple people for subjects,
treating them with understanding

PLATE 132 · NOLDE, EMIL · *Windmill on Shore* · LITHOGRAPH · 1929(?) · 23⅞″ x 30¹⁵⁄₁₆″ · Museum of Modern Art, New York (Gift of Mrs John D. Rockefeller, Jr)

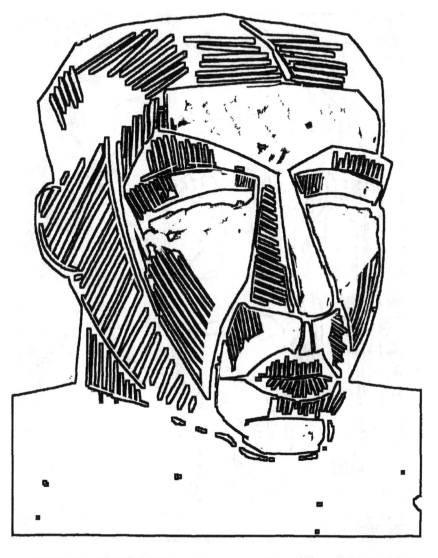

PLATE 133 · SCHMIDT-ROTTLUFF, KARL · *Melancholia* · WOODCUT · c 1919 · 15″ x 12¼″
Fogg Museum, Harvard University

The impact of this bold head is immediate It is akin to the best of powerful sculpture By some wizardry
the artist convinces us that this massive monumental head could not be more solid were it carved out
of granite

PLATE 134 · NOLDE, EMIL · *The Prophet* · WOODCUT · 1912 · 12⅝″ x 8⅞″ · National Gallery of Art, Washington, D C (Rosenwald Collection)

Perhaps no other single Expressionist print is as deeply emotional, as insistently dramatic, as obviously intense as this powerful head. Nolde heightened the tension through the technical device of a sharp contrast between the pure ungraded blacks and the pure untouched white of the paper. No buffers here for timid eyes This is true also of his impressive landscape (Plate 132)

PLATE 135 · BECKMANN, MAX · *Self-Portrait with Graver* DRYPOINT · 1917 · 11¾" x 9⅜"
Museum of Modern Art, New York (Gift of Edgar Kaufmann, Jr)

Beckmann did a self-portrait almost every year As in the case of Rembrandt, they are images of psychological penetration This and Plate 139 are from *Gesichter,* a portfolio of nineteen etchings published
by the Marees-Gesellschaft, Munich, 1919

PLATE 136 · HECKEL, ERICH · *Portrait of a Man* · COLOR WOODCUT · 1919 · 18¾″ x 12⅞″
Museum of Modern Art, New York

In this remarkable colored print the intensity is modified by a brooding quality.

PLATE 137 · FRASCONI, ANTONIO · *Self-Portrait* WOODCUT · 1950 22½" x 7½" · Fogg Museum, Harvard University

Frasconi, now in his middle thirties, is an artist of significant stature Born in Uruguay, the son of Italian parents, he is one of the most industrious and versatile of the younger generation of American artists To emphasize his worth I have placed his penetrating self-portrait facing that of an acknowledged master work

In this juxtaposition it holds its own, revealing his distinguished capacity in the woodcut medium Note the precision with which the block is cut, the undeniable style

PLATE 138 (opposite) · KIRCHNER, ERNST LUDWIG · *Portrait of Schames, the Dealer* · WOODCUT · 1917 22¹³⁄₁₆" x 10³⁄₁₆" Museum of Modern Art (Gift of Curt Valentin)

Disturbed in his youth by prevalent academic sterility, Kirchner turned for inspiration to the Sixteenth Century giants of Germany — to Durer and Cranach, in their woodcuts This portrait is the most effective of Kirchner's brilliant, intensely individualized woodcuts It is unusual in design and characterization, proof that he carries forward the great German woodcut tradition

Hans Carl Valentin und dein, dein "schwere Kirchner
März 38

PLATE 139 · BECKMANN, MAX · *Descent from the Cross* · DRYPOINT · 1918 · 12⅛″ x 10⅜″
Museum of Modern Art, New York (Gift of Mrs. Bertha Slattery Lieberman)

We omit Beckmann's disturbing, and sometimes sadistic prints in the belief that this moving Deposition, like the portraits, reveals more worthily his profound penetration, his power, his serious role in Twentieth Century art. He once said to Perry Rathbone "I have come to realize that Christ is everything"

PLATE 140   BECKMANN, MAX · *Boy with Lobster*   DRAWING, CHARCOAL AND GOUACHE · 1926
23¾″ x 17⅞″ · Mr and Mrs Richard S Davis, Wayzata, Minnesota

PLATE 141 · CORINTH, LOVIS *Self-Portrait* DRAWING, CRAYON · 1924 · 12½″ x 9¹⅜₁₆″ · Fogg
Museum, Harvard University

This rapidly drawn self-portrait, one of many by Corinth, illustrates his power of rendering a face with
psychological penetration learned from a study of Rembrandt It is an example of highly emotional,
slashing, independent German Expressionism

156

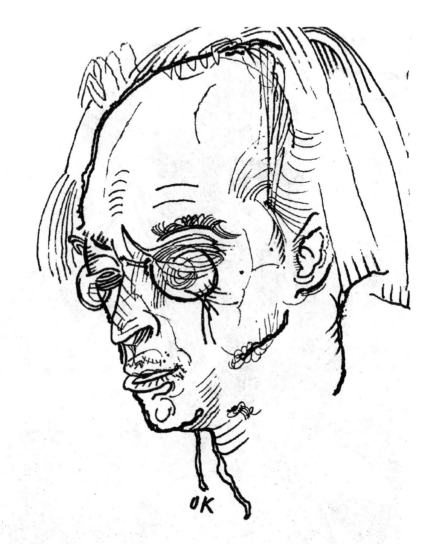

PLATE 142   KOKOSCHKA, OSKAR · *Portrait of the Poet, Herwarth Walden* · DRAWING, PEN AND
INK · 1910 · Fogg Museum, Harvard University

PLATE 143 · KOKOSCHKA, OSKAR · *Resurrection* · LITHOGRAPH · (From *Bach Cantata* portfolio)
1914 · 17⅝" x 13⅜" · Museum of Modern Art, New York

More visionary, more imaginative than Barlach is the Austrian Expressionist, Oskar Kokoschka Contrast the brightly illumined lithograph of the *Resurrection* with the portrait drawing of the poet-critic, *Herwarth Walden* (Plate 142), in which the very quality of the rapidly drawn lines reflects tension and excitement.

PLATE 144 · LEHMBRUCK, WILHELM *Prodigal Son* DRYPOINT · c 1912 · 11¾" x 7⅞" · Fogg
Museum, Harvard University

Lehmbruck, the sculptor, is also a subtle draughtsman—an admirer of Maillol He is a late German
romantic, dedicated to the pursuit of beauty. There is in his work a note of melancholy, an aristocratic
touch that sets him apart from the savage romanticism of Kirchner and Schmidt-Rottluff, an innate
refinement quite absent in Barlach and Beckmann Lehmbruck delights to carve figures of extreme
elongation, a characteristic apparent also in his sensitive prints and drawings.

PLATE 145 · KOLLWITZ, KATHE · *Death Reaches for a Child* · LITHOGRAPH · 1934-35 · 20″ x 14⅞″ · Fogg Museum, Harvard University

PLATE 146 · KOLLWITZ, KATHE · *Self-Portrait* · LITHOGRAPH · 1924 · 17″ x 12″ · Fogg Museum,
Harvard University

Kathe Kollwitz made more than fifty self-portraits. This is the head of an observant, silent woman, dedicated to recording the life of the downtrodden There is a quality akin to sculpture in this moving, seared
countenance The emotional impact is immediate The last of her great print sequences of eight lithographs
was entitled *The Theme of Death*—a theme that haunted her imagination (Plate 145)

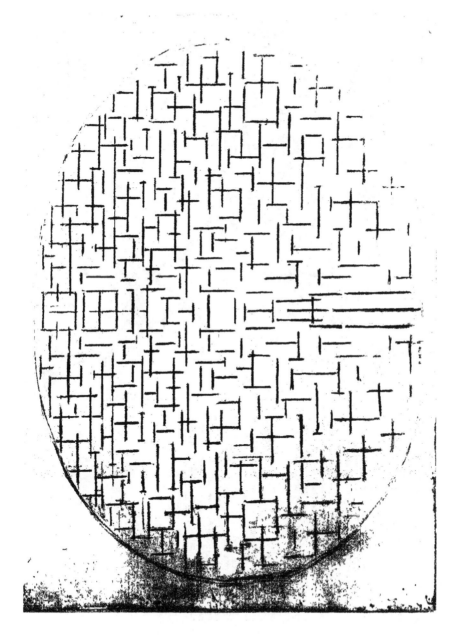

PLATE 147 (opposite). MONDRIAN, PIET
Pier and Ocean DRAWING, CRAYON AND PENCIL
WITH BLACK AND WHITE WASH · 1914 · 34⅜" x
44". Museum of Modern Art, New York (Mrs
Simon Guggenheim Fund)

Mondrian, an abstractionist, is likely to be remembered longest because as leader of the *de
Stijl* group, founded by Theo van Doesburg in
Holland in 1917, he chose, like Kandinsky (Plate
148), to remove from his pictures almost every
suggestion of reality. But there the similarity between the two ends. In his paintings Mondrian is
geometrical, substituting for reality carefully balanced rectangular forms composed in asymmetric
balance. When he uses color he limits himself to
the primary hues: red, blue, and yellow.

PLATE 148 (right). KANDINSKY, WASSILY
Abstraction · COLOR LITHOGRAPH · c 1922 · 10⅜"
x 9⅞". Busch-Reisinger Museum, Harvard University

This is a typical work by Kandinsky. In this im-
provisation, rhythmically arranged, we have visual evidence of Kandinsky's belief (as set forth in
his *The Art of Spiritual Harmony*, 1912) in *absolute abstraction*, in order to achieve something
akin to absolute music. There is here complete
divorce from actuality, from reliance on nature

PLATE 149 · GROSZ, GEORGE · *Portrait of Anna Peter (Artist's Mother-in-Law)* · DRAWING, PENCIL
c 1926 · 26⅜″ x 21″ Museum of Modern Art, New York (Gift of Paul Sachs)

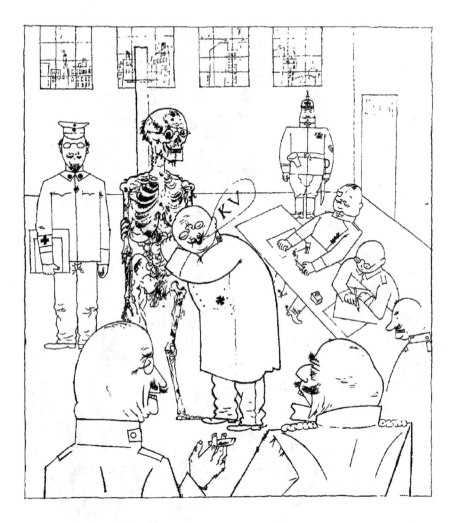

PLATE 150   GROSZ, GEORGE · *Fit for Active Service*   DRAWING, PEN, BRUSH, AND INDIA INK
1918 · 14⅝" x 13⅜" · Museum of Modern Art, New York

It is hard to believe that this drawing is by the same hand that made the solid traditional portrait on the opposite page

This mordant, crisply drawn, satiric work is a bitter indictment of war It was made in days of disillusionment and defeat before Grosz migrated to America As is the habit of Expressionists, Grosz emphasizes to the point of caricature the people he portrays, thus increasing horror and emotional tension.

PLATE 151 · DIX, OTTO · *Head of a Woman* DRAWING, BLACK AND WHITE CHALK · 1932 · 22⅜"
x 18½" · Busch-Reisinger Museum, Harvard University

Once again a great tradition plays its role in this powerful, solid drawing We are reminded instantly of
Dix's German forebear, Matthias Grünewald (c 1465-1528)

Chapter 6
ITALY IN THE
TWENTIETH CENTURY

THE earlier of two Twentieth Century Italian movements of international significance was *Futurism*, born under the *literary* leadership in 1909 of the poet-agitator, F T Marinetti, and in 1910 of the painter-sculptor Boccioni (Plates 154, 156, 157) and his associates, Carrà, Russolo, Balla, and Severini (Plate 155). They all extolled in the visual arts, the dynamism of the machine age At its best the movement was shortlived. Even so, its influence had a greater impact upon European art than any except that of Cubism and perhaps Fauvism

The various *Manifestoes of Futurism*, the first of which was published in Paris in 1909 by Marinetti (later an ally of Mussolini), are helpful reading if you wish to understand the bombastic emphasis on energy and danger for its own sake, the beauty of speed and the glory of war The Manifesto bursts with grandiloquent sentences like this·—"It is in Italy that we launch this Manifesto of violence, destructive and incendiary, by which we this day found Futurism, because we would deliver Italy from its plague of professors, archaeologists, tourist guides and antique dealers. . . ."

And then in 1910 there appeared over the signatures of Boccioni, his teacher Balla, and his fellow student Severini, the *Manifesto of Futurist Painting,* a cry of rebellion addressed to the young artists of Italy, couched once again in orotund terms. This Manifesto, significant for our purposes, reads in part:—"Our ancestors drew their artistic material from the religious atmosphere that weighed upon their souls and in the same way we must draw our

167

inspiration from the tangible miracles of contemporary life, from the iron net of speed that envelops the earth. from ocean liners, from dreadnaughts, from marvelous flights that plow the skies, from the dark daring of underwater navigators, from the anguished struggle of the conquest of the unknown

We propose   to rebel against the tyranny of the words *harmony* and *good taste*, expressions so elastic that with them one might easily demolish the work of Rembrandt, Goya and Rodin .   We propose to render and glorify the life of today, incessantly and tumultuously transformed by the victories of science.   ."

Flamboyant as this philosophy is, I wish to stress something else that has little to do with it·—the exhilarating revival of distinguished draughtsmanship in Italy. The age-old Italian instinct for drawing has remained alive The reproductions in this chapter, whether they be by men labeled Futurist or anything else, all bear eloquent testimony to the vitality of draughtsmanship

Few Twentieth Century artists have produced drawings finer in quality than the Futurists and their fellow countrymen

Until recently we had known only by hearsay the notable painting and drawing, the monumental sculpture of *Umberto Boccioni* (1882-1916) Now, thanks to the drawings at Yale University and to the distinguished examples of his work in the Museum of Modern Art, New York (Plates 156, 157), we are able to see and hence evaluate the work of this original, bold leader of Futurism It was Boccioni, author and propagandist, who wrote the 1910 Manifesto and who showed the work of the Futurists in Paris and London, besides creating the only important sculpture (Plate 156) by any member of the group

"Of all the futurists," says Marcel Duchamp, "Boccioni was the most gifted, and his premature death [at thirty-three] was certainly a reason for the break-up of the movement in its further development "

The drawing reproduced in Plate 154 is a superb preparatory study for the most important painting by a Futurist, as impressive a work of art as any in the whole field of modernism Even though it is a document of basic importance in a movement of brief duration, its quality transcends the limitations of any school, and even of its own epoch.

The Futurists did not exhibit at the Armory show of 1913 My generation had its first opportunity in 1917 to see *Gino Severini's* work (b. 1883)

(Plate 155) at an exhibition arranged at Gallery "291,' presided over for long years by Alfred Stieglitz, that extraordinary discoverer of talent in the early decades of this century and, in his foresight, comparable only to Ambroise Vollard in France.

Italian by birth, Severini resided in Paris but maintained his striking independence His affiliation with the modern French School started early through association with Picasso and Braque as well as with Dufy, Léger, and Gris whose color he, in turn, influenced For six years, starting in 1916, he was absorbed by theoretical studies and mathematics which served as a background for a book he published in 1922

The Sitwells* were among the first to appreciate Severini and commissioned him to do frescoes and mosaics at their Florentine palazzo and later in their London home Severini also decorated several

MODIGLIANI PORTRAIT OF A YOUNG WOMAN PENCIL. 1919(?)
FOGG MUSEUM

*Edith Sitwell (b. 1887), Osbert Sitwell (b 1892), Sacheverell Sitwell (b 1900) all grew up at the family estate at Renishaw Park in England, built in the Seventeenth Century. They are witty, satirical poets and writers of novels, plays, and short stories The youngest is best known for his art criticism and lyric poetry.

churches in Switzerland in 1924 He designed the mosaics for the University of Padua and for the palaces of various Italian patrons

Severini, one of the original signers in 1910 of the *Manifesto of Futurist Painting*, never yielded his independence to group aims, never lost interest in the design and color of Seurat's works, and is nearly as much identified with the geometric abstract Cubism of Picasso and Braque as with Futurism, a label he used even in his 1917 show in New York

The other movement I referred to at the start of this chapter was the *Scuola Metafisica* which, with di Chirico as leader, was in sharp opposition to Futurism The *Scuola Metafisica* stresses the mystic content of the world of dreams.

Giorgio di Chirico (b 1888), called by Guillaume Apollinaire the most astonishing painter of his generation, is the brilliant Italian spokesman for that dream world which found common cause with Surrealism In di Chirico's art (Plate 158) massive buildings set in deserted squares project a profound and unmistakable silence The immobile forms of his fantastic architecture create this enigmatic quality, the stillness of this master of mystery His finest painting is suffused with an unearthly light that exerts a hypnotic effect Like Klee, he is a precursor of Surrealism Although Klee and di Chirico were outside the movement, they were both particularly admired by the Dadaists

Amedeo Modigliani (1884-1920) (Plate 152), one of the towering Italian artists of the Twentieth Century, a victim of tuberculosis, who worked at fever heat throughout his short and turbulent life, was always desperately poor He went to Paris in 1906 in the decades when Fauvism and Cubism were born Modigliani was denied even limited recognition until just one year before he destroyed himself at thirty-six

Modigliani always drew He was one of the few inspired draughtsmen of modern times In all his works the linear basis of his art is what first strikes us; the exquisite, fluent, significant outline Years ago when I acquired this slight, rapid sketch (p 168), I was at once struck by his power to reduce details to the merest essentials Even in his painting and in his sculpture, influenced by Brancusi, he seems to have thought first in line, whether rendering a human head sadly, or a sensuous nude These were his preoccupations as an artist.

I find in his drawings many influences that carry us down through the ages to the perplexing present —Egyptian low reliefs, primitive African sculpture

In his nudes his disciplined line reminds us of the early Italians, of Botticelli. But there are more recent influences —the calculated distortions of Cézanne (Plate 30), the austerity of Cubism, the draughtsmanship of Toulouse-Lautrec (Plate 54) at his simple best He was also aware of the rounded contours in the perverse but decorative drawings of the Englishman Aubrey Beardsley (Plate 164) Modigliani made many subtly individualized portraits of artists and writers like Plate 153, as well as frankly erotic nudes

Giacomo Manzù (b 1908) is a distinguished sculptor, an incisive draughtsman in the great Italian manner Manzù and Marini are both gifted individualists quite untouched by Futurism

Whether in his fluent sculpture or in his clean-cut graphic work, or in his drawings of clerics (Plate 162), Manzù might well pass for a man of the Renaissance On the other hand, the widely traveled *Marino Marini* (b 1901) in his vigorous stylized horses and riders (Plate 163) reminds us of Chinese prototypes

Both have added the most authentic luster to the revival of art in Italy, contemporary in its most meaningful sense.

MARINI   HORSE AND RIDER   INK AND GOUACHE   1951
CURT VALENTIN GALLERY, N Y

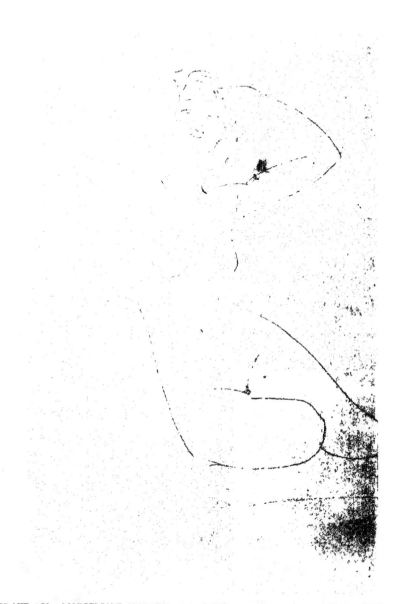

PLATE 152 · MODIGLIANI, AMEDEO · *Seated Nude* · DRAWING, PENCIL · c.1918 · 17⅜″ x 11″
Museum of Modern Art, New York

Note the fluent outline in this, one of the finest of Modigliani's drawings of the nude, in which the disciplined line calls to mind Botticelli's illustrations for Dante

PLATE 153 · MODIGLIANI, AMEDEO · *Portrait of Mme Zborowska* · DRAWING, PENCIL · 1918
11⅛" x 7⅜" · Museum of Art, Rhode Island School of Design, Providence

This drawing in the usual mannerist elongation of the features is a characteristic Modigliani portrait. As in his impressive sculpture the influence of African Negro prototypes is startling The sitter is the wife of his friend and dealer, the Polish poet who arranged Modigliani's first exhibition at the Paris gallery of the forward-looking Berthe Weill.

PLATE 154 · BOCCIONI, UMBERTO · *Study for "The City Rises"* · DRAWING, CRAYON AND CHALK
1910 · 22½″ x 33½″ · Vico Baer, Milan

Boccioni, the brilliant leader of the first Futurist group in Italy (1910-15), made this handsome drawing as a preparation for what I consider his greatest painting It is a work of marked emotional intensity. The violent strains and stresses of the two heavy plunging horses are suffused with intense energy.

172

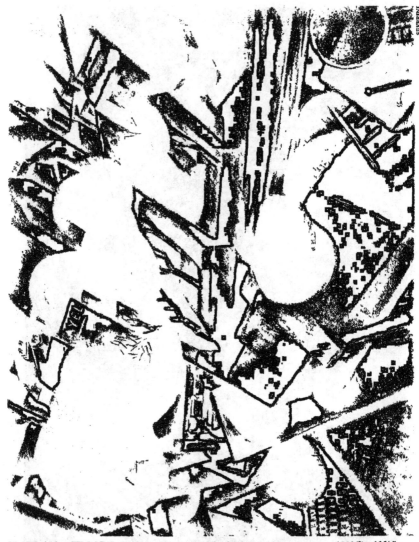

PLATE 155 · SEVERINI, GINO · *The Train in the City* · DRAWING, CHARCOAL · 1913(?) · 19⅝″ x 25⅝″ · Metropolitan Museum, New York (Alfred Stieglitz Collection)

This is a perfect example to illustrate the Futurists' preoccupation with the problem of recording speed, that disturbing symptom of our modern age.

"Futurism," says James Thrall Soby, "was essentially a crossbreeding of Impressionism with Cubism: motion from one and form from the other."

173

PLATE 156 (above right) · BOCCIONI, UMBERTO · *Unique Forms of Continuity in Space* · BRONZE
1913 · Height 43⅛″ · Museum of Modern Art, New York (Acquired through the Lillie
P. Bliss Bequest)

PLATE 157 (above left) · BOCCIONI, UMBERTO · *Muscular Dynamism* · DRAWING, CHARCOAL
(Study for the statue, *Unique Forms of Continuity in Space*) · 1913 · 34″ x 23¼″
Museum of Modern Art, New York

The Futurists grappled with the problem of representing forms in motion Like the Cubists, they moved
around an object, surveyed all sides of it in order to analyze, to dissect its form, its structure. The drawing,
Muscular Dynamism, takes on full significance only when seen in juxtaposition with the magnificent
bronze for which it is a study In the bronze, dynamic movement is miraculously realized.

174

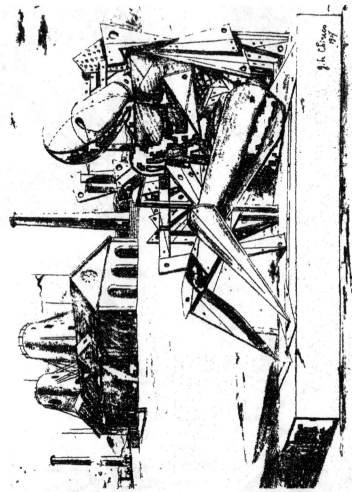

PLATE 158 · DI CHIRICO, GIORGIO · *Solitude* · DRAWING, PENCIL   1917 · 8¾″ x 12½″ · Paul W. Cooley, West Hartford, Connecticut

How admirably the introspective Italian master has named this haunting drawing in which he suggests not only solitude but silence and melancholy

"What is so interesting about the drawing," Soby wrote me, "is that it is so complete a summary . . . of his entire early iconography, with a deserted square, a mannequin, still-life elements, a factory chimney, and so on Also . . the drawing did appear in the book which really started the international fame of the 'metaphysical school' of di Chirico and Carlo Carrà (Ferrara, 1917). So much for pedantry, to which I sometimes think those of us who work in the contemporary field are more susceptible than anyone else, perhaps because we miss time's healing certainty in our judgments."

It is obvious that di Chirico was, like Klee, a precursor of Surrealism

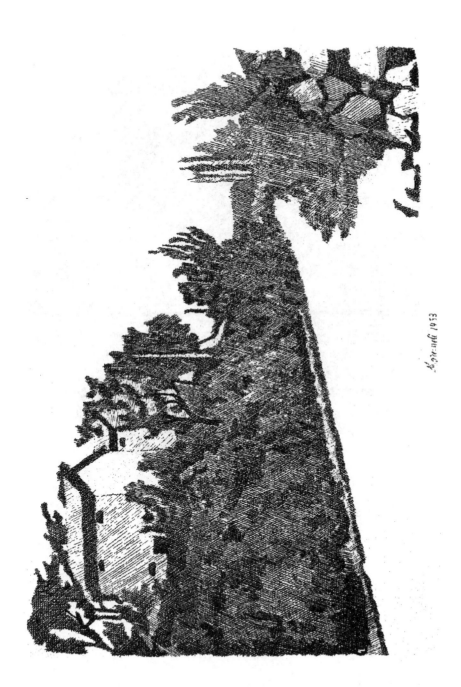

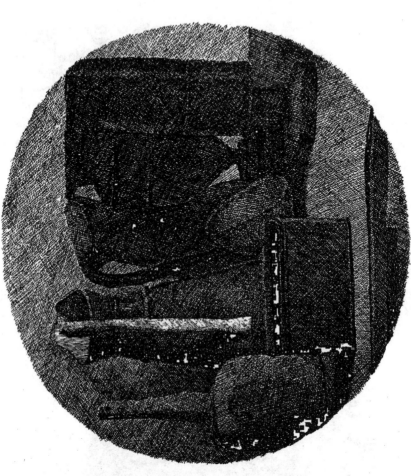

PLATE 159 (opposite) · MORANDI, GIORGIO · *Landscape* · ETCHING 1933 · 8¹⁵/₁₆″ x 11¹⁵/₁₆″ · Museum of Modern Art, New York

PLATE 160 (right) · MORANDI, GIORGIO · *Oval Still Life* · ETCHING 1945 · 10½″ x 11¾″ · Museum of Modern Art, New York (Gift of James Thrall Soby)

Morandi, one time member of the *Scuola Metafisica*, is today more appreciated in his native land than abroad. From a technical point of view he is interesting as an innovator. There is in his prints a sensitive balancing of shapes and forms, a capacity to render enveloping atmosphere

PLATE 161 (opposite) VESPI-
GNANI, RENZO · *Three Hanging
Men* · DRAWING, PEN AND INDIA INK
1949 · 13" x 8¾" · Mr and Mrs. R
Kirk Askew, Jr , New York

Like so many fine Twentieth Century Italian drawings this work, in
the great tradition, reminds us of
similar drawings by Pisanello and
Rembrandt

PLATE 162 (right) · MANZU,
GIACOMO *A Clerical* · DRAWING,
PEN AND INK · Owned by the artist

Manzù is, like Modigliani and Boccioni of an earlier generation, one
of the distinguished sculptors of
contemporary Italy He is noted for
his bas-reliefs His sculptures of
clericals reveal a tender piety This
drawing, worthy of the great Italian
draughtsmen of earlier days, is a
step in his thinking for a piece of
sculpture.

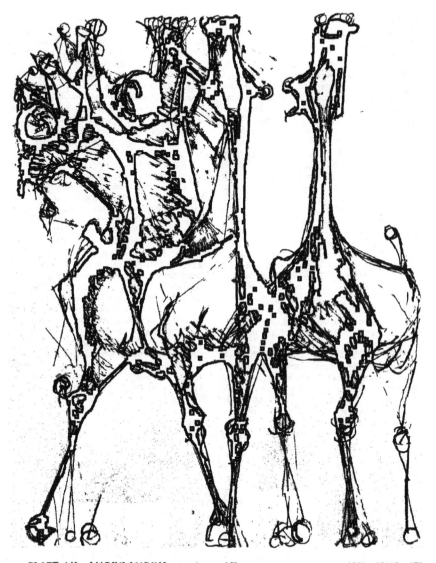

PLATE 163 · MARINI, MARINO · *Acrobats and Horses* · COLOR LITHOGRAPH 1952 · 22¼" x 17"
Fogg Museum, Harvard University

What is it that carries conviction in this lively recent lithograph of *Acrobats and Horses*, distorted but unified? It is the telling shorthand of taut, jet-black lines which suggest to perfection the attitudes and gestures of acrobatic riders

Chapter 7
ENGLAND

THE choice of reproductions in this chapter must be limited to draughtsmen who either felt the impact of Continental work or who per contra exerted an influence abroad comparable to that exercised by John Constable (1776-1837), at the Salon of 1824, on French painters

It would be a delight to dwell on such Nineteenth Century ancestors of modern art in England as William Blake (1753-1828), Thomas Bewick (1753-1828), J M W Turner (1775-1851), the illustrators John Leech (1817-1864) and Charles Keene (1823-1891), Sir John Tenniel (1820-1914), George du Maurier (1834-1896) and Sir Max Beerbohm (b 1872) They like Edward Lear (1812-1888) (p 182) established a tradition which enchants us Where else but in Anglo-Saxon hands will you find nonsense in line and verse that continues to amuse and delight the world, except in the drawings for Max and Moritz and the Fliegende Blätter by the German poet-illustrator Wilhelm Busch (1832-1908)?

Samuel Palmer (1805-1881), a romantic revered by lovers of English art, is illustrated (Plate 166) in a little known drawing of unusual character

Palmer (Plate 168) inspired John Piper (b 1903), a one-time abstractionist who has more recently turned romantic recorder of English architecture in sensitive prints and watercolors and in 1952 produced the remarkable variation on the theme of Giorgione's Tempest (Plate 169)

Some twenty years ago I studied the work of Aubrey Beardsley (1872-1898) in which the fin de siècle spirit of the 90's finds its most striking representation I knew well a distinguished group of his drawings in the strange New York apartment of an ardent collector who appreciated the macabre tone of the illustrator's work Such elegant black drawings on snow-white paper were the sole adornment on the jet black walls of this collector's living room

In a review of The Limit by Ada Levenson, friend of Oscar Wilde and of Aubrey Beardsley, the following perceptive statement was recently made by John Mason Brown —"On many counts she deserves remembrance as one of those figures who though minor, are minor in a major way." Beardsley, the sophisticate, deserves remembrance, for of him it is also true that —"The world into which . .

[he] leads us is a vanished universe "

Drawings by Beardsley exert a compulsion of their own because of their crisp linear finality (Plate 164), their balance of blacks and whites, their atmospheric elegance

I wonder whether Beardsley drawings influenced Picasso in his pure line illustrations as they undoubtedly did Toulouse-Lautrec and other French artists? I ask the question because Beardsley's drawings were reproduced about 1900 in a Catalan weekly which also published some early illustrations by Picasso before he left Barcelona for Paris

Walter Richard Sickert (1860-1942) was a witty conversationalist, prolific writer, and painter of an often vulgar world Sickert admired Charles Keene In advance of his countrymen he appreciated Whistler, whose Arrangement in Black and Grey Sickert took to France for exhibition at the Salon of 1883 The trip stimulated his interest in the Impressionists and above all, Degas Sickert repudiated Whistler when he fell under Degas' spell, yet he was unable to give his own figures (Plate 167) the convincing reality that marks even the slightest sketch by the French master Life does not throb in Sickert's human beings He just missed endowing his figures with the pulsating vitality, punctuated by gesture, that glorifies similar subjects by the French master

The War and Post-War production of contemporary English artists is not sufficiently appreciated because inadequately shown in our museums More is the pity, for, internationally viewed, the English revival in the graphic arts is almost as impressive as the Italian Reluctantly, I omit examples of the work of a whole group of contemporary Englishmen — Wyndham Lewis, Duncan Grant, Paul Nash, Stanley Spencer, John Tunnard, Edward Burra, and Ben Nicholson

I single out just two English contemporaries of impressive stature: — Henry Moore, audacious sculptor, powerful draughtsman, and Graham Sutherland, graphic artist of originality and daring palette

Henry Moore (b 1898) is a giant in the field of English art, a true creative genius of our time He is endowed with acute powers of observation His warmth won me years ago We were "in tune" from the moment when I called for him at the railroad station in Boston in 1946 He politely expressed his love for art museums but was impatient to visit first the Peabody Museum of Archaeology and Ethnology at Harvard. The afternoon at the Peabody

CALICO PIE

was memorable As we went from room to room, Moore "devoured" sculpture with his eyes He repeatedly touched Central American stones and Mayan objects that impressed him. He taught me to "see" sculpture as never before In watching him it was clear why he projected massive forms based on his observation of human beings His *forms* (Plate 171) are revolutionary creations carved out of massive, oddly shaped, weighty stones As we moved slowly from object to object there was one constant refrain —"truth to material", "truth to material." He was intrigued by Negro, by Mexican, by Oceanic art but, most surprisingly of all, by Eskimo handicraft. The words "material," "simplicity," "vitality" illumined his perceptive comments Only our Max Weber, two decades ago, had spoken to me with equal conviction and, strangely enough, both men talked about the art of Masaccio (1401-1429); also about the art of primitive peoples; about Picasso.

No wonder an artist with Moore's broad ranging interests and with so striking, so persuasive a personality exerts a deep influence on his contemporaries.

Moore is a bold, imaginative artist who respects *"material"* whether stone, wood, or metal His inspirations are deep rooted. They stem primarily from nature, from traditional as well as strangely varied artistic sources

Moore is the son of a Yorkshire miner During the bombing of London he gave impressive proof of his originality, his love of his fellow men Commissioned by the War Artists' Committee at the instigation of the distinguished connoisseur Sir Kenneth Clark, Moore recorded in a series of touching underground shelter drawings (Plate 170) the ruthless impact of war on human beings James Johnson Sweeney is right in stressing the fact that while Moore's humanity is more assertive in such drawings than in his earlier and later work, the *forms* are still a sculptor's forms. Sweeney refers to the drawings as —"Michelangelesque in their power—perhaps better like Masaccio in their

*"Calico Pie is a poem which suggests autumn leaves fluttering to the ground No one could have written it but Edward Lear.
"If you were once a child whose spirits flagged for days, yet rose at a remembered scent, a scrap of song, what he says should affect you If you are now old, you must know how little there is left to grasp of all there was—of all which might have been Last but not least, do you believe in fantasy—in humour that is subtly complex? Lear loved to invent words as simple as their sound, and others with overtones
' When you are weary with complexity, stark reality, and pressure, he leads you off towards the delicious world of dreams. It is a child's world, too, where simplicity is essential, and relationships exist between incongruous things .
"Here is what Edward Lear wrote and drew for children . . . far away and many years ago."—Philip Hofer

182

JOHN JAMES JOYCE CRAYON 1930 MRS W MURRAY CRANE, N Y

simple monumentality--a return to his early Florentine enthusiasm At the same time there is a nightmare quality, a haunted quality with which his emotion has dyed these papers . "

An aid in understanding Moore's *forms,* taken from nature as sources of suggestion, is through a study (Plate 171) of his drawings, which he looks upon as stepping stones in the creation of his sculpture

Graham Sutherland (b 1903) is a surprising colorist, an artist of feeling turned naturalist His exciting approach to segments of nature, free from what he terms *superficial reality,* deserves far more attention than he has received in America His early small, etched romantic landscapes and his watercolors were in the Samuel Palmer tradition which influenced Piper as well as other English artists of the present generation

In the last twenty years, however, Sutherland has blazed an imaginative trail entirely his own, even though affected by Picasso's creations, notably the *Guernica* Sutherland delights in inventing *forms* (Plate 173) as does his friend Henry Moore in sculpture However, Sutherland's forms are usually based on *details* of objects in nature, not like Moore's, which are based on the human figure Sutherland is fascinated by palms, thistles, gourds,

root forms (Plate 172) fallen trees, boulders, and insects His exciting series of thorn tree sketches executed in dashing color and nervous line, should be thought of as connected with, or as a prelude to, his ambitious 1943 undertaking--a dramatic *Crucifixion* for the Church of St Matthew, Northampton, England, the same church for which Henry Moore was commissioned to carve his monumental *Madonna and Child* Sutherland's tense and moving *Crucifixion* is dramatic with little regard for ' formal ' beauty. In this, as in most of his paintings and drawings, a tense line heightens the quality of his draughtsmanship, strikingly suggestive of the emotional, expressionist Isenheim Altar of Matthias Grunewald (c 1455-1528)

Sutherland's artistic roots are nourished not only by Grünewald, one of his favorite masters, but among his English forebears, Blake, Turner, Samuel Palmer, and Paul Nash Yet Sutherland has evolved a personal idiom He arrests our attention through his vigorous drawing and by his unexpected use of blues, yellows, and pinks

Once again tradition and example have exerted their influence on a distinguished contemporary not to bind or hamper, but to free him for the conception of the new and the challenging that the great of every era must find for himself and his generation

PIPER REGENCY SQUARE AQUATINT AND ETCHING 1939

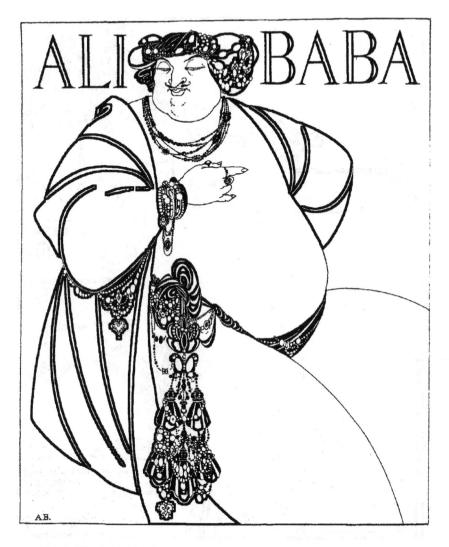

PLATE 164 · BEARDSLEY, AUBREY · *Ali Baba* · DRAWING, INK · C 1894 · 9⅞₁₆″ x 7¹¹⁄₁₆″ · Fogg
Museum, Harvard University

This swank, sophisticated, decorative drawing has in it more than linear distinction and a masterly use of
black and white Exotic suavity and elegance are tellingly rendered It is a personal, expressive mode,
perfectly adapted to the illustration of Oscar Wilde's *Salomé* or the pages of the *Yellow Book* Beardsley
in his daring drawings is the supreme representative of the '90's His work is evocative of an entire period
in English art and literature With Lautrec he represents the *Art Nouveau* movement in graphic design

184

PLATE 165 · VALLOTTON, FELIX · *The Flute* · WOODCUT · 1896 · 12¼″ x 9⅞″   Museum of
Modern Art, New York (Gift of Victor S. Riesenfeld)

This woodcut by a Swiss is placed in the English Chapter, opposite the Beardsley, for obvious and self-
explanatory reasons. Vallotton was a friend of Vuillard and Bonnard (pages 63-4 and Plates 57-8).

PLATE 166 · PALMER, SAMUEL · *Leaf from a Sketch-Book* · DRAWING, PEN AND INK · 1824
8⅜" x 7½" · Victoria and Albert Museum, London

Poetic vision is implicit in this fine sketch as in all of Palmer's work

PLATE 167 · SICKERT, WALTER · *"My Dream* ." · ETCHING · 1922 · 11¹¹/₁₆" x 7¾" · Metropolitan
Museum of Art, New York

Even though Sickert was profoundly influenced by French art and more particularly by Degas, whom he
venerated, he spoke of himself as a pupil of Whistler His etching technique substantiates the statement

187

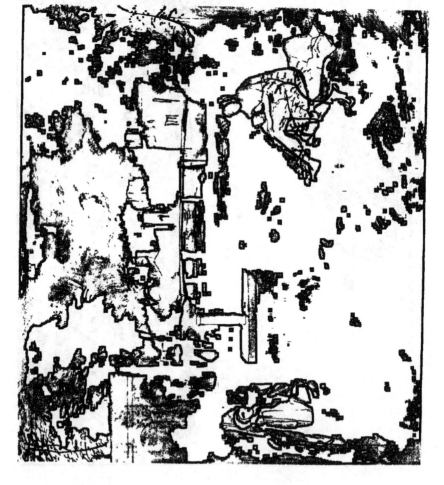

PLATE 168 (opposite) · PALMER, SAMUEL *Cornfield by Moonlight with Evening Star* WATERCOLOR, GOUACHE, AND PEN c 1830 · 7¼" x 11¾" Sir Kenneth Clark, London (Courtesy Durlacher Brothers)

One of Palmer's remarkable drawings of a moonlit landscape, showing the influence of William Blake

PLATE 169 (left) · PIPER, JOHN *Copy of Giorgione's "Tempest"* DRAWING, WASH 1952 15" x 15" Fogg Museum, Harvard University

Not only is this handsome drawing a variation on the well-known painting by Giorgione (1478-1510), but in it we also see striking reminders of Palmer's tree drawing

PLATE 170 · MOORE HENRY · *Woman Seated in the Underground* DRAWING, CHALK, PEN AND INK WITH WATERCOLOR · 1941 · 18½″ x 14¾″   Tate Gallery, London

This is one of the finest underground bomb shelter drawings done during World War II, when material for sculpture was scarce.

PLATE 171 · MOORE, HENRY · *Three Standing Figures* · DRAWING, WATERCOLOR AND CRAYON
1948 11½″ x 9½″ · Fogg Museum, Harvard University

As in his sculpture, the holes are for purpose of contrast They enhance the three-dimensional quality of the form, the organic shape Moore is mistakenly credited with the invention of the use of organic and hollowed-out forms which, as Soby has pointed out, were invented by the modern Belgian sculptor, Georges Vantongerloo

PLATE 172 · SUTHERLAND, GRAHAM · *Blasted Oak* · DRAWING, PEN AND WASH   1941   15″ x 12″
Sir Colin Anderson, London

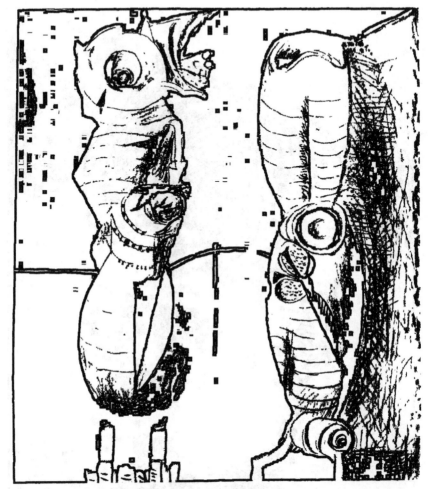

PLATE 173 · SUTHERLAND, GRAHAM   *Study for Standing Forms* · DRAWING, INK AND CRAYON
1950 · 22½" x 17¾" · Fogg Museum, Harvard University

"People ask about my 'Standing Forms' What do they mean? They do not, of course, *mean* anything
The forms are based on principles of organic growth (with which I have always been preoccupied) To me
they are monuments and presences   "—Graham Sutherland over B B C , September 1952

"   . the microscope and telescope," says Sir Kenneth Clark, "have so greatly enlarged the range of our
vision that the snug, sensible nature which we can see with our own eyes has ceased to satisfy our imagina-
tions We know that by our new standards of measurement the most extensive landscape is practically the
same size as the hole through which the burrowing ant escapes from our sight We know that every form
we perceive is made up of smaller and yet smaller forms, each with a character foreign to our experience
.   . One of the disconcerting things in Mr Sutherland's work is the disappearance of a humanist scale—
the way in which a thorn tree or a group of dead thistles suddenly assumes colossal proportions   .."

PLATE 174   POSADA, JOSE GUADALUPE · *Calavera Zapatista (Death as a Zapatista)* · RELIEF
ENGRAVING ON METAL · C 1910 · 8⅝" x 8¾" · Museum of Modern Art, New York

In this famous print Posada combines political caricature with the dance of death tradition so popular in
modern Mexico The Zapatistas were followers of Emilio Zapata, the Agrarian leader in the Mexican
revolution which began in 1910, three years before Posada's death Rivera, Orozco, Siqueiros all made
portraits of Zapata in their lithographs and murals

194

Chapter 8
MEXICO

THE best graphic works of the Western Hemisphere have their roots in the traditions of European art

José Guadalupe Posada (1851-1913), popular Mexican illustrator, made line cuts for Penny Broadsheets (Plate 174) depicting the life, interests, and superstitions of the poor He is the vital creator of a type of genre art in Mexico Though less distinguished than Goya, he calls to mind the Spaniard's remarkable prints. Posada attracted a host of younger followers to his folk art

Mexican mural painting, which burgeoned under government approval after the Obregon Revolution, is of important communal significance The aspirations of the nationalist fresco painters were stated in 1922, in the *Manifesto of the Syndicate of Technical Workers, Painters, and Sculptors*—a manifesto very different from the 1910 manifesto of the Italian Futurists.

The Mexican manifesto repudiated "so-called easel art" as "aristocratic" These resounding words were used —"We hail the *monumental* expression of art because such art is *public prop-*

erty" Painted on the walls of public buildings, it was popular art for the masses Its chief standard bearers were Rivera, Siqueiros, and Orozco.

Diego Rivera (b. 1886) (Plate 176), *José Clemente Orozco* (1883-1949) (Plate 175), and *David Alfaro Siqueiros* (b 1898) (Plate 178) are the acknowledged leaders of the most powerful school of mural painting in the Western World. based on a thorough understanding of the true *fresco* (painting on wet plaster) tradition of Italy, but used in Mexico in the service of radical social and economic ideas Their studies made of the aesthetics and forms of Italian mural painting are more important even than their use of fresco Siqueiros who now prefers duco to fresco has also been much influenced by surrealism

Though Mexican mural painting and Mexican graphic art are largely political in subject, the politics of the leading artists differ Rivera though not a success in the U S S R is a Communist whereas Orozco is opposed to all authoritarian dogma—in Guadalajara one can see his great mural in which the cross, the swastika and the hammer-and-sickle are jumbled together with equal suspicion and contempt In his art he expresses his passionate concern for the poor and oppressed without involving himself in the political exploitation of their misery.

Jean Charlot (b. 1898) is Paris-born We couple his name with that of Rivera and Orozco Charlot painted with the two giants on their overwhelmingly expressive projects so full of content In his weighty, moving lithograph of *Mother and Child* (Plate 177) the influence of his 1926 stay in Yucatan persists If there were no other evidence, this print alone would justify us in considering him the leader of color lithography in the Western World

195

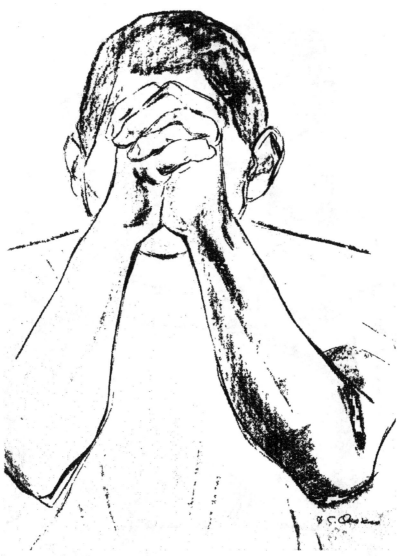

PLATE 175 · OROZCO, JOSE CLEMENTE · *Figure with Clasped Hands* · DRAWING, CRAYON · C 1923
25¹³⁄₁₆″ x 18¹¹⁄₁₆″ · Fogg Museum, Harvard University

This calm, monumental drawing illustrates the type of distinguished draughtsmanship that gives solid form
to the visions that Orozco creates, even if here there is little hint of the intense emotion, the symbolic moral
protest that characterize the master's painting, such as his *Martyrdom of St Stephen.*

PLATE 176 · RIVERA, DIEGO · *Sleeping Woman* · DRAWING, PENCIL · 1921 · 23″ x 18″ · Fogg
Museum, Harvard University

Powerful draughtsmanship such as this is used by Rivera in his mural painting.

PLATE 177 · CHARLOT, JEAN · *Mother and Child* · COLOR LITHOGRAPH · 1934 · 27″ x 11″ · Museum of Fine Arts, Boston

In this weighty, moving, simplified picture we see in both the style and the serious point of view the all-pervading influence of Rivera and Orozco, whom Charlot assisted in their large and powerful decorative schemes in Mexico There are evidences here also of his stay in Yucatan in 1926

PLATE 178 · SIQUEIROS, DAVID ALFARO · *Moisés Sáenz* · LITHOGRAPH · 1931 · 21½" x 16¼"
Museum of Modern Art, New York (Inter-American Fund)

In this anguished head the artist delivers his message with a ringing blow, without restraint That is characteristic of all the work of Siqueiros, a leader of the modern Mexican renaissance In much of his work there are thinly veiled reminders of Pre-Columbian sculpture

199

PLATE 179 · CASTELLANOS, JULIO · *The Injured Eye* · LITHOGRAPH · 1935 · 18¼″ x 10½″
Museum of Modern Art, New York (Inter-American Fund)

This accomplished, realistic work reflects Castellanos' ever-present sympathy for the masses as well as his technical skill.

PLATE 180 · MEZA, GUILLERMO · *Giantess* · DRAWING, PEN AND INK · 1941 · 25⅝″ x 19⅞″
Museum of Modern Art, New York (Gift of Edgar Kaufmann, Jr.)

There is little in this powerful, plastic, impressive drawing, in which scale is perfectly realized, to suggest
Meza's Surrealist preoccupations

Chapter 9
UNITED STATES

NO gulf separates American art from the other cultures considered in earlier chapters I shall try, however, to call attention in the text and in the captions to certain specifically American nuances and overtones

We have left for last the consideration of American graphic art, for thus only can we visualize in proper perspective and with necessary humility the inescapable link between European and American art

You may find it fascinating to see how, after long devotion to a realist tradition, we have absorbed the influence of new European movements, shaping them to our needs Have we as yet produced any work as important in quality or in originality as that by such prolific and versatile men of genius as Cézanne, Seurat, Picasso, and Matisse?

The United States was long isolationist in art as in politics We were preoccupied with developing a vast continent We took little note of the currents and counter-currents the ferment in European art In cityscape pictures the natural bent of our artists in the Nineteenth Century was to depict in a traditional realist American mode, the varied, teeming life of the melting pot. The landscape painters were frankly lyric, sentimental and romantic

A change took place in the 90's due to the widely acclaimed painting of Whistler and Sargent even though they were both such confirmed expatriates that they were more at home in England than in their native land.

James Abbott McNeill Whistler (1834-1903) learned the etcher's technique making maps for the United States Coast Survey As etcher he was compared, by American collectors at least, to Rembrandt and Goya —an overstatement that, even after all these years, is annoying, since Rembrandt and Goya were two of the greatest artists who ever lived and surely the *unequaled* masters of etching of all time

Whistler went abroad to paint. On reaching Paris, he was influenced by Courbet and Manet He was admired by Degas and Fantin-Latour In London he crossed swords with Ruskin, which led to the famous law suit. Whistler was a caustic critic, a prince of aesthetes, a reckless, irritating wit, an all-round stormy petrel, and a lover of Japanese objects

Enthusiasm for Whistler's works, paintings and prints (Plate 182) alike, almost universal in my youth, has since been tempered To many contemporary eyes, brought up on "stronger meat," he seems thin, too exquisite, too precious But that does not take account of the fact that as an individualist as an independent, his paintings reflect an interest in form and in decoration in the truly modern meaning of those words, that in the most fundamental sense his interests make him an American ancestor of modern art. The great public uninfluenced by changing fashion and theories is still hypnotized by his name Quite rightly they acclaim his Louvre masterpiece which Whistler called (significantly from a modern point of view) *Arrangement in Black and Grey* Actually it is a portrait of his mother It was acquired for $800 by the French Government after going about unwanted for many years But four decades later, one of the most popular pictures in the world, it was valued at a half-million dollars

Whistler's influence on the cityscape print is far from negligible, but above all else, we should remember that he insisted on *freedom* for the artist

SARGENT VERNON LEE PENCIL 1889 ASHMOLEAN MUSEUM, OXFORD UNIVERSITY

HOMER THE HERRING NET CHARCOAL AND WHITE CHALK C 1885 COOPER UNION MUSEUM, N Y

John Singer Sargent (1856-1925) was like Whistler, an expatriate He was a fashionable, unimaginative painter He was not at his best in his academic portraits in oil nor in his overrated Boston and Cambridge murals But his watercolors and his early pencil portraits show evidence of his great gift and enormous facility

John Ciardi, the poet, makes a distinction between our expatriates and our native American artists, particularly useful at this point He says — "Now and then, as in the best of Longfellow and in such native idylls as Whittier's 'Telling the Bees' (and certainly in parts of 'Snowbound') the richness of a native feeling emerges whole and unselfconscious   often, however, the American poets seem to have it as their major business to prove their culture was as wide, their vocabulary as Latinate, their sensibility as nice, as that of, say, an Oxford don "*

*Mid-Century American Poets edited by John Ciardi New York, Twayne Publishers, Inc , 1950, pp. ix-x

Ciardi's comments about expatriates seem to me to apply to Whistler and Sargent His remarks about Longfellow and Whittier have equal validity for some of our best men — Winslow Homer, Eakins, Bellows, Sloan, and Hopper

Winslow Homer (1836-1910) was a Yankee of seafaring ancestry Like Eakins, the sober realist, and Ryder the visionary, Homer was untouched by French Impressionism although he went to the International Exhibition in Paris in 1867 Homer's realism was American He never lost interest in form Critics and public alike take pride in his achievement Never in eclipse, he is today acclaimed as an American dramatic realist His works are accorded respect and admiration because of his powerful directness of vision —on the stormy coast of Maine or its more tranquil countryside, on the hurricane-swept beaches of Florida, on the lakes and trout streams in the heart of the Adirondacks When into such unspoiled scenes any living thing is introduced, the heart and eye are satisfied, be-

203

cause of the technical skill and the love with which man and nature are joined in convincing unity

Homer's long apprenticeship started in Civil War days as a faithful recorder of camp life Through woodcuts and engravings of soldiers or of Negroes. of school scenes or of children at play (p 239) his honest drawings were reproduced in popular magazines like *Harper's Weekly* Such commissions strengthened his inborn capacity as a draughtsman They prepared him for his subsequent technical accomplishments in watercolor, as in oil After 1876 he dedicated his talents to painting Homer lived and worked in England, during two years, close to the angry pounding sea, just as in his home at Prout's Neck, Maine Late in life he voiced a prophecy that has come true —' You will see in the future I will live by my watercolors "

Thomas Eakins (1844-1916), whose name we bracket with that of Homer, was acclaimed only after his death as one of our great American realists The two artists were very different in outlook, practice, and training Eakins, a powerful, conservative portrait painter of rare distinction, took for his subjects the serious people in his immediate milieu Always an artist of probity, he was austere and cerebral. He was interested in perspective, anatomy, and scientific truth.

Homer worked out of doors Eakins, whether indoors or out, collected his data and then with deliberation brought his meticulous paintings to completion in his studio, whether he chose for subject matter Dr Gross in his clinic (Plate 183) or John Biglen (Plate 181), the professional oarsman, rowing on the still Schuylkill River as it flows through his native Philadelphia.

Eakins has left us no prints and but few drawings Those we have are forthright and uncompromising, as are his solid portraits of penetrating depth, on which his fame rests

In 1908 there occurred an artistic event still vividly remembered by the older generation William Glackens (Plate 187), Maurice Prendergast (p. 205), John Sloan (Plate 185), George Luks, Ernest Lawson, Everett Shinn, and their leaders, Robert Henri and Arthur B Davies, rebelled against the National Academy This revolt was brought into focus by their exhibition at the Macbeth Gallery as the rebel *Eight*. They were stigmatized by the academicians as the "Ash Can" School because some of them chose their subject matter from the seething slums of New York Their aim was to liberalize American art

John Sloan (1871-1951) (Plate 185), lover of

New York, painter, etcher, author, and teacher. was at no time an ivory tower artist He was a city realist in art as in life, developing his technique and skill by long hard work on a Philadelphia newspaper He never studied in Europe, but as Daumier for the newspaper *Charivari*, as Homer for *Harper's Weekly*, as Ben Shahn in the poster field today— Sloan worked for the leading popular magazines

He was thirty when he started to exhibit For twenty years thereafter he failed to sell a picture Late in life, as the beloved dean of American artists he won financial reward, personal honors, and the recognition that he deserved as an independent of integrity and character

George Bellows (1882-1925) (Plate 184), beloved human being, distinguished draughtsman, was also, like his gifted painter friend Eugene Speicher, an enthusiast for boxing and baseball Bellows came to New York from Ohio to study with the then influential teacher, Robert Henri He became a happy member of the "Ash Can" group which was stimulated by noise, by crowds, by tenements, by streets, by the waterfront, by bars, by the prize ring, and by the slums

Bellows' famous, well composed print of *A Stag at Sharkey's* (Plate 184), both in its subject matter and in its basic design, is one of the most effective lithographs left us by this exuberant realist—a typical work close to the heart of America

An event more significant for the future of American art than any efforts of *The Eight*, who held the center of the stage in New York for about five years, was the first and little understood exhibition of the work of Henri Matisse at the unorthodox "291" Gallery, so named from the number of Steichen's Fifth Avenue studio This gallery owed its vitality to the genius of the artist-photographer, Alfred Stieglitz, inspired by Edward Steichen The Matisse exhibition at "291" heralded the coming of other shows at that exciting little gallery They served to educate us visually in the advanced work of the moderns —the Americans, Marsden Hartley, John Marin (Plate 192), Max Weber (Plate 189a, b), and the Europeans, Toulouse-Lautrec, Picasso, and other Cubist and Expressionist experimenters

However, the first time that the great public— apart from the limited group that frequented "291" — felt the impact of the varied European movements was at the vast and revolutionary Armory show of 1913

Only a group of our artists, then young, a few dealers, like de Zayas and Charles Daniel; a few open-minded critics, like Pach, McBride, Wright Field, and Watson, a few independent collectors, like Quinn, Lillie Bliss, and Arensberg had anything good to say about the memorable event which puzzled the crowds that milled about the 69th Regiment Armory, New York Denunciation was passionate and almost universal

Nothing is more illuminating as a reflection of the temper of the time than what ex-President Theodore Roosevelt, an enlightened but critical layman, then wrote —"The recent 'International Exhibition of Modern Art' in New York was really noteworthy   No similar collection of the works of European 'moderns' has ever been exhibited in this country The exhibitors were quite right as to the need of showing to our people in this manner the art forces which of late have been at work in Europe, forces which cannot be ignored

"This does not mean that I in the least accept the view that these men take of the European extremists whose pictures were here exhibited It is true, as the champions of these extremists say, that there can be no life without change, no development without change, and that to be afraid of what is different or unfamiliar is to be afraid of life It is no less true, however, that change may mean death and not life, and retrogression instead of development. . . There was one note entirely absent from the exhibition and that was the note of the commonplace   .

"For all of this there can be only hearty praise But this does not in the least mean that the extremists   are entitled to any praise, save, perhaps, that they have helped to break fetters. Probably in any reform movement, any progressive movement, in any field of life, the penalty for avoiding the commonplace is a liability to extravagance It is vitally necessary to move forward and to shake off the dead hand, often the fossilized dead hand, of the reactionaries, and yet we have to face the fact that there is apt to be a lunatic fringe among the votaries of any forward movement   Take the picture which for some reason is called 'A Naked Man Going Down Stairs.' There is in my bathroom a really good Navajo rug which, on any proper interpretation of the Cubist theory, is a far more satisfactory and decorative picture .   I was interested to find that a man of scientific attainments who had likewise looked at the pictures had been struck, as I was, by their resemblance to the later work of the palaeolithic artists of the French and Spanish caves .   to be found in a recent number of the 'Revue d'Ethnographie.' .   This stumbling

effort in his case [the palaeolithic artist] represented progress, and he was entitled to great credit for it Forty thousand years later, when entered into artificially and deliberately, it represents only a smirking pose of retrogression, and is not praiseworthy   the exhibition contained so much of extraordinary merit that it is ungrateful even to mention an omission   I am not speaking of the acknowledged masters, of Whistler, Puvis de Chavannes, Monet, nor of John's children, nor of Cézanne's old woman with a rosary; nor of Redon's marvellous color-pieces—a worthy critic should speak of these All I am trying to do is to point out why a layman is grateful to those who arranged this exhibition "*

While Theodore Roosevelt was far more open-minded and generous than other people at the time, it is also true that on many of his points critics and laymen today would disagree

Because the art he failed to comprehend has become widely accepted let us now turn to the illustrations of American graphic works created in large part after the Armory show.

It will be recalled that earlier in the narrative,

PRENDERGAST ORANGE MARKET COLOR MONOTYPE, C 1910
MUSEUM OF MODERN ART, N Y

*The Works of Theodore Roosevelt, National Edition, vol XII, "Literary Essays." New York, Charles Scribner's Sons, 1926, pp 147-151.

speaking of Degas, it was urged that we be as tolerant as catholic in taste, and as understanding as he was in his open-minded attitude about Twentieth Century works of art

As you look at the individual pictures, whether they are conservative or radical, it may be useful to keep in mind certain accepted criteria of artistic quality Is there structural clarity of form? Is there clear distinction of planes? Is there flexibility and sensitiveness of touch? Is there feeling for the medium? Is there suggestive power? Is there expressiveness? Is there artistic economy? Is there originality of concept? Try these tests for yourselves in the pictures that follow Obviously not every test just cited can be applied to every picture

John Marin (1870-1953), on his return to America after six years in Europe, was shown by Alfred Stieglitz at "291" and regularly thereafter It was Stieglitz who opened our eyes early in the century to Marin's gift as a watercolor painter

"Marin fits perfectly," Soby has written, "an ingrained, romantic image of the gifted Yankee,

laconic, profound, fiercely independent, honest, gentle and proud " Marin loved the watercolor medium He took for his themes hectic New York streets, skyscrapers (Plate 192), mountain landscapes (Plate 191), or scenes on his well-loved coast of Maine His early cityscapes show the influence of Whistler. In 1910 his semi-abstract, pulsating, expressive style developed rapidly Stimulated by the thinking of Cézanne and then of Picasso and Braque, he formed his own style He should not be pigeonholed with any group He is always his own man He is little understood abroad, where the belief appears to be current that we overrate his resources

We illustrate Marin with a work reminiscent of Cézanne (Plate 191), a firm, calm, impressive semi-abstraction, and also by one of his improvisations on a New York theme (Plate 192)

Charles Sheeler (b. 1883) (Plates 195, 197) and *Ben Shahn* (b 1898) (Plate 208) have both at times accepted Twentieth Century industrial patronage The Metropolitan Museum held an exhibition of

FEININGER LEHNSTADT WOODCUT 1919

contemporary art, a few years ago, sponsored by the Pepsi-Cola Company, and more recently a group of pictures was shown at the Massachusetts Institute of Technology—works commissioned by the Standard Oil Company of New Jersey These pictures convey a sense of the far-flung empire of the petroleum industry This certainly is "art with a function," art intended to instruct Whatever the underlying motive of industrial patrons may be, it is important to keep in mind that the artist is asked to accept the commission with the understanding that he is to paint or draw specific subject matter, but he is given complete freedom to work in his own personal style In this age some of our best artists like Sheeler and Shahn have, in fact, found great industrial plants stimulating

They have produced pictures of factories in which the lessons of Cubism are not lost, or in Shahn's case they have produced magnificent posters, for the O W.I , for labor unions, for radio broadcasting companies Ben Shahn's *Welders* may be compared to the work of the great Italian Fifteenth Century fresco painter, Piero della Francesca Tradition is now at the service of indus-

try, even in the hands of one of our great socially minded artists

Lyonel Feininger (b 1871) "Feininger's art," says Frederick S Wight, "is composed of opposites —on the one side, reticence, withdrawal and discipline, on the other, sensibility and human warmth ."

Music plays a subtle role in his background as in that of Paul Klee There is order in Feininger's work akin to that in musical composition, which he has successfully incorporated into his disciplined painting in watercolor and line

He with Klee and Kandinsky, you will recall, was associated with Walter Gropius at the famous Bauhaus in its great days. There Feininger was resident teacher for over twenty years He is fundamentally American in his art (Plate 196) in spite of almost fifty years spent abroad Sent to Germany to study music, he promptly turned to the graphic arts instead, producing cartoons for Berlin and Paris papers As early as 1906 he drew "comics" for the *Chicago Tribune* From such beginnings he progressed, in a combination of precise drawing and painting, to severe, angular representations of

207

houses and to pictures of sea, sky, and ships. These are not transcripts of nature but rather a combination of Cubist and abstract designs based on nature

Stuart Davis (b 1894) grew up in conservative surroundings His father as art director of the *Philadelphia Press* had employed Sloan and Luks before they joined *The Eight* in New York The Armory show, in which Davis exhibited, shocked him into a new appreciation of painting based on the picture as a reality in itself, not just the record of a visual impression The stimulus to turn "modern" Davis received in studying the work of Gauguin, van Gogh, and Matisse at the Armory show Thus began his determination to develop a pictorial philosophy of his own, which took final shape during his two years in Paris (1928-1929), where he observed the methods employed by Toulouse-Lautrec, Seurat, Leger, Picasso, and Aubrey Beardsley Such facts, unfortunately, do not help us very much to understand the particular work illustrated on page 207, an apparently simple geometrical abstraction with its strange, vital, linear motion, its merest suggestion of "davits" as we know them.*

A statement by Stuart Davis himself may cast light on this and on other puzzling abstract pictures —"So many people think a picture is a replica of a thing or a story about some kind of situation To an artist, on the other hand, it is an object which has been formed by an individual in response to emotional and intellectual needs His purpose is never to counterfeit a subject but to develop a new subject " Now, is not that just what Davis has done here? "Davits" were simply his inspiration He did not imitate them Out of them he developed an attractive abstract design entirely his own

Alexander Calder (b 1898) (Plate 201), a brilliantly ingenious sculptor, is known chiefly as the inventor of "mobiles"—capricious wire, wood, and metal arrangements In Europe, as in America, he is appreciated as the most original of the younger American artists Although his technique is more solid, due to his interest in abstract design, he reminds one inevitably in his studied simplicity, in his touch of fantasy, in his many waggish creations of animals, of Edward Lear. "If he [Calder] had not been an American," says the astute English art critic Eric Newton,** "he would not have had the vitality, the sense of play, and the engineer's love

of metal that started him off and if he had not gone to Paris in his formative years, he might have remained a playboy all his life He is a product of American vigor and French education That makes him more robust than Klee, more practical than Miro His humor is broader than theirs He has a less elusive and more direct appeal "

I have watched the growth of *Jack Levine* (b 1915) (Plate 204) from his early boyhood As a disciple of Denman Ross and Harold Zimmerman, he was trained as a draughtsman in the great tradition of the old masters From that springboard he has developed a personal, modern idiom in which drawing is still at the base of his original creations He is aware of the uses to which distortion, abstraction, expressionism can be put He either uses them or experiments with them but is not enslaved by modern trends and, like the great innovators, the rebels of the Nineteenth and Twentieth Centuries, he haunts museums and learns his lessons well

He uses distortions and enlargements of shape deliberately and consciously to accelerate the tempo of his impact In his own words, he seeks "to distort images in an attempt to weld the drama of man and his environment " More convincing, however, than any of his words are the works themselves in which he comments on the foibles of his contemporaries with caustic irony. An interest in Soutine and Rouault seem to me implicit in his work He reacts to the oppressive problems of our day with profound cynicism.

Max Weber (b 1881) (Plate 189a, b) is, like Matisse, Rouault, Picasso, Villon, and Maillol, one of the grand old men still active in our time

Weber is, I am sure, unaware that some thirty

BASKIN. PORCUPINE WOODCUT 1951

*"Davit—projecting curved arms of timber or iron used with tackle to raise or lower a boat as from the deck to water "—*Webster's Dictionary*
**The New York Sunday Times*, August 10, 1952

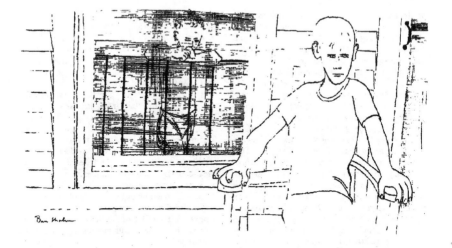

SHAHN BOY ON PORCH INK 1946 DR COTTER HIRSCHBERG, DENVER

years ago he taught me a valuable lesson I have tried to keep it in mind whenever I have failed to understand the work of a pioneer One Sunday morning a neighbor telephoned that he would like to bring Max Weber to "Shady Hill" to see me I hesitated for I feared there was little, if anything, in my collection that I could show the artist who is today the dean of American moderns; who had but recently returned from Paris where he had persuaded Matisse to turn teacher for a brief period, who was interested in the *Fauve* movement as in distortion and later on in abstraction However, we met. I watched his roving eye. As in the case of Henry Moore we were in tune. When he left, after many hours, I realized that rarely, if ever, had I met an artist so informed, so deeply aware of the great tradition of drawing and painting He has continued to be an artist of astonishing originality, deeply versed and appreciative of the art of the past, sympathetic and understanding of every valid development in the art of the present. He is a dashing colorist who has never lost the emotional intensity of his race

Stanley William Hayter (b. 1901). Hayter must be included in even a short account of Twentieth Century graphic art because he is an influential teacher, an original creative artist, master prac-

titioner, appreciated for his technical innovations His Atelier 17 in Paris opened in 1924 It was visited by artists of such stature as Picasso, Miró, Kandinsky, Chagall, and Calder Hayter, an Englishman, greatly influenced New York artists in the 1940's

Many collectors of the older generation will fail to understand why certain skillful, orthodox engravers and a host of artists whose works were popular in their youth have been omitted Of all these favorites of a bygone day only Meryon and Whistler have been included because more than the others they still exert an influence on present-day artists.

And I have excluded some, I must avow, because though I have lived long, through generations of painters, both remembered and forgotten, my perspective has changed and I see them through the eyes of this day.

As to many artists of the present, lack of space precluded their inclusion I list some of them here — Barnett, Beal, Benton, Berman, Bloom, Capp, Curry, Dehn, Dickinson, Gropper, Hartley, Kent, Kuniyoshi, Luks, Mangravite, MacIver, Manship, Pascin, Pereira, Robinson, Spencer, Stuempfig, Thurber, Watkins, Wengenroth, Wood, Young, Zerbe, and Zorach

209

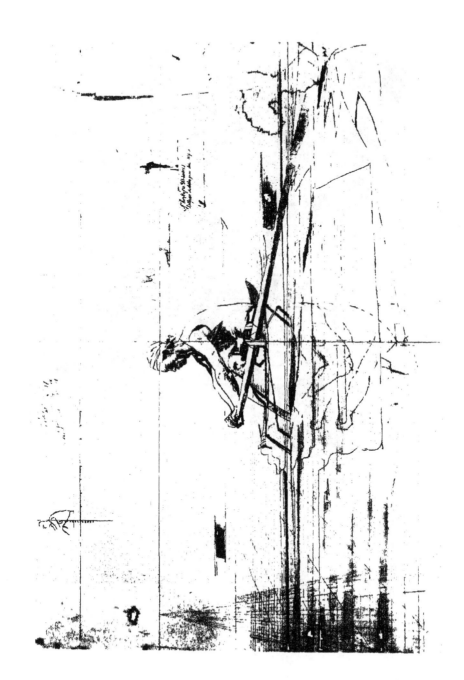

PLATE 181 (opposite) · EAKINS, THOMAS · *Perspective Drawing of John Biglen in a Single Scull* · DRAWING, PENCIL AND INK · c.1874 · 32" x 48" · Cornelius V. Whitney, New York

Eakins used this structural method in planning with care the skeleton of the design for his finely composed painting, a treasure of the Metropolitan Museum, New York

PLATE 182 (right) · WHISTLER, JAMES A McNEILL · *Black Lion Wharf* · ETCHING · 1859 · 6" x 8¹⁵⁄₁₆" Fogg Museum, Harvard University

Whistler is master of the etching medium This is one of the sixteen etchings of the *Thames Set*, which he started in 1859 and issued in 1871. They are all fine in draughtsmanship and done in a mode made famous by Meryon.

The *Black Lion Wharf* is crisp and sharp because the surface of the metal plate from which the picture was printed was wiped so that ink remained only in the lines

PLATE 183 · EAKINS, THOMAS · *Gross Clinic* · DRAWING, INDIA INK WASH · 1875 · 25⅝" x 19⅛"
Metropolitan Museum, New York

This is a copy by Eakins of his famous painting Light helps to emphasize the design Everything is tellingly rendered The firmly modeled features, the impressive brow, the beautiful silvery hair underline the personality of the great surgeon Was Eakins influenced, as Degas certainly was, by Holbein's astute practice of placing the subject in his accustomed setting?

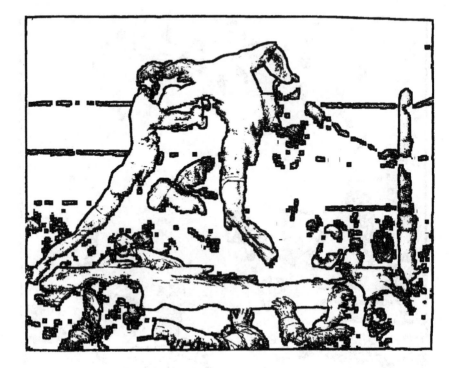

PLATE 184   BELLOWS, GEORGE · *The Stag at Sharkev s* · LITHOGRAPH · 1917 · 18¾" x 24" · The
Albert H Wiggin Collection in the Boston Public Library

This picture reflects preoccupation, in the early years of the century, with the American Scene *The Stag at Sharkey's* is the best-known lithograph by Bellows, a follower of *The Eight* Bellows loved to watch the exciting fights at Sharkey's Athletic Club in New York These boisterous, rough-and-tumble occasions were for men only, hence the "stag" at Sharkey's The prize fighters are caught in action and placed in the rectangle to perfection The lithograph illustrates Bellows' skill in rendering lusty, mundane American scenes, as typical in character as our national conventions with their noisy, exuberant crowds

213

PLATE 185 (above) · SLOAN,
JOHN   *Turning Out the Light*
ETCHING · 1905 · 4¾" x 6¾"
Museum of Modern Art (Gift of
Mrs John D Rockefeller, Jr)

PLATE 186 (left) · HOPPER,
EDWARD · *Evening Wind*
ETCHING · 1921   7" x 8¾"
Museum of Modern Art (Gift of
Mrs John D Rockefeller, Jr)

It is difficult to believe that early in the century a work like *Turning Out the Light* by Sloan, a member of *The Eight*, reflecting a mood as does the Hopper, should have been looked upon as radical

Hopper, completely American, is akin to Sloan in his choice of subject matter This straightforward, unembroidered, tender picture, so poetic in feeling, was made by Hopper only a few years after he took up etching Through subtle magic we are made to share the restlessness of a city dweller on a hot and humid summer night

PLATE 187   GLACKENS, WILLIAM   *Washington Square* · DRAWING, PENCIL AND WASH TOUCHED
WITH WHITE OVER BLUE CRAYON OUTLINES · 1913 · 24⅝" x 18¼" · Museum of Modern
Art, New York (Gift of Mrs John D Rockefeller, Jr.)

With skill Glackens records the varied attitudes and movements of children and grownups in an animated
scene of gay holiday-making

215

PLATE 188 · STERNE, MAURICE · *Italian Beggar* · DRAWING, PENCIL · 1906 · 16¾" x 14¾" · Professor and Mrs Charles A Robinson, Jr , Providence

No school can claim Sterne or Lebrun (Plate 205)—master draughtsmen Sterne has drawn inspiration from long sojourns in Italy, India, Burma, Java, Bali, and America His work, like Lebrun's, always experimental and yet traditional, has grown out of his early studies of Fifteenth Century Italian giants Mantegna, Pollaiuolo, Piero della Francesca—and Cézanne They are both of their time but refreshingly independent Their styles have changed much, but they have never cut their roots with the past

PLATE 189A (left) · WEBER, MAX · *Man Reading* · COLOR WOODCUT · 1918 · 4¾₁₆″ x 1⅞″ · Museum of Modern Art, New York (Gift of Mrs. John D. Rockefeller, Jr)

PLATE 189B (right) · WEBER, MAX *Figure* · COLOR WOODCUT · 1918 · 4⅜₁₆″ x 2″ · Museum of Modern Art, New York (Gift of Mrs John D Rockefeller, Jr)

A fascinating quality, inherent in all of Weber's original painting, is the feeling for color harmony Today many printmakers use color, but few achieve a harmony comparable to his In Weber's accomplished decorative woodcuts, skillfully placed in the rectangle of the paper, we see the influence of African Negro sculpture

217

PLATE 190 (above) · CEZANNE, PAUL · *View of Mt. Ste.-Victoire* · WATERCOLOR · c. 1886 · 14¼"
    x 19⅞" · Henry P McIlhenny, Philadelphia

PLATE 191 (below) · MARIN, JOHN · *White Mountain Country* · WATERCOLOR · 1927 19⅛" x 24"
    Fogg Museum, Harvard University

Note the firm, impetuous, characteristic, sharp-angled, slashing strokes realized with clarity by Marin's
fluent brush

PLATE 192 (right) MARIN, JOHN *Wool-worth Building, No 4* · ETCHING · 1913 · 12⅞" x 10½" · Museum of Modern Art, New York (Gift of Mrs John D Rockefeller, Jr)

PLATE 193 (below) · DELAUNAY, ROBERT *Eiffel Tower* · DRAWING, PEN AND INK · 1910 21½" x 19⅜" Museum of Modern Art, New York

These works by Cézanne, Delaunay, and Marin taken together tell their own story Marin, a Yankee in outlook and character, is fully aware of European trends, as the juxtapositions illustrate

PLATE 194 · DEMUTH, CHARLES · *Acrobats* · WATERCOLOR · 1920 · 13" x 7⅞" · Museum of Modern Art, New York (Gift of Mrs John D Rockefeller, Jr)

Demuth is one of the classicists of modern American painting whether in his architectural subjects or in his late exquisite, meticulous still-lifes, or best of all in his figure pieces of vaudeville performers such as these drawn in nervous lines combined with color and the use of dark areas that remind us of both Beardsley (Plate 164) and Lautrec (Plates 54, 55)

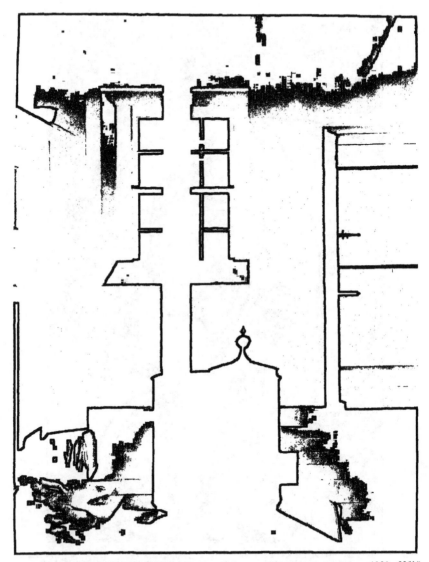

PLATE 195   SHEELER, CHARLES · *Interior with Stove* · DRAWING, CONTE CRAYON · 1932 · 28⅝"
x 20¾" · Capt. Edward Steichen, New York

This carefully drawn interior illustrates Sheeler's ability to achieve an effect of abstraction in a realistic
picture. He is a distinguished photographer as well as draughtsman and painter Boats, farm buildings
and skyscrapers (Plate 197), rendered with clarity and precision, interest him particularly.

221

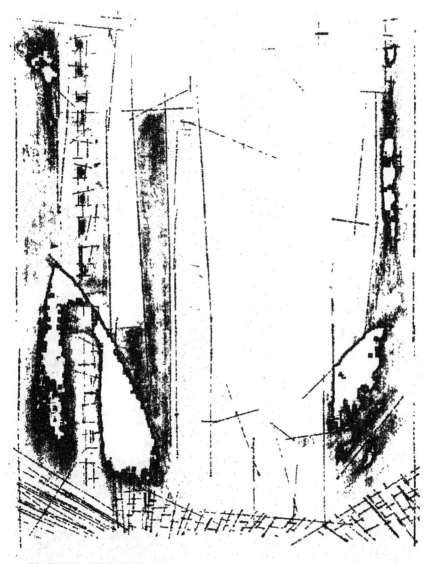

PLATE 196 · FEININGER, LYONEL · *Skyscrapers* · LITHOGRAPH · 1952 11″ x 8½″ · Fogg Museum,
Harvard University

Feininger, still a serene creator at over eighty, proves in this print the continuing vitality of Cubism, which
influenced him in 1912. This poetic variation on the theme of modern skyscrapers is a symbolic rather
than a literal interpretation, when compared with Sheeler's *Delmonico Building.*

222

PLATE 197 · SHEELER, CHARLES · *Delmonico Building* · LITHOGRAPH · 1926 · 10½" x 8½"
Fogg Museum, Harvard University

223

PLATE 198 (opposite) BURCH-FIELD, CHARLES · *The East Wind* · WATERCOLOR · 1918 · 18" x 22" Museum of Modern Art, New York (Gift of Mrs W. Murray Crane)

Burchfield has for some thirty years been recognized as one of our most accomplished watercolorists. He is best known for his portraits of drab Victorian houses, which he endows through some magic of vision and brush with character and distinction. He has, however, never abandoned his early lyric fantasies, in character akin to *The East Wind*. It is such work that best reflects his personality.

PLATE 199 (right) · GRAVES, MORRIS · *Blind Bird* · GOUACHE · 1940 30½" x 27" · Museum of Modern Art, New York

This is a strange, haunting bird of mystery, the type of Graves gouache drawing that Oliver W. Larkin has described so well as "forlorn birds enmeshed in white threads of moonlight."

This is a whimsical, but fundamentally serious, sketch It is not like the familiar, rollicking *New Yorker* type of drawing done in wiry lines, in which Steinberg lampoons American foibles Here the action of a musician is closely observed and set down with economy of means on a sheet of music. We suppress a smile as we share the absorption, the mood of the performer Steinberg carries forward in Twentieth Century terms the activity of such artistic forebears as Longhi (1702-85), Ghezzi (1674-1755), and Daumier (1808-79).

PLATE 201 · CALDER, ALEXANDER · *The Hostess* · WIRE CONSTRUCTION · 1928 · Height 11¼″
Museum of Modern Art, New York (Gift of Edward M M Warburg)

This drawing in wire is witty, waggish, and sophisticated The characterization is based on keen observation and endless practice; an ingenious invention by a shrewd Yankee tinker.

In these pictures, which face each other, we see the mature humor of their creators In spirit and fantasy Steinberg and Calder can well be compared to Klee and Miró

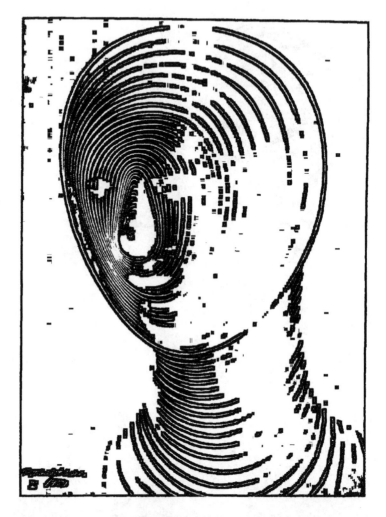

PLATE 202 (opposite) · TCHELITCHEW, PAVEL · *Portrait of Nikolas Kopekin* · DRAWING, SILVER-POINT · 1937 · 18⅞" x 12⅜" · Fogg Museum, Harvard University

PLATE 203 (above) TCHELITCHEW, PAVEL · *Head* DRAWING, BEIGE PENCIL · 1950 · 19¾" x 13¾" · Mr and Mrs R. Kirk Askew, Jr , New York

Note the precision of line in the portrait of *Kopekin*, drawn in the exacting medium of silverpoint, which does not permit of correction Note also in the *Head* that it is done in a continuous, unbroken line similar to heads by the engraver Mellan in the Seventeenth Century. These two drawings are, for our purposes, in the absence of color, more significant than studies for Tchelitchew's fantastic, brilliant paintings, *Phenomena* and *Hide and Seek*, which illustrate his other abiding interest—multiple images and the metamorphoses to which he subjects realistic forms.

229

PLATE 204 · LEVINE, JACK · *Ruth Gikow* · DRAWING, PENCIL · 1948   11″ x 8¼″ · Fogg Museum, Harvard University

Levine's bitter social comment and the caricatured types in his paintings, brilliant in color, do not prepare one for this recent reflection of the gentler side of his nature, which we need to know if we are to evaluate justly an individualist who is steeped in the art of the past. The drawing bears comparison with Plate 25, a lithograph by Toulouse-Lautrec

PLATE 205 · LEBRUN, RICO · *Beggar Woman* · DRAWING, INK AND CHALK · 26″ x 20″ · Arthur Sachs, Paris

PLATE 206 · BLUME, PETER *The Rock* · DRAWING, PENCIL · 1942 · 18¼″ x 22¼″ · Mr and Mrs.
Millard Meiss, New York

In *The Rock* we have a drawing beautiful in tone, rich in meticulous detail Though often fantastic or
ambiguous in his subject matter, Blume has never associated himself with the Surrealists. *The Rock* is an
early study for a large and complex painting of the same title

PLATE 207 · WYETH, ANDREW · *Beckie King* · DRAWING · 1946 · 30″ x 36″ · Dallas Museum of
Fine Arts

Wyeth, a penetrating observer who captures moods, gives proof in *Beckie King*, as in all of his portraits,
of the gulf that separates such a drawing, produced by a sensitive artist, from even the best photograph.
There are in his Twentieth Century realistic works attractive reminders of the sharp vision of both Homer
and Eakins in the Nineteenth Century

233

PLATE 208 · SHAHN, BEN *Girl Jumping Rope* · DRAWING, INK · 1943 · 21½″ x 29½″ · James Thrall
Soby, New York

Ben Shahn speaks in an idiom that is unmistakably American These drawings rise above mere factual
reportage His interest in recording mood adds significance to his works and would have been appreciated
by Corot, Manet, and Degas Shahn has used his disciplined gifts in the service of social commentary,
satirical propaganda, and commercial advertising.

PLATE 209 · SHAHN, BEN · *Man Picking Wheat* DRAWING, INK · 38″ x 25″ · Fogg Museum, Harvard University

The contrast between the delicate stalks of wheat and the heavy hands that pluck them is striking

235

PLATE 210 · HAYTER, STANLEY WILLIAM · *Tarantelle* · ENGRAVING AND ETCHING · 1943 · 21⅝"
x 13" Museum of Modern Art, New York (Edward M M Warburg Fund)

236

Chapter 10
TECHNICAL PROCESSES

As I pointed out at greater length in an earlier book* the word "draw" means:—to drag a pen or other instrument over a surface, leaving a mark behind it To draw is to outline; to delineate, to represent a form or shape by lines or by means of light and shade alone or within a simple outline —in short, to make a picture by such means To draw lines or outlines is a way to express ideas—the grammar of art Drawing is, indeed, the fundamental element in all great picture making, just as grammar is at the root of all good writing An artist's line has fundamental significance when it reveals form or design.

My pet slogan continues to be what it has always been —the eye is best trained through an intimate knowledge of the finest of a genre Understanding and discrimination, that is, *connoisseurship*, can only be developed by repeated contact with the best visual images produced in the draughtsman's *own* language How, if we continue to rely chiefly on those who would lull us with words, can we hope to *see?*

The instinct for *quality* has made for the success of the great collectors. They have, as a rule, relied upon their direct reaction to the isolated object. Often they have preceded, indeed formed, the critics The drawings and prints selected for reproduction in this book were not chosen because of their rarity, but because, whether slight, quick sketches or finished designs, they give evidence, through their technical excellence, of the translation of the vision of the artist into graphic language.

A brief account of how drawings and prints are made may prove helpful

Silverpoint (Plate 202), the favorite tool used by artists in Italy, in the Netherlands, and sometimes in Germany, in Mediaeval and Renaissance times, yields delightful, delicate results This exacting method is rarely used today If the artist does

BIDDLE GEORGE SANTAYANA LITHOGRAPH 1952

It is in his drawings that the artist makes his most spontaneous statements and enables us to follow his thought in the very act of creation Long before Ingres (Plate 1), one of the remarkable draughtsmen of the Nineteenth Century, insisted that drawing is the probity of art, Vasari had said in the Sixteenth Century·—"drawing . . is the necessary beginning of everything [in art], and not having it one has nothing."

*The Pocket Book of Great Drawings, Pocket Book No 765

GREENE. TWO BOYS, INK 1952 FOGG MUSEUM

employ it, he coats his paper with a thin ground of powdered bone, mixed with gum water, and on such a surface (sometimes colored) he makes his drawing The result is a pale, gray line which is attractive by virtue of its crispness and clarity In silverpoint drawings unity is achieved because of the harmony between the sharp, sensitive strokes and the paper on which the artist works In Flanders, in the Fifteenth Century, in the period from Van Eyck to Memling, we find that *silverpoint*, the most common of the metal points used for drawing, was the favorite tool

Pen and ink is a mode widely used by present-day artists as by the old masters The sharp point of pen or quill results in precise clarity (Plate 15) Subtle gradations are rarely feasible with pen alone and when such gradations are desired, the artist tends to supplement his line with brush strokes (Plate 19) of the same color Another variation in pen drawing, illustrating the power that can be achieved by this mode, we observe in the work of van Gogh (Plate 40)

Drawings with *charcoal* (Plate 50), *black and red chalk* (Plate 75), and *pencil* (Plate 65) offer an impressive variety of work, since with these, sharpness or delicate gradations of tone can be achieved Our contemporary artists use pencil for

SPEICHER PORTRAIT OF A GIRL CHARCOAL. FOGG MUSEUM

rapid notation and for sketching (Plate 203), but only rarely do they use the hard chalk with which Raphael, Michelangelo, Holbein, Rubens, and Watteau enchant us

Since with *pastel* an artist is enabled to employ a full range of colors it is perhaps stretching a point to include it here among the processes of drawing rather than of painting Pastel is included, however, because it is akin to soft chalk Starting with the French Impressionists, in the Nineteenth Century, both pastel and charcoal came once again to be favored materials

We think, quite rightly, of *original Drawings* as unique We ought, however, to include *Prints* as an important category in the field of drawing Prints, although not unique, are none the less original and autographic A print is one of many *impressions* of an original drawing *pulled* multiple times from an engraved and inked hard surface of either wood, metal or stone, on which the artist has drawn his picture or on which some other craftsman has transferred an artist's design

In prehistoric times an unknown artist, in addition to drawing and painting on the walls of caves, used a sharpened stone to incise a design on a bone The result was what we commonly call a drawing If we imagine such an incision inked and paper pressed into the incised lines, we have an impression from the incised primitive drawing—a *print*

It follows from these simple, preliminary hints that he who would increase his enjoyment of every type of drawing—prints which are multiplied drawings or so-called *original*—that is, unique drawings — ought to give some thought to the various *processes* that artists employ in duplicating their drawings, that is, in making prints

The study of drawings, in any form, is an absorbing subject, for it touches our daily lives more than any other form of art I have found drawings and prints fascinating since early boyhood First I copied Kate Greenaway Then for many years I cut out printed pictures from Harper's and other magazines—pictures by Timothy Cole, Kruell, and Winslow Homer (pp 203, 239) These cherished pieces of paper I pasted from baseboard to ceiling on the walls of my small New York bedroom That was my first well-loved and instructive art gallery I came to realize how near prints are to literature; how they enliven our reading each day, how in its long history art has after all been *story-telling* art

The reader would do well to take another look at the pictures in this book, so as to note that the different techniques used, result in rendering pictures that have a *special* character of their own You will observe that in Plate 182 the etcher, who works, as we shall see, under peculiar restrictions imposed by the copper plate, secures a picture which when printed differs in character from one more freely drawn (Plate 22) on a lithographic stone

In describing the various processes used by artists to *pull* drawings from engraved surfaces, we shall not discuss *states, condition, margins*—all dear to the heart of the specialist, the collector, the curator, and the dealer We shall merely address ourselves to the question of *how prints are made,* describing some only of the fundamental processes of printmaking, because as a teacher I realize that most laymen are curious about the know-how of making prints

I will not attempt a description of the various mixed methods, variations on fundamental processes or new techniques which have been recently developed The would-be practitioner should consult technical manuals A few books listed in the *Bibliography* (p 259) may prove useful to the layman, especially an article by Una E Johnson, which is invaluable and suggests the frequent variety of present-day procedures

No detailed explanation of the fundamental print process is necessary Mr. Ture Bengtz of the Department of Drawings and Graphic Arts at the Museum of Fine Arts, Boston, has permitted the reproduction of a series of his photographs which are admirable, self-explanatory, visual demonstrations (Plates 211-222.)

BECKMANN SELF-PORTRAIT WOODCUT 1922

I · THE RELIEF METHOD
(Woodcut—Wood Engraving)

(a) The *Woodcut* (Plate 211) is the oldest of the graphic arts, practiced in the Eighth Century in China to illustrate Buddhist texts and in Europe in the Fifteenth Century chiefly for manufacture and distribution of inexpensive religious images The first European woodcuts were for textile designs In woodcut the artist works on a plank of soft wood cut along the grain He draws his picture on the wood, those parts of his design which are not to print black are cut away with a sharp knife or gouge The drawing then stands out in relief as in type The surface of the block is inked, covered with a sheet of paper and run through a press. The inked design is thus transferred to the paper and the resulting picture (that is, the print) is itself called a woodcut.

HOMER RAID ON A SWALLOW COLONY WOOD ENGRAVING 1874

(b) *Wood Engraving* (Plates 212, 213), a variation of woodcut, was invented in the Eighteenth Century In wood engraving, the artist works on the hard end of the block with a metal tool called a burin or graver, which has a lozenge-shaped point. The wood employed is always a hard wood (as opposed to woodcut), usually boxwood The actual

239

block is engraved crosswise rather than plankwise with the grain The printing process is the same as in woodcut. The resulting picture when transferred to paper is itself called a wood engraving To bring out the delicacy and precision of line, the block is printed by press, usually under great pressure In the middle of the Nineteenth Century, before the invention of photomechanical engraving, wood engraving was widely used for reproductions in books and magazines, as in the Winslow Homer which appears on the preceding page

II · THE INTAGLIO* METHODS
(Engraving on metal, Drypoint, Etching, Aquatint, and Mezzotint)

(a) In the graphic process of *Engraving on Metal* (Plate 214) the picture is made by cutting into the polished surface of the plate with a burin or engraving tool which is pushed before the hand As the aim of line engraving is clarity of line, the burr is removed with a scraper The printing process is the same as in etching and drypoint, and the resulting picture transferred to the paper is itself called an engraving

(b) The graphic process of *Drypoint,* though frequently spoken of as drypoint-etching, is in fact not etching. It is a form of intaglio engraving often used to reinforce etching The lines are *scratched* into the metal plate with either a pointed piece of steel or a diamond point This tool is drawn across the plate It is not pushed before the hand The point raises a shaving called *burr* This burr, which holds ink, is left along the line or furrow and is not scraped away as in line engraving on metal Drypoint is often used to reinforce a plate that has already been etched In the printing of a drypoint, because of the burr, a rich velvety effect is attained

(c) The graphic process of *Etching* originated in the shops of armorers It was used for picture making as early as the Sixteenth Century Rembrandt in the Seventeenth Century was the greatest of all etchers In etching, the lines are not cut with a burin, but are bitten or etched (literally—to eat in) by acid. A polished metal plate (usually copper) is covered with a protective film called the etching ground This ground resists the action of acid ** It is applied (Plate 215) by bringing a silk bag filled with a wax composition in contact with the heated plate The wax, melted by the heat,

MERYON LE STRYGE ETCHING 1853*

penetrates the bag and is then spread evenly on the plate with a dabber or roller The plate is then smoked so that the artist may see his drawing as he makes the lines that lay bare the metal. The drawing finished, the *back* of the metal plate *must* be sealed off before the plate is placed into an acid bath (Plate 216) Wherever the needle has laid bare the protected surface, the acid does its work—its biting—by attacking the metal The darkness or depth of the etched line depends on the length of time the plate is bitten The plate is now ready for printing which is the reverse of printing a woodcut or wood engraving As we noted, the lines in woodcut or wood engraving are in relief and only they, as in type, are inked In an etching, an engraving on metal, or drypoint, the lines are cut into or eaten into the metal and the ink is forced *into* the lines. This done, the plate is wiped clean (Plate 217) with a cloth, always a fine, soft cloth, usually silk, or with the palm of the hand, and hence the ink remains only in the bitten lines or furrows. A damp sheet of paper is put on top of the plate and both are run through a press under very heavy pressure The damp paper is forced into the ditches or furrows—the lines—which alone, in the wiping process, have retained ink As the pressure in the press is re-

---

*So called from the Italian word meaning to "cut in "

**Of course the acid can be applied directly to the plate with a brush as in the Rouault (Plate 72)

*Meryon, the most distinguished of cityscape artists, said of this devil in stone "The monster is mine and that of the men who built this tower of St. Jacques He means stupidity, cruelty, lust, hypocrisy. They have all met in that one beast "

240

leased, the ink is sucked out of the incised lines, leaving an *impression,* a print of the etching, on the paper A print thus made (Plate 218) is itself called an etching

(d) *Aquatint,* an etching process in which line and tone are combined, is a variation of pure etching just described. The tone or tint is obtained by biting, not through a smooth solid ground of wax, but through a porous ground formed of sand or of some powdered resinous substance coated evenly over the surface of the plate In this variation of

GOYA HUNTING FOR TEETH AQUATINT C 1797

etching the surface of the copper plate, being only partially protected, enables the acid to find its way through the porous ground and into the background, as into the lines Almost at its inception, Goya (Plate 5) was master of aquatint, using it constantly for beautiful tone effects akin to the washes of watercolors.

(e) *Mezzotint* (Frontispiece). An artist's aim in using the process of mezzotint (one of the tone processes used freely in the Eighteenth Century for reproductive purposes and rarely used today) is to produce a picture which is rich and *velvety* in *tone,* rather than to supplement line, as in aquatint.

Instead of working from a clear base to dark lines or shadows, as is usual in engraving, the artist who uses mezzotint reverses the process and proceeds from a dark base to the highlights The dark base is secured through the use of a tool with sharp, tiny, cutting teeth called a *Rocker* which is placed in the hand at right angles to the plate and rocked all over the surfaces of the plate, abrasing it evenly. If the plate were inked at this stage, it would merely result in an even all-over black or brown piece of paper without any design. The picture is made, however, through the removal of the burr with a mezzotint scraper To secure the lighter portions of the design and where highlights are needed the plate is burnished so thoroughly that no ink whatever can be retained At this point the artist is ready to ink and pull his print in the usual way.

III · LITHOGRAPHY
The Surface Method (Planographic)

Lithography, the third graphic process, was invented in 1798 by Aloys Senefelder, a German The principle of this surface method is based on the antipathy of grease and water In lithography (Plates 219-222) the artist draws with a greasy chalk on the grained surface of a heavy slab of porous Bavarian limestone The stone is then moistened Wherever there is grease the water is repelled A greasy ink is rolled over the surface Where there is a greasy mark or line the grease on the roller is attracted Where the stone (or its substitute, a prepared zinc or aluminum plate) is damp and clean, the grease is repelled Paper is placed on the stone or metal plate and run through a press A duplicate of the surface drawing on the stone or plate adheres to the paper This completely autographic process has made it a favorite among many of the great painters and draughtsmen of the Nineteenth and Twentieth Centuries

A discussion of technical processes cannot close without some mention of new directions in graphic techniques Experimentation is an important aspect of Twentieth Century printmaking Particularly in the United States, much attention has been devoted to new possibilities of familiar media as well as to the development of completely new methods Traditional approaches have been re-evaluated and in some cases revolutionized, although in the long history of printmaking it is seldom that a "new" discovery has not previously been attempted by someone else.

The application of textures (cloth, paper, wire)

241

has become a standard device employed by many American etchers, lithographers and woodcutters. Today's frequent use of soft-ground etching not only permits the use of textures but permits a freedom of drawing perhaps impossible with the traditional etching needle Many woodcuts are actually engraved on linoleum and composition-board—even lucite and slate have been used for similar effect. Serigraphy, prints made through screens of silk, is a graphic medium recently perfected in the United States. Several printmakers are experimenting with processes based on the chemistry of plastics And to engrave on metal, not only the burin but any tool that incises can be used—from the diamond to the dentist's drill

Today color has assumed an unprecedented importance in printmaking As William S. Lieberman has said· "Boldness of scale and the use of color are two striking characteristics of recent prints This departure from the long tradition of black and white, as well as the development of prints of larger size, suggests that many recent prints deliberately assume some of the aspects of painting "

MAILLOL WOMAN IN WIND LITHOGRAPH

PLATE 211 (above) · Using a gouge on a WOODCUT (All photographs for Plates 211 through 222 courtesy Ture Bengtz)

PLATE 212 (below left)   Using a burin on a WOOD ENGRAVING

PLATE 213 (below right)   Using a loupe for enlarging detail on a WOOD ENGRAVING

PLATE 214 · Using a burin on a COPPER ENGRAVING

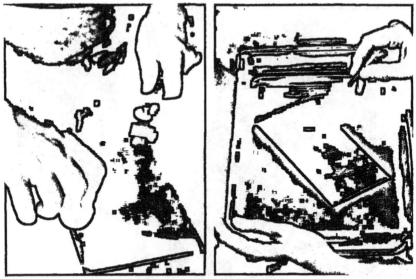

PLATE 215 (above left) · Applying the ground—ETCHING
PLATE 216 (above right) · Biting the copper plate—ETCHING
PLATE 217 (below left) · Wiping the copper plate—ETCHING
PLATE 218 (below right) Pulling the proof—ETCHING

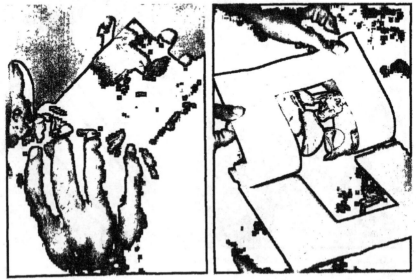

PLATE 219 (above left) · Graining the stones—LITHOGRAPHY
PLATE 220 (above right) · Rolling up the stone—LITHOGRAPHY
PLATE 221 (below left) · Stone in press—LITHOGRAPHY
PLATE 222 (below right) · Pulling the proof—LITHOGRAPHY

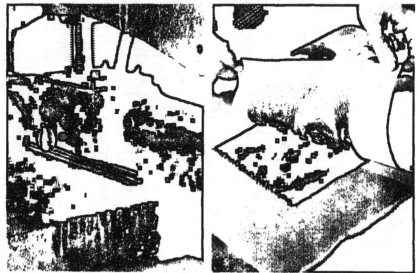

SHAHN ORCHESTRA CHAIRS—EMPTY SERIGRAPH 1951

Biographies

BARLACH, ERNST *(bar'-lakh)*
(German 1870-1938) PLATE 131, p 125
Sculptor, graphic artist, writer Born Wedel, Holstein 1888-94, attended School of Applied Design, Hamburg, and Academy, Dresden 1895-96, studied in Paris 1899-1900, studied at the Academy, Hamburg, and in Berlin 1906, traveled in Russia 1907, settled in Gustrow, Mecklenburg, to begin his career as sculptor and dramatist. 1910, in Florence Returned to Gustrow Under Hitler his sculpture was cast out of German museums, his dramas banned Illustrated his own poetic dramas such as *Der Tote Tag*, 1912, *Der Arme Vetter*, 1918, *Die Echten Sedemunds*, 1920 Influenced by Mediaeval art and Gothic sculpture Died Rostock

BASKIN, LEONARD
(American 1922-) p 208
Sculptor and graphic artist Born New Brunswick, N J 1940-41, studied at New York University School of Architecture and Allied Arts 1941-43, Yale University School of Art 1949, received BA New School for Social Research 1950, Academy of La Grande Chaumière, Paris, and 1951, Accademia delle Belle Arte, Florence 1937-39 apprenticeship with sculptor, Glickman 1940, Honorable Mention Prix de Rome 1947, received William Comfort Tiffany Fellowship, 1953 Guggenheim Fellowship Taught arts and sculpture, Worcester Museum Teaches at Smith College, Northampton, Mass

BEARDSLEY, AUBREY VINCENT
(English 1872-1898) PLATE 164
Draughtsman and illustrator Born Brighton. 1881, moved to Epsom 1883, family moved to London Known as infant musical genius Admired Kate Greenaway Decorated menus and invitation cards 1884, returned to Brighton Left school and entered architect's office, London 1889, worked for the Guardian Fire and Life Insurance. Serious illness started 1891, began to illustrate Marlowe, Congreve, etc Joseph Pennell and J M Dent were instrumental in introducing his art to the public Copied Greek vases in British Museum and studied in National Gallery, Knew Watts and Burne-Jones 1892, attended Brown's night school 1893, began to publish his drawings Designed first cover for the *Studio Magazine* 1894, illustrations for Wilde's *Salome* and drawings for the *Yellow Book* 1895, stopped contributing to *Yellow Book* 1896, began to illustrate for the *Savoy* Became severely ill in Brussels Retired to Bournemouth 1897, moved to Paris Illustrated the *Rape of the Lock* Died Mentone, France, of tuberculosis Admirer of Mantegna, Crivelli and the Japanese

BECKMANN, MAX *(bek'mahn)*
(German 1884-1950) PLATES 135, 139-40, pp 127, 239
Painter, graphic artist, writer Born Leipzig 1900-03, studied at Weimar Academy 1903-04, traveled to Paris and Florence In museums admired Rembrandt, Piero della Francesca, Signorelli and the Post-Impressionists 1906, received first prize at German Artists League, Weimar Joined Secessionist movement 1909, began first lithographs illustrating mythological and Biblical subjects 1911, resigned from Secession Although not member of *Die Brucke*, his art is expressionist in larger sense Admired Delacroix and El Greco 1914, served in Army Field Hospital Corps 1915 became ill, went to Frankfort-on-Main to convalesce Resumed painting 1921-22, wrote four plays Was exponent briefly of the Neue Sachlichkeit (New Objectivity) movement 1925, professor at Frankfort Art School Strong influence of Northern Gothic art Expressed in painting his horror of war and the bitterness and disillusion of post-war Germany 1929, received Second Prize Carnegie International Exhibition 1930, large retrospective exhibition, Basle 1929-32, in Paris Attacked in Frankfort and Berlin by the Nazis 1936-47, took refuge in Amsterdam 1939, received first prize Golden Gate International Exposition, San Francisco 1947, came to U S Appointed professor, School of Fine Arts, Washington University, St Louis 1947, retrospective exhibition, City Art Museum, St Louis Died St Louis

BELLOWS, GEORGE WESLEY
(American 1882-1925) PLATE 184
Painter, draughtsman, lithographer Born Columbus, Ohio, son of architect and builder At Ohio State University a crack baseball player Studied with Robert Henri, N Y 1913, Member of National Academy With others founded Society of Independent Artists and New York Society of Painters Taught at Art Students League Spent summers at Woodstock, N Y Began his lithographs about 1916 Certain stiffness in some of his work due to use of Jay Hambidge's theory of "dynamic symmetry" Keen interest in athletics, especially prize fighting. Subject matter came from American scenes of city and country life Died New York

BIDDLE, GEORGE
(American 1885-) p 237
Painter, graphic artist, critic Born Philadelphia Studied Harvard University, then Paris, Spain and Munich After First World War, spent two years in Tahiti Began lithography in 1914 Has painted murals in Washington, D C, Rio de Janeiro and Mexico City Extensive travels, most recently in Italy 1952 Lives in Croton-on-Hudson, N.Y

BLUME, PETER
(American 1906-) PLATE 206
Painter and draughtsman Born Russia. 1911, came to America and educated in Brooklyn, N Y Studied at night at Educational Alliance, Art Students League, and Beaux-Arts Ran subway newsstand to earn living Worked in jewelry factory and

247

as lithographer's apprentice 1930, one-man exhibition, Daniel Gallery, N Y 1932, to Italy on a Guggenheim fellowship (renewed in 1936) 1934, *South of Scranton* took first prize at Carnegie International Exhibition 1937, one-man exhibition, Julien Levy Gallery Lives Gaylordsville, Conn.

BOCCIONI, UMBERTO *(bawt-cho'-nee)*
(Italian 1882-1916)   PLATES 154-57, p 167
Painter and sculptor Born Reggio in Calabria 1898-1902, studied at Brera, Milan, and was pupil of Balla in Rome Traveled in Russia and France before settling in Milan, 1907 Organizer of Futurist movement and signed the *Manifesto of Futurist Painting*, 1910 Exhibited with Futurists in Europe and America Active sculptor and painter Author of theoretical writings including a *Manifesto of Futurist Sculpture* (1912) and a work entitled *Pittura, Scultura Futuriste* (1914) Wounded in World War I Died, 1916

BONNARD, PIERRE *(bon-nar')*
(French 1867-1947)   PLATES 57 58
Painter, graphic artist, illustrator Born at Fontenay-aux-Roses of bourgeois family Studied at Academy Julian with Vuillard, Roussel, Bouguereau Member of the Nabis group Exhibited with Impressionists and Symbolists at Père Tanguy s shop and at Vollard's and Durand-Ruel's, 1893-1899 Actually far removed from the theories of Serusier and Maurice Denis 1895, exhibited stained glass at Societe Nationale des Beaux Arts with Denis, Lautrec, Serusier, Vallotton, etc 1899, dedicated himself to painting. Took part with Emile Bernard, Signac, Vuillard and Denis in the exhibition "Hommage a Odilon Redon," organized by Durand-Ruel Influence of these artists evident in work of first period during which he was decorator of stage settings, furniture Made many lithographs, posters, and book illustrations Vollard one of his first patrons About 1910 began to spend much time at Montval 1902, illustrated *Daphnis et Chloe* 1907, visited Belgium and Holland, Germany, England, Spain, Tunisia and Algeria At end of his life spent winters in the Midi at Le Cannet and summers in Paris and Vernon 1946, illustrated the *Crépuscule des Nymphs* by Pierre Louys Died at Le Cannet The same year an important retrospective exhibit at the Orangerie. The Museum of Modern Art, N Y, large exhibition in 1948

BRAQUE, GEORGES *(brahk)*
(French 1882-)   PLATE 91, p 97
Painter, sculptor and graphic artist Born Argenteuil, son of house painter At Havre, Braque was apprentice of house painter. 1902-04, went to Paris to study painting at Ecole des Beaux-Arts Traveled with Friesz to Antwerp, 1906, and to L'Estaque, 1907 1908, met Picasso and saw *Les Demoiselles d'Avignon* His geometric landscapes refused by Salon d'Automne of 1908 Exhibited at Kahnweiler Gallery From 1910 until World War I evolution of his art closely connected with Picasso's. During World War I was mobilized and later wounded 1917, began to paint again New tendency in his art appeared, the painterly awareness of object itself and its natural properties This evolution came to a climax in 1922-23 and continued until 1929 during which time he painted nudes as well as still lifes. From 1930 on he moved away again from nature under the influence of Picasso Composed cartoons for tapestries Began to engrave on plaster Lived frequently at Varangeville Exhibited paintings and sculpture at Salon d'Automne of 1943 1945, a Braque-Rouault exhibition at Tate Gallery Exhibition at Museum of Modern Art, N Y, 1949

BRESDIN, RODOLPHE *(bres-dan')*
(French 1825-1885)   PLATE 46
Draughtsman, etcher, lithographer Born Ingrande Taught engraving to Redon, with whom he shared admiration for Rembrandt. A gifted recluse Until recently too little known. Died Sèvres

BURCHFIELD, CHARLES
(American 1893-)   PLATE 198
Watercolorist and Painter Born Ashtabula Harbor, Ohio Started as accountant 1912, entered Cleveland School of Art. 1916, first N. Y exhibition 1921, moved to Buffalo from Salem, Ohio 1929, moved to Gardenville, N Y 1930, exhibition Museum of Modern Art, N Y Most noted as watercolorist His middle period one of realistic and romantic representations of American Victorian architecture Imagination and lyricism of his early style revived in recent works Lives at Gardenville

CALDER, ALEXANDER
(American 1898-)   PLATE 201; p. 1
Sculptor, graphic artist, book illustrator Born Philadelphia, son and grandson of sculptors 1919, graduated from Stevens Institute as mechanical engineer, 1923, studied painting Art

Students League, N Y 1926, went to Paris, first exhibition of paintings Made first wire sculpture and animated toys 1928, one-man show, Weyhe Gallery Returned to Paris, met Miro and Pascin Spent time alternately between Paris and N Y Knew Léger, van Doesburg, and Mondrian 1931, illustrations for *Fables of Aesop* 1932, first exhibition of mobiles. 1933, traveled to Madrid, Barcelona 1938, stage designs and first American retrospective exhibition, Springfield, Mass 1943, exhibition Museum of Modern Art, N Y 1944, illustrations for *Fables of La Fontaine* Mobile for Terrace Plaza Hotel, Cincinnati 1947, with Leger exhibited in Berne and Amsterdam 1948, travel in Brazil, California, Mexico 1950, returned to Paris Traveled to Lascaux caves, Brittany, Finland, Sweden 1951, exhibition Museum of Modern Art, N Y One of few American artists of the 20th Century to achieve international reputation 1952, Grand Prize for Sculpture, Venice, Biennial Lives Roxbury, Conn.

CASSATT, MARY *(kas-sat')*
(American 1845-1926)   PLATE 26
Painter and graphic artist Born Pittsburgh, Pa 1851-56, lived in Paris with parents, who were of French ancestry 1856-68, studied drawing, Philadelphia Academy of Art 1868, went to Europe to study, visiting Parma, Italy, where her interest was Correggio Later went to Madrid, Antwerp and Holland copying old masters. 1874, permanent residence in Paris where she studied under academician, Charles Chaplin Influenced by Manet, Degas, and Japanese prints Exhibitor at Paris salons during 70 s 1877, joined Impressionists and exhibited with them in 1879-81 and 1886 1879, first met Mr and Mrs H O Havemeyer Began to concentrate on graphic arts, especially etching, soft ground, and drypoint 1890, established summer residence at Chateau de Beaufresne near Paris Same year attended Japanese Exposition at Beaux-Arts with Degas, who admired her work 1891, first one-man exhibition, Durand-Ruel, Paris 1893, started decorations for Women's Building, Columbian Exposition, Chicago 1897, toured Europe with Mrs. Havemeyer, helping build her collection 1899, returned to America briefly 1904, received Lippincott Prize, Pennsylvania Academy, Phila 1909, made Chevalier of Legion of Honor, Paris, and associate National Academy of Design 1926, recipient Gold Medal of Honor, Pennsylvania Academy Blind in old age, she died at Mesnil-Theribus in 1926 The author of many prints, a field in which she made important technical innovations in aquatint and color printing

CASTELLANOS, JULIO *(kah-stel-yah'-naw ss)*
(Mexican 1905-1947)   PLATE 179
Painter and draughtsman, stage designer, graphic artist Born Mexico, D F Studied at Academy of Fine Arts (San Carlos) 1925-27, traveled in Europe, South America and U S A Important member of artistic generation following Rivera and Orozco Fresco in the Primary School of Coyoacán

CÉZANNE, PAUL *(say-zahn')*
(French 1839-1906) PLATES 30, 32-34, 190, p 35
Painter, draughtsman, graphic artist Born Aix-en-Provence, son of a banker Attended Aix schools excelling in Latin and mathematics Long friendship with Zola Studied art at Aix Academy after Zola left for Paris Father insisted he study law at Aix University but finally allowed his son to go to Paris to paint 1861, Paris, attended Academy Suisse with Pissarro Constantly visited Salon and Louvre After four months returned, discouraged, to Aix and became briefly a bank clerk. 1862, returned to Paris Constantly rejected by the Salon Came to know Manet, Pissarro, Degas, Renoir and others of the Cafe Guerbois group 1870, left Paris for L'Estaque on the Mediterranean 1872, moved to Pontoise with Hortense Fiquet and their son, Paul Worked closely with Pissarro, from whom he received first methodical training Painted at Auvers-sur-Oise Encouraged by Dr Gachet, amateur artist-collector, the doctor of van Gogh. 1874, exhibited two landscapes at first group showing of Impressionists. Public and critics failed to realize his artistic stature Retired to south where he began to modify Pissarro s teachings During mid-80's his style became as geometrical as his famous remark "Treat nature by the cylinder, the sphere, the cone " During 80 s often visited Monticelli in Marseilles and was visited by Renoir His friendship with Zola ended 1886 Gauguin and Signac bought his work In the 90's Cézanne devoted much time to portrait and figure painting though still life and landscape were never neglected Theme of the *Bathers* became of vast importance Divided time between Aix and Paris Met Rodin, Mary Cassatt, Clemenceau and worked with Monet 1895, Vollard gave him an exhibition from which Renoir and Degas bought works 1895, two of his paintings entered the Louvre 1899, exhibited at Salon des Indépendants. After 1900, a more restless, fluid and less three-dimensional style evolved 1905, exhibited Salon d'Automne. Died Aix.

248

CHAGALL, MARC *(sha-gal')*
(French 1889-   )   PLATES 127-30. p 128
Painter, graphic artist, stage designer Born Vitebsk, Russia, of poor family 1907 on, began to paint Attended school St Petersburg. Pupil of Léon Bakst 1910, went to Paris where he knew Leger and Modigliani Refused at Salon d'Automne but continued to exhibit at Salon des Independants Knew Delaunay, Max Jacob, Apollinaire and others In 1914, with aid of Apollinaire, had large comprehensive exhibit in Berlin which had repercussions on style of Expressionists During World War I obliged to return to his native land 1917, at outbreak of Russian Revolution named Commissioner of Art at Vitebsk and founded in that city a State Academy 1920 went to Moscow to paint mural for State Jewish theatre, also sets and costume designs 1922, traveled to Berlin to regain his paintings from the 1914 exhibition, to discover they had been confiscated or sold Returned to Paris 1931, made trip to Egypt and Palestine Many book illustrations including those for the *Fables of La Fontaine*. Left France during German Occupation Came to U S 1941 1946, exhibition Musuem of Modern Art, N Y On return to France a comprehensive exhibition took place at the Musée National d Art Moderne Lives at Vence

CHARLOT, JEAN *(shar-lo')*
(American 1898-   )   PLATE 177
Painter, writer, graphic artist Born Paris of partially Mexican parents Arrived Mexico, 1921 Became U S citizen 1939 One of first to experiment with encaustic and fresco at the Preparatoria Staff artist with Carnegie Archaeological Expedition, Chichen Itzá, 1926-29 Book illustrator Has lived in U S since 1929, and taught at Art Students League, N Y, and University of Georgia where he decorated Fine Arts and Journalism Buildings with large frescoes

DI CHIRICO, GIORGIO *(kee'-ree-co)*
(Italian 1888-   )   PLATE 158
Painter, graphic artist, stage designer Born Volos, Greece, of Italian parentage Studied art at Volos, Athens and Munich 1911-15, worked and exhibited Paris 1915, returned to Italy Entered army same year During World War I met Carrà, with whom he launched the *Scuola Metafisica* Spent post-war period in Rome and Florence Returned to Paris, 1925 In late 1920's broke with Surrealists whom he had influenced Has lived in Italy since 1940

CORINTH, LOVIS *(ko-rinnt')*
(German 1858-1925)   PLATE 141
Painter and graphic artist Born Tapiau, Prussia, son of a tanner At 17 studied at Academy of Königsberg, then Weimar and finally Munich Academy In Antwerp influenced by Flemish colorists, especially Rubens 1884-87, attended the Academy Julian, Paris Bouguereau one of his masters. 1887-90, returned to Königsberg 1890, Munich, 1901, Berlin, where he opened private art school largely attended by women Successor to Max Liebermann as president of the Berlin Secessionists In Paris influenced by Courbet, Manet and Impressionism Particularly interested throughout his life in Rembrandt Nudes, religious subjects, portraits (often self-portraits) were favorite themes 1911, severe illness impaired his health and work 1925, died of second attack of apoplexy 12 years after his death his paintings were removed from German museums and exhibited in the 'Degenerate Art Show" in Munich

COROT, JEAN BAPTISTE CAMILLE *(ko-ro')*
(French 1796-1875)   PLATE 18
Painter, draughtsman, graphic artist Born Paris, son of a milliner Early schooling at Rouen Returned to Paris, 1812 When he failed to succeed in trade, his parents permitted him, at 26, to study painting Worked in studios of Michallon and Bertin, followers of David's neo-classicism 1825, left Paris for Italy, residing in Rome for 3 years. 1827, sent to Paris several works of his Italian period 1829, returned to Paris Exposition of 1864 won Cross of Legion of Honor for *View of the Forest* of Fontainebleau Found ready market for his etchings and paintings. Participated actively in resisting enemy during the Franco-Prussian War Friend of Daumier Except for two later trips to Italy (1834, 1843), his life uneventful at Fontainebleau and Ville d'Avray where he died

DALI, SALVADOR *(dah'-lee)*
(American 1904-   )   PLATE 108
Painter and draughtsman Born Figueras, Spain Attended Academy of Fine Arts, Madrid, from which twice expelled Describes his artistic evolution as running course of "impressionism, divisionism, futurism, constructivism, scientific cubism, magic realism, abstract irrationalism surrealism" Influenced by di Chirico, Miró, Tanguy, Art Nouveau, etc Collaborated with Luis Buñel on scenarios of two surrealist films (*Le Chien Andalou* and the *Golden Age*) produced by Studio 28 1939, he moved to the U S where allied himself with the

Surrealist group which included Andre Breton 1941, exhibition Museum of Modern Art, N Y Remains active as painter and advertising artist Has worked with Walt Disney on several animated cartoons

DAUMIER, HONORÉ *(dome-yay)*
(French 1808-1879)   PLATES 13-14
Painter, sculptor, graphic artist Born Marseilles, son of a glazier 1816, went to Paris with his family Studied painting with Lenois and lithography with Ramelet One of the greatest draughtsmen of 19th Century, he was influenced by Michelangelo and Rembrandt Author of about 4,000 lithographs for papers *Charivari, Caricature* and others Produced countless drawings and about 200 paintings Passionate realist, his subjects range from affectionate humor, searing satire of the human comedy, to tragic seriousness Died as a blind old man in a cottage given him by generous Corot in Valmondois

DAVID, JACQUES LOUIS *(dah-veed')*
(French 1748-1824)   PLATES 3-4, p 260
Painter and draughtsman Born Paris Entered Academy Art School at 18 First master, J M Vien 1774, won Prix de Rome Began as history-painter Court painter to Louis XVI 1784, Member of the Academy, same year commissioned to paint *Oath of the Horatii* 1791, returned to Rome 1792, became Deputy of the Convention and voted for King's death Member of Comité de l'Instruction and of the Commission des Arts Abolished the Academy while art dictator of the Republic 1794-95, after fall of Robespierre was attacked in the Convention and imprisoned in the Luxembourg. Retired from politics and was given studio by the Directorate Napoleon appointed him First Painter of the Emperor and commissioned him to paint imperial ceremonies Under Napoleon, David endeavored to become art dictator once again but without success 1816, exiled by Louis XVIII for signing the Acte Additionel Spent last nine years of his life in Brussels where he died.

DAVIS, STUART
(American 1894-   )   p 207
Painter, lithographer, draughtsman Born Philadelphia Moved to East Orange, N J, 1901 1910, studied with Robert Henri in N Y 1913, exhibited Armory Show when only 19 1916, exhibited with Independents 1918, map-maker for Army Intelligence Department 1923, visited New Mexico. 1928, went to Paris 1929, lived in N Y and Gloucester, Mass. 1931, taught at Art Students League 1934-39, active in Artists Congress 1940, began to teach at New School for Social Research 1946, exhibition Museum of Modern Art, N Y Meticulous abstract painter in colors of high intensity Murals in Rockefeller Center, WNYC, N Y, and Indiana Univ Lives in N Y

DEGAS, HILAIRE GERMAIN EDGAR *(de-gah')*
(French 1834-1917)   PLATES 22, 24, 28
Painter, sculptor, draughtsman, graphic artist Born in Paris, son of family of bankers Attended Lycee Louis Le Grand Short period as student at law school 1854, attended Ecole des Beaux-Arts 1865, met Ingres, became his pupil 1856-57, lived in Rome and Naples where he studied early Italians, Raphael and other 16th Century masters Copied Mantegna, Clouet, Holbein, Poussin and others at Louvre 1870, served in National Guard during Franco-Prussian War After war spent some time in New Orleans with relatives Until 1876 sent his work to the official Salon Became member of the Cafe Guerbois group of painters and writers 1874 on, exhibited with Impressionists except in year 1882 His individual style always separated him from the group Frequent travels in Italy, England, Belgium, Holland and Spain Constant visitor at circus, café-concert, race tracks and opera Was keenly interested in Japanese prints and in photography Degas experimented in many graphic media—etching, drypoint and lithography, as well as drawing and pastel His late pastels, daring in composition and brilliant in color, influenced Gauguin, Toulouse-Lautrec and Picasso Died almost blind

DELACROIX, FERDINAND VICTOR EUGÈNE *(de-la-krwa')*
(French 1798/99-1863)   PLATES 8, 12
Painter, draughtsman, graphic artist Born at St Maurice, Charenton, near Paris Early schooling at Bordeaux Lifelong interest in music Attended Collège Louis-Le-Grand in Paris and met Gericault. 1816, began study at Ecole des Beaux-Arts Entered Guérin's studio Frequent visitor at Louvre where he admired old masters and English painters, Hogarth, Rowlandson and the landscapists 1821, at age of 23, painted the renowned, romantic *Dante and Virgil* which was exhibited at Salon of 1822 It aroused conflicting appraisal, but was later purchased by the state Left studio of Guérin because of dissatisfaction with academic restrictions. Began to write his famous *Journals* Influenced by paintings of Constable as well as of Rubens Visited England in 1825 where he met Lawrence

249

Ardent admirer of the theatre, especially Shakespeare, Byron and Goethe About 1827, produced group of lithographs illustrating Faust, Hamlet and other dramas 1832, went on diplomatic mission for Louis Philippe to Morocco Influence of contact with Orient very strong Received many commissions to decorate public buildings including Louvre, Hôtel de Ville, Ste Sulpice, Libraries of Luxembourg and Chamber of Deputies Left over 9,000 sketches Died of a chest ailment

DELAUNAY, ROBERT-VICTOR-FÉLIX (de-lo-nay')
(French 1885-1941)   PLATE 193
Painter and draughtsman Born Paris Attended schools at Bourges and Paris. Worked for 2 years at Academy of Theatre Design at Belleville Earliest landscape and portrait style was in the pointillist technique 1905 on, his art developed under influence of neo-impressionism, Henri Rousseau, Metzinger and cubist group, including Apollinaire 1909, lived at Chaville, influence of Cezanne is evident 1911, 'tower' period, exhibited at 1911 Salon des Indépendants 1912, period of cities ' 1911-13, "the windows," a period dubbed by Apollinaire cubisme orphique " "Circular forms" was name given style of 1914 Until 1930, variations of this last style 1914, trip to Spain and Portugal Designs for Diaghilev ballet and mural decorations for San Francisco Fair Participated in Cubist International Show, 1925 1930-35, new rhythmic style Deco rated Railroad Palace and Palace of Air at Paris Exposition, 1937 Died Montpellier

DEMUTH, CHARLES HENRY
(American 1883-1935)   PLATE 194
Painter and draughtsman Born Lancaster, Pa Studied under Chase at Pennsylvania Academy of Fine Arts 1904, and again during 1912-14, lived in Paris studying at Academy Colarossi Strongly influenced by Cubism Close friend of Marcel Duchamp although he modified this influence Returned to U S 1917-18, painted series of architectural subjects, inspired by Cubism Illustrated in watercolor works of Balzac, Zola, Poe and Henry James 1917-19, vaudeville, night life and architectural subjects. After 1920, made mostly still-life and beautiful flower pieces Died Lancaster 1950, exhibition Museum of Modern Art, N Y

DERAIN, ANDRÉ (de-ran')
(French 1880-   )   PLATE 79 end page
Painter, draughtsman, graphic artist Born Chatou-sur-Seine Studied at Polytechnical School At 15 began to paint Attended Academy Carriere and met Matisse. 1899, met Vlaminck, shared a studio at Chalou, 1901-02 Spent much time painting landscape 1905, painted with Matisse at Collioure Exhibited Fauve landscapes at Salon d Automne, 1905 1905-08, Fauve period followed by landscapes which record Céret and Martigues 1907, associated with Kahnweiler 1910, visit to Spain 1912, returned to Paris and began to experiment with figure painting 1913, spent summer at Martigues with Vlaminck At outbreak of World War I at Avignon with Picasso and Braque Mobilized 1920, worked on landscapes of the Midi and of Italy Still-lifes and portraits take large place in his oeuvre 1931, Paul Guillaume gave him exhibition Post-war preoccupation with nude, many sanguine drawings. Interested in theatre design Since early 1900's has isolated himself from group exhibitions Received two important one-man shows in France, 1916 and 1931 Woodcut illustrations for Apollinaire's L'Enchanteur Pourrissant, 1909, Max Jacob s Les Oeuvres Burlesques et Mystiques, and an edition of Pantagruel, Skira, 1945

DESPIAU, CHARLES (des-pee-o')
(French 1874-1946)   PLATE 80
Sculptor and draughtsman Born Mont-de-Marsan, son of a plasterer Paris, studied at Ecole des Arts Decoratifs and at Ecole des Beaux-Arts 1898, work accepted at the Salon Worked in studio of Rodin, with whom he collaborated over period of years Influenced by classical Greek sculpture Especially well known for his portrait heads and busts Died Paris.

DIX, OTTO (diks)
(German 1891-   )   PLATE 151
Painter and graphic artist. Born Unterhaus, 1891 1905-10, mural-decorator's assistant 1910-12, attended Dresden School of Arts and Crafts and Academy Fought in World War I Post-war period spent in Dusseldorf, Berlin and Dresden where he became professor at the Academy Influenced in early work by Italian Quattrocento Series of war etchings are unforgettable

DUFY, RAOUL (doo-fee')
(French 1877-1953)   PLATE 78
Painter, draughtsman, illustrator Born at Havre Studied at Ecole des Beaux-Arts, Havre, where Friesz also a pupil 1910, went to study at Ecole des Beaux-Arts, Paris, and in studio of Bonnat. Came in contact with art of Impressionists and

Cézanne and influenced by Matisse, Monet, Jongkind, van Gogh, and Lautrec Made frequent visits to Havre and Côte d Emeraude, Normandy, where he painted landscapes and regattas. Began to exhibit at Salons in 1901 1908, began to develop theories of tonal and formal relationships akin to those of certain Cubists such as Herbin and Valmier Worked on many decorative projects and often designed silks and textiles for Bianchini and dress designer Paul Poiret Influenced after war by Chinese painting Decorative style in watercolor and gouache developed Continued to make designs for ceramics, tapestries and textiles Designed large mural, L'Histoire de l Electricité a travers les Ages, for Pavilion of Electricity at Exhibition of Arts and Techniques, 1937 1952, visited U S Died France

EAKINS, THOMAS
(American 1844-1916)   PLATES 181, 183
Painter, sculptor, draughtsman Early education Central High School, Phila Early showed aptitude for drawing and science Studied at Pennsylvania Academy of Fine Arts and anatomy at Jefferson Medical College under famous surgeon, Pancoast 1866, France Studied at Ecole des Beaux-Arts under Gérôme. 1868, traveled in France, Switzerland, Italy, Germany 1869, in studio of Bonnat Same year traveled in Spain, deeply impressed by Velasquez 1870, returned to America 1874, began to exhibit watercolors in N Y 1875, painted the Gross Clinic 1880, Member of National Academy During 80's developed an interest in photography Taught at Pennsylvania Academy of Fine Arts and Philadelphia Art Students League His penetrating, sympathetic, realistic portraits little appreciated in his own time Loved sports, especially rowing, swimming and baseball Died Phila

ENSOR, JAMES SYDNEY (en'-sor)
(Belgian 1860-1949)   PLATES 117-19
Painter and graphic artist Born Ostend, Belgium 1877-80, studied at Brussels Academy under Portaels 1880, returned to Ostend 1881, exhibited at Brussels Salon 1882, exhibited at Paris Salon 1884, his work was rejected by Brussels group This was followed by formation of group known as Les XX 1886, first etchings 1889, Les XX refused his important painting The Entry of Christ into Brussels and same group voted to expel him 1896, one-man show Brussels 1898, exhibition in Paris under auspices of magazine La Plume 1913, first catalogue of his prints, published by Garvens-Garvensburg, Hanover, Germany 1914-18, remained in Ostend 1921, received retrospective exhibition in Antwerp During 1921 collected writings were published 1927, large exhibition in Hanover 1929, large retrospective exhibition in Brussels 1932, Musee National du Jeu de Paume exhibited his work 1939, second large exhibition in Paris under auspices of Gazette des Beaux-Arts 1939-45, spent war years in Ostend which suffered severe bombing 1946, National Gallery, London, large exhibition Died Ostend 1950, large group of his works shown at Biennale, Venice 1951-52, retrospective exhibition at the Museum of Modern Art, N Y

FEININGER, LYONEL
(American 1871-   )   PLATE 196, p 206
Painter and graphic artist Born N Y of German parents, both musicians 1887-88, pupil at School of Decorative Arts, Hamburg, 1888-90, at Academy, Berlin 1906, returned to Paris Weekly comic page for Chicago Tribune (1906-07) Influenced later by Cubism 1908, in Berlin 1919, became professor at Bauhaus in Weimar and Dessau 1931, traveled to Brittany and Northern France Large retrospective exhibition, Berlin, 1931 and Museum of Modern Art, 1944 Art condemned by the Nazis 1937, left Germany for U S Lives in N Y C and Conn

FORAIN, JEAN LOUIS (fo-ran')
(French 1852-1931)   PLATE 29
Painter and graphic artist Born Rheims Studied under Jacqueson de la Chevreuse and later under sculptor, Carpeaux Influenced by Goya, Rembrandt, Manet, and Degas French satirist renowned for paintings and prints of social, political and legal world in Paris Contributed to French newspapers and journals for thirty years Admired by Degas and Toulouse-Lautrec Died Paris Prolific works in fields of drawing, lithography and etching

FRASCONI, ANTONIO (frass-ko'-nee)
(Uruguayan 1919-   )   PLATE 137
Graphic artist Born Montevideo, Uruguay, of Italian parents Frasconi has been given one-man shows in Montevideo, Mexico, Weyhe Gallery, N Y Represented in group exhibitions in U S, South America and Europe Received Inter-American Guggenheim fellowship, 1952 One of the artists who has given new impetus to woodcutter's art, in color and in black and white Has to his credit some 260 woodcuts produced in about ten years.

LA FRESNAYE, NOEL FRANCOIS ROGER ANDRÉ DE
(la-fray-nay') (French 1885-1925) PLATE 85
Painter, sculptor, draughtsman, graphic artist Born Mans of
aristocratic family Attended Academy Julian where he met
Segonzac Studied with Maurice Denis and Sérusier Later became interested in Cubist movement under Picasso and
Braque 1910-13, exhibited at Salons d Automne and Indépendants with cubists Developed personal style in landscape
Also active in sculpture 1913-14, period of beautiful still-lifes
Entered World War I as infantryman Managed to keep up his
draughtsmanship while at front. Contracted pneumonia 1918
and spent years at Grasse combatting tuberculosis Influenced
by the Classic world as well as by Quattrocento and later
Renaissance arts Died at Grasse.

GAUGUIN, PAUL *(go-gan')*
(French 1848-1903) PLATES 43-45, p 37
Painter, sculptor, graphic artist Born Paris Spanish-Peruvian
heritage Spent childhood in Peru Early ambition to be sailor
1871, became stockbroker 1873, began to paint Pissarro intro-
duced him to Impressionist group 1883, abandoned social and
family ties to devote himself to painting 1886, left for Pont-
Aven, Brittany 1887, went to Martinique Impact of these
trips separated him from Impressionism 1888, made second
sojourn in Brittany with E Bernard and Serusier Friend of
Symbolists and leader of Synthetist movement Visited van
Gogh at Arles 1891-93, left France for Tahiti Returned to
France 1894, again left for Tahiti 1895 Died in Marquesas
Collected works of Manet, Monet, Cezanne, Sisley, Pissarro,
and Renoir He opened up new fields in graphic arts

GÉRICAULT, JEAN LOUIS ANDRÉ THÉODORE
(zhay-ree-ko') (French 1791-1824) PLATES 7, 9-11
Painter, draughtsman, graphic artist Born Rouen Early
schooling at Collège Louis-Le-Grand Love for horses throughout his short life Left school at 17 to study under Carle
Vernet, spent period in studio of neo-classicist Guerin, pupil
of David Ardent copyist at Louvre where he most admired
Caravaggio, Rubens, and Rembrandt 1816-18, visited Florence
and Rome where he fell under spell of Michelangelo His
painting, *The Raft of the Medusa*, one of most important
paintings of the Romantic movement 1820-22, visited England
where he admired work of Turner, Constable, Lawrence, and
English watercolorists Returned to France where two years
later he died as result of fall from horse Author of many
lithographs and drawings

GLACKENS, WILLIAM JAMES
(American 1870-1938) PLATE 187
Painter and illustrator Born Philadelphia Studied Pennsyl-
vania Academy of Fine Arts Illustrator for Philadelphia
newspapers 1895, went to Paris. Illustrated for *New York
Herald* and *New York World* First exhibited with *The Eight*
War staff artist of *McClure's* magazine during Spanish-Ameri-
can War Died N Y.

VAN GOGH, VINCENT *(van khokh)*
(Dutch 1853-1890) PLATES 37-42; p 37
Painter, draughtsman, graphic artist Born Groot Zundert,
Brabant, son of clergyman At 16 employed by Goupil, art
dealers Began letters to his brother, Theo Visited museums
studying Rembrandt, Hals, Ruysdael, Reynolds, Gainsborough,
Turner, Old Crome, Constable, Millet, and Corot Avid reader
of Bible, Michelet and Dickens Schoolteacher in England
Returned to Holland, worked in book shop Began to prepare
for university, to study theology Again suffered failure and
second breakdown Worked among miners in Borinage, Belgium 1877-78, determined to become painter Miners his first
models He copied reproductions of Millet's works 1885, year
of his father's death, van Gogh's first major work appeared,
the *Potato Eaters* 1886 87, in Paris Attended Cormon's art
school Met Toulouse-Lautrec and Emile Bernard, later Pissarro, Monet, Seurat and Gauguin Exhibited in art shop of Père
Tanguy with Cezanne and Renoir 1888-89, Arles There his
friends were Postmaster Roulin and Milliet the Zouave Was
visited by Gauguin and at this time they quarreled and van
Gogh cut off his own ear Van Gogh was taken to hospital His
painting and drawing reached a climax in which he freed himself from influence of Impressionists Nature and Japanese
prints were his deepest inspirations 1889-90, St Remy, where
he lived at Asylum of St Paul Alternating periods of good
health and depression Worked feverishly Homesickness for
Holland increased Drew often from memory Copied engravings after Rembrandt, Delacroix and Millet, but these "copies"
were original interpretations Public recognition of his art
began 1890 Invited to exhibit with the XX group in Brussels
1890, Auvers, where he lived under care of Dr Gachet
Committed suicide 1929 and 1936, retrospective exhibitions
Museum of Modern Art, N Y

GOYA Y LUCIENTES, FRANCISO JOSÉ DE *(go'-ya)*
(Spanish 1746-1828) Frontispiece, PLATES 5-6, pp 6, 241
Painter, draughtsman, graphic artist Born Fuentodos. Studied
painting under Jose Luzán in Saragossa, and under Francisco
Bayeu in Madrid At 25 went to Rome 1775, commissioned by
Royal Manufactory of Tapestries to paint cartoons Studied
old masters at Prado especially Velasquez, after whose work
he made series of etchings Goya's early painting and etching
has much of the rococo spirit 1789, became first court painter
Early influence of Tiepolo and Rembrandt in his first major
graphic series, *Los Caprichos* (The Caprices) (c 1799) Effects
on Goya of French invasion of Spain (1808-12) led to his
graphic series, *Disasters of War* (c 1810-1820). First published,
1863 1824, left Spain for France unable to tolerate political
persecution of his native land Mastered lithography at end of
his long and prolific career. One of the most penetrating of all
portraitists, superb draughtsman and innovator in graphic arts
Goya s art cannot be over-estimated in its tremendous influence
on the 19th and 20th Centuries Died Bordeaux, France

GRAVES, MORRIS
(American 1910-) PLATE 199
Painter and draughtsman Born Oregon Paints usually in
gouache and watercolor Traveled in Japan, Puerto Rico, and
Europe Admires Oriental art and religion Lives near Seattle

GREENE, STEPHEN
(American 1918-) p 237
Painter and draughtsman Born New York City 1936-37,
studied National Academy, N Y 1939-42, attended William
and Mary College and Iowa University, studying painting
1943-45, lived in N Y 1945-46, returned for Master's Degree
to Iowa University 1946-47, taught at Indiana State University 1947-52, taught at Washington University, St Louis, and
at Parsons School, N Y Three one-man exhibitions, Durlacher
Bros , N Y 1952, received fellowship for study at American
Academy, Rome

GRIS, JUAN *(greess)*
(Spanish 1887-1927) PLATES 104-05
Painter, draughtsman, graphic artist Born Jose Victoriano
Gonzalez in Madrid. Castilian and Andalusian heritage
Studied in Madrid, but was obliged to leave his studies to help
provide for his large family 1906, went to Paris where he met
Picasso Made drawings for *Le Temoin* and *L'Assiette au
Beurre* Began to exhibit his paintings in 1910 and immediately
became involved in Cubist movement 1912, exhibited at Salon
des Independants 1913, went to Ceret with Picasso, Braque,
Max Jacob, and others. During early months of War in 1914,
he went to Collioure with Marquet and Matisse Suffered from
pleurisy and convalesced at Beaulieu and Ceret. 1922, established himself in Boulogne-sur-Seine, spending winters in the
Midi Chiefly known as painter and illustrator 1924, stage designs and costumes for three Diaghilev ballets, illustrated Max
Jacob's *Ne coupez pas Mademoiselle* (1921), and Gertrude
Stein's *A Book concluding with a Wife has a Cow, A Love
Story* (1926) Died Boulogne-sur-Seine

GROSZ, GEORGE *(grohss)*
(American 1893-) PLATES 149-50
Painter and graphic artist Born Berlin Grew up in small garri-
son town where he observed military and bourgeois life
1909-12, pupil at Dresden Academy 1913-14, student at
School of Industrial Art Post-war period lived in Berlin
1920, traveled to Italy, 1922, Russia, 1924, 1925, 1927, France,
1929, England Illustrated for German periodicals and
L'Illustration Influence of the War, as on Dix, was profound
Founded satirical reviews with the photo-monteur Heartfield
and the editor Herzfelde, the most important being the *Platte*
Participated in the Dada movement Was one of the members
of the *Neue Sachlichkeit* Went to U S after Hitler regime
came into power Taught at Art Students League, N Y 1937,
awarded a Guggenheim Fellowship His style has changed
since arrival in America. The vitriolic draughtsmanship seems
to have relaxed

HAYTER, STANLEY WILLIAM
(English 1901-) PLATE 210
Painter, graphic artist, author Born London Studied King's
College, University of London Founder of Atelier 17, Paris,
a studio which flourished between 1927 and 1939, and attracted
many artists including Picasso, Miró, Kandinsky, Calder and
Tanguy 1940, Atelier 17 moved to New York where it has
continued to influence graphic artists. 1940-45, Hayter was
instructor of etching and engraving at New School for Social
Research, N Y Author of *New Ways of Gravure* (see Bibliog)
Lives in Paris.

251

HECKEL, ERICH (hek'-l)
    (German 1883-   )   PLATE 136
Painter and graphic artist. Born Döbeln. Studied architecture, Dresden, 1904 1905, gave up architecture to form, with Kirchner and Schmidt-Rottluff, the *Brücke* group 1906, in preparing first exhibition of *Brücke* group in Dresden met Nolde and Pechstein 1910, went to Italy and traveled to Mortzburg with Otto Mueller, who joined the *Brücke*, 1911 1912, participated in Exposition of Sonderbund at Cologne met Franz Marc, Feininger, and others 1913, when *Brücke* group was dispersed went to the fjord of Flensburg During World War I served as a volunteer hospital attendant in Belgium, 1915, met Beckmann in Flanders 1926, traveled to Rhône Valley, Provence, England, and Paris 1927, visited Denmark and Sweden 1929, returned to Provence, Pyrenees, and Aquitaine 1930, again in Sweden

HOMER, WINSLOW
    (American 1836-1910)   pp 203, 239
Painter and graphic artist Born Boston Apprenticed to lithographer, Buffard, Boston Began to illustrate for *Ballou's Pictorial* and *Harper's Weekly* 1859, studied in N Y at National Academy of Design Commissioned by *Harper's Weekly* to cover Lincoln's inauguration and Civil War scenes 1867, went to France 1864, member of National Academy 1876, gave up illustration to devote himself to painting 1881, visited England Here began his intense absorption in marine subjects Painted in White Mountains, Adirondacks, Gloucester, Mass , and in Maine 1883, lived at Prout's Neck, Maine 1884, went to Nassau Died Prout's Neck.

HOPPER, EDWARD
    (American 1882-   )   PLATE 186
Painter and graphic artist Born Nyack, N Y 1900-05, attended Chase School under Robert Henri and Miller 1906-07, lived in Paris where influenced by Impressionism 1909-10, spent summers in Europe Until 1924, earned his living as illustrator 1924, exhibition of water colors, N Y. Gave up commercial work and returned to oil painting Lives in N. Y

INGRES, JEAN AUGUSTE DOMINIQUE (ang'gr)
    (French 1780-1867)   PLATE 1, p 7
Painter, draughtsman, graphic artist Born Montauban, son of a sculptor At 11, student at Academy of Fine Arts, Toulouse, where he distinguished himself, especially in draughtsmanship 1797, arrived Paris and became pupil of David Attended Ecole des Beaux-Arts and Swiss Academy Began to make pencil portraits. Won Prix de Rome, 1801, leaving for Rome, 1806 His art strongly influenced by Raphael 1824-34, lived in Paris, the recipient of honors and commissions 1825, elected member of Academy of Fine Arts, Paris, began long career as teacher Became director of the Academy, 1829 1834, returned to Rome as director of French Academy At Universal Exposition of 1855, about seventy of his paintings were exhibited Died 1867 at age of 87, having been honored by two emperors, Napoleon I and Napoleon III Influenced Degas and Puvis de Chavannes. On his death the Ingres Museum was founded in Montauban.

JOHN, AUGUSTUS EDWIN
    (English 1878-   )   p 183
Painter and graphic artist Born Tenby, Wales 1896-99, studied at Slade School, London. Traveled, Europe 1901-02, taught at University of Liverpool Returned to London where he became prominent portrait painter World War I, official artist with Canadian Corps. Visited U S 1928, member Royal Academy Prolific in fields of landscape, still-life, watercolor, etching, lithography as well as portraiture. Lives in England.

KANDINSKY, WASSILY (kan-din'-skee)
    (Russian 1866-1944)   PLATE 148
Painter and graphic artist Born Moscow Early childhood in Italy. School years in Odessa. At 18 studied political economy and law in Moscow Left Moscow to study painting in Munich. 1902-03, opened his own art school 1902, member of Berlin Secessionists and exhibited at Salon d'Automne, Paris 1903-04, traveled in Tunisia and Kairuan, 1905, visited Rapallo, 1906, Sèvres, 1907, Berlin 1908, returned to Munich 1908-1912, president of the Neue Künstlervereinigung in Munich Wrote *Concerning the Spiritual in Art*, published in 1912. 1911, made his first abstract painting 1912, formed with Franz Marc the *Blue Rider* group. Shortly came to know Klee 1913, published *Klänge*, a book of poetry and woodcuts, exhibited at Armory Show, N Y 1914, returned to Russia and published autobiography. Became member of art section of Popular Commissariat of Public Instruction, then professor at Academy, Moscow 1919, director of Museum of Pictorial Culture 1920, professor at University of Moscow 1921, founded Academy of Artistic Sciences 1921, returned to Berlin 1923, vice-president of Société Anonyme, N Y Professor at Bauhaus, Weimar and Dessau, 1922-33 1934 until his death, lived in Paris

252

Widely traveled in Europe and Middle East 1952, retrospective exhibition, Institute of Contemporary Art, Boston

KIRCHNER, ERNST LUDWIG (keerkh'-ner)
    (German 1880-1938)   PLATE 138, p 126
Painter, sculptor, graphic artist Born Aschaffenburg 1901, studied architecture in Dresden Leading spirit of *Brucke* group, which he founded with Heckel and Schmidt-Rottluff, 1905 Painted outside Dresden with Pechstein and Heckel near lake of Moritzburg Made poster and a number of other graphic works for *Brucke* group 1911, went to Berlin 1914, entered military service Suffered from tuberculosis Convalesced first at Königstein, in 1916 went to Davos, Switzerland Earliest artistic influences came from van Gogh and Munch, and Russian novelist Dostoyevsky Editor of *Chronik der Brücke* in which he tells that his artistic inspirations came from 15th and 16th Century German woodcutters, African Negro sculpture, and sculpture of Pacific Islands Later felt impact of Picasso's art Committed suicide, Davos First major showing of his painting in this country at Busch-Reisinger Museum, Harvard University, 1950-51

KLEE, PAUL (klay)
    (Swiss 1879-1940)   PLATES 120, 122-26
Painter and graphic artist Born near Berne Father Bavarian musician, mother French Studied Munich, 1898, and visited Italy where he was interested in early Christian, Saracen, and baroque art In Naples was fascinated by the zoological laboratory, Oceanographic Institute 1903-06, lived partly in Berne 1903, made first engraving Took courses in anatomy Studied Goya, Blake, Beardsley, Ensor, and Redon, and authors Hoffmann, Poe, Gogol, and Baudelaire Illustrated Voltaire's *Candide*, 1911-12 1905, short trip to Paris After 1906 went to Munich where he remained till 1920 Admired Cézanne and Matisse 1912, joined *Blue Rider* group with Kandinsky and Marc. Exhibited with them in 1912 and at Sturm Gallery, Berlin, 1913 1912-13, visited Paris where he met Rousseau, Picasso, Delaunay and Apollinaire 1914, traveled to Kairuan 1916, entered military service 1920-29, professor at Bauhaus in Weimar and Dessau 1926, founded with Kandinsky, Jawlensky and Feininger the *Blaue Vier* 1930, professor Dusseldorf Academy Anticipated work of Paris Surrealists Admired art of children and primitive peoples. Died Locarno. 1930 and 1941, exhibitions Museum of Modern Art N Y

KOKOSCHKA, OSKAR (ko'-kosh-ka)
    (Austrian 1886-   )   PLATES 142-43
Painter and graphic artist Born Pöchlarn, Austria Father a Czech, trained as goldsmith Despite poverty, parents instilled love for philosophy, music and literature 1904, received scholarship at Vienna School of Arts and Crafts, remaining three years 1908, published first illustrated book, *The Dreaming Boys* First Vienna exhibition, showed graphic art, sculpture and painting Some of these works so radical he was dismissed from school, but quickly championed by progressives 1910, visited Berlin, came to know some of founders of Expressionism Nolde, Kirchner, Heckel In Berlin, under sponsorship of publisher-critic Herwarth Walden, began to illustrate for magazine *Sturm* Returned to Vienna, 1911, subject to virulent criticism as well as praise 1914, two lithograph series appeared, *The Fettered Columbus* and *The Bach Cantata* Wounded 1916, went to Dresden to convalesce Worked with intensity in literature, painting, illustration, and became professor at Dresden Academy, 1920-24. Left Dresden 1924, exploring Switzerland as well as France, Holland, London, North Africa, and Near East 1931, returned to Vienna and to political upheavals which eventually caused him to depart in 1934 for Prague 1934-38, battled against forces of Nazism, which labeled his art "Degenerate " Left Prague in 1938 and lived in England throughout World War II 1948, Institute of Contemporary Art, Boston, gave first retrospective exhibition in America Bulk of graphic work created in Vienna, Berlin and Dresden before World War II Three posters, *La Pasionara, Help the Basque Children,* of 1937, and *Remember the Children of Europe Who Will Starve This Winter,* of 1945, testify to his still potent ability in the graphic arts

KOLLWITZ, KATHE SCHMIDT (koll'-vitss)
    (German 1867-1945)   PLATES 145-46
Graphic artist and sculptor Born Königsberg, Prussia. Brought up in atmosphere of stern religious thought and high social principles Studied etching under Rudolph Mauer. 1888, Art School, Berlin. Influenced by writings of Zola and Ibsen 1891, after marriage, began to devote herself to etching Strong influence of Rembrandt. 1894-98, first print cycle, *The Weavers,* inspired by Hauptmann's play 1902-08, second series, *Peasant War,* again developed a social theme. These years saw single prints, including self-portraits First decade of 1900's, began to experiment with lithography World War I years, in which she suffered a personal loss In death of a son, mark her

important early sculpture Tragedies of post-war Germany led her to create some of most powerful posters, lithographs and woodcuts in new monumental, more abstract style 1923, *Krieg* series of woodcuts 1933, expelled from Berlin Academy for anti-Nazi sympathies 1934-35, last great print series, *The Theme of Death* Last years of her life devoted to sculpture One of the few 20th Century woman artists to achieve stature of greatness Her sculpture, prints and drawings reflect her sympathy with plight of fellow man in modern times Died Moritzburg

LEAR, EDWARD
(English 1812-1888)   p 182
Poet, humorist watercolorist, draughtsman, illustrator Born Highgate, London At 15 earned his living doing advertisement sketches for shops, painting fans and screens Made anatomical drawings for hospitals and doctors 1831, employed by Zoological Society Engaged by Earl of Derby at private menagerie, Knowsley Continued to illustrate books for zoologists 1837-41, traveled in Southern Europe, Italy and Albania Made topographical landscapes Was briefly drawing master to Queen Victoria Admired by Tennyson and Ruskin 1846, *The Book of Nonsense* was published Spent much of his later life in Italy and traveling in Calabria, Sicily, Malta, Greece and Near East. Died San Remo, Italy

LEBRUN, RICO (le-brun')
(American 1900-   )   PLATE 205
Painter and draughtsman Born Naples, Italy Studied art in Naples Served in Italian army during World War I 1924, came to U S to establish branch of Naples stained glass factory in Springfield, Ill 1925, came to N Y 1935-37, received Guggenheim Fellowship Taught Art Students League, N Y, Chouinard Art Institute, Los Angeles, and Sophie Newcomb College, New Orleans.

LÉGER, FERNAND (lay-zhay')
(French 1881-   )   REAR JACKET
Painter and graphic artist Born Argentan Came to Paris in 1898 Worked as architectural designer and retoucher of photographs 1901-03, attended courses under Gérôme at Ecole des Beaux-Arts 1908, reacted strongly against Impressionism Met Archipenko 1910, through Kahnweiler, came to know art of Braque and Picasso 1912, began to exhibit at Gallery Kahnweiler Mobilized during World War I. Machinery of war had powerful effect and stimulated him to create a kind of "Mechanical Dynamism" which he later applied to treatment of the human form 1917-23, period "mécanique " 1924, traveled to Venice and Ravenna to see mosaics 1924-25, painted series of animated landscapes but gradually by 1925 abandoned the dynamic for static manner of painting. 1925, painted murals for the Exposition of Decorative Arts, Paris alone. Active in cinema research 1924, was author of cinema *Ballet Mécanique* 1931, visited N Y 1933, visited Greece 1937 marked new abstract phase 1940, again visited America where his painting became more primitive in technique. Spent years 1941-46 as teacher After war returned to France. 1945, Galerie Louis Carré held retrospective of his work since 1918 1952, created mural designs for Assembly Building of the United Nations, N, Y Lives in France.

LEHMBRUCK, WILHELM (lame'-brook)
(German 1881-1919)   PLATE 144
Sculptor, painter, graphic artist Born Duisburg-Meiderich, Germany, son of Ruhr miner Began to draw and carve in youth, copying pictures from school books 1895-99, attended Art School, Düsseldorf 1901-09, student at Academy, Düsseldorf 1905, visited Italy 1910-14, lived in Paris 1912, second trip to Italy Influenced by Rodin and Maillol Early work reveals some influence from Italian Renaissance. His art suggests relationships to Gothic elongated sculpture as well as to Blue Period of Picasso 1914-17, lived in Berlin Member of Berlin Academy 1917, lived in Zürich and Berlin 1919, committed suicide, Berlin

LEVINE, JACK
(American 1915-   )   PLATE 204
Painter and draughtsman Born Boston, of Lithuanian parents Attended children's classes of Museum of Fine Arts, Boston, from 7 - 10 years of age Harold Zimmerman, painter, and Denman Ross, of Harvard University, encouraged and taught Levine in his youth. Worked for the W.P.A. 1937, exhibited at Whitney Museum and Museum of Modern Art, N Y Served in Army during World War II 1947, traveled in Europe 1950-51, received Fulbright Award 1952, one-man show, Institute of Contemporary Art, Boston. Lives in N. Y.

LIPCHITZ, JACQUES (leep-sheets')
(French 1891-   )   PLATE 112
Sculptor and graphic artist. Born Druskeniki, Polish Lithuania. Early schooling in Vilna. 1909, Paris, studied at Academy

Julian, commercial workshops, and Ecole des Beaux-Arts Early influence of Archipenko, African Negro sculpture and Cubism (1913-17) 1911-15, used the prism and sphere as basic forms for sculpture Close friend of Gris and admired Rodin 1924 on, exhibited with Société Anonyme 1927, first "open" sculpture of twisted cast bronze strips. 1941, came to U S 1946, revisited France As exemplified in his sculpture *Prometheus*, in Rio de Janeiro, exploits in modern manner psychological roots of mythology His works, during World War II, reflect return to an old interest in plant forms but with surrealist undertones His most recent sculpture often planned for open air Lives in N. Y.

MAILLOL, ARISTIDE (my-) oll')
(French 1861-1944)   PLATES 75, 83-84, p 242
Sculptor and graphic artist Born Banyuls Early education at Banyuls and Perpignan 1882-87, studied at Ecole des Beaux-Arts, Paris, under Cabanel and Gérôme. Knew Gauguin and Bourdelle at this time Studied tapestry making and Gothic tapestries at Cluny Museum Briefly had his own tapestry workshop at Banyuls. 1895, returned to Paris where he met Vuillard, Bonnard, Matisse and Nabis group 1899-1900, defective eyesight turned him to sculpture 1902, included in one of Vollard's exhibitions where his work met approval of Rodin. 1908, traveled to Greece with Count Kessler, German collector and amateur typographer who later published Maillol's *Eclogues of Vergil* 1912, received commission for *Fame*, a memorial to Cezanne 1919-23, war memorials for Céret and Port-Vendres 1925, first exhibition in U S at Albright Art Gallery, Buffalo, and Brummer Gallery, N Y Died Banyuls

MANET, EDOUARD (mah-nay')
(French 1832-83)
PLATES 17, 19-20, pp 9-11, 258-59
Painter and graphic artist Born Paris, son of a magistrate 1847, failed examination for naval school, visited South America 1850, entered studio of Couture Admired Delacroix 1856, traveled in Belgium, Holland, Germany, Italy 1860, joined Café Guerbois group including Zola, Duranty, Duret, Degas, Renoir, and later joined by Cezanne, Sisley, Monet and Pissarro 1861, Salon accepted two of his paintings Published nine engravings in 1862 In same year, *Déjeuner sur l Herbe* appeared at Salon des Refusés Championed by his friends, Baudelaire, Zola and Mallarmé. 1867, Paris World's Fair, Manet exhibited fifty pictures 1868, visited London. Berthe Morisot and Eva Gonzalez entered his studio as pupils. Admired great Spanish masters, especially Velasquez and Goya. 1870, Franco-Prussian war, Manet remained in Paris 1871, made trip to Holland, keen interest in Hals, painted *Bon Bock* 1874, painted with Monet at Argenteuil 1879, *The Execution of Maximilian* was first Impressionist painting to be exhibited in U S 1882, received Cross of Legion of Honor Died Paris

MANZÙ, GIACOMO (mahn-tzoo')
(Italian 1908-   )   PLATE 162
Sculptor and draughtsman Born Bergamo Self-taught sculptor, occasional student at Academy of Verona 1930, moved to Milan First important one-man exhibition, Galleria della Cometa, Rome, 1938 Received grand prize for Italian sculpture at Venice Biennial Exposition, 1948 Lives in Milan.

MARIN, JOHN
(American 1870-1953)   PLATES 191-92
Watercolorist, painter, etcher Born Rutherford, N J Worked in architects' offices as a young man. 1888, earliest watercolors. 1899-1901, studied at Pennsylvania Academy of Fine Arts under Anshutz 1901-03, studied at Art Students League, N Y 1905-09, Europe, where he lived in Paris and traveled to Italy, Holland, Belgium, England. 1909, first exhibition at Stieglitz' "291" Gallery Returned to U S. 1910-11, again in Europe-Paris, Tyrol, Grenau. 1911 on, lived in U S. 1936, exhibition Museum of Modern Art, N. Y Lived in Cliffside, N J, and Maine Died Cape Split, Maine.

MARINI, MARINO (ma-ree'-nee)
(Italian 1901-   )   PLATE 163; p 169
Sculptor, draughtsman, graphic artist Born Bergamo Studied painting and sculpture at Academy of Fine Arts, Florence. Visited Paris during 1928-38 Traveled throughout Europe Frequent exhibitor at European centers First prize for sculpture at Roman Quadrennial Exposition, 1935, and later in Paris, 1937. Lives in Milan

MARQUET, ALBERT (mar-kay')
(French 1875-1947)   PLATE 74
Painter and draughtsman Born Bordeaux. 1890, Paris Attended the Ecole des Arts Decoratifs and the Ecole des Beaux-Arts. 1894, entered studio of Gustave Moreau where he met Matisse. Earned his living decorating stuccoes of the Grand Palais, 1900 Frequent sketcher in streets, was also constant copyist at Louvre, of Chardin, Claude Lorrain and Poussin Influence of van Gogh 1904, painted frequently with

Matisse One of first *Fauves* to achieve success 1908-10, worked at Academy Ranson Painted many views of Paris 1912-13, traveled with Matisse to Tangiers. Continued to travel in search of new landscape themes, Naples, Hamburg, Rotterdam, Rouen, Dunkerque, Norway Paris and the Seine constant themes of inspiration After 1908 *Fauve* period came to an end, and style became more calm and subdued in color Fond of watercolor and etching 1940, made another trip to Algiers. Met Gide and Saint-Exupery Visited Russia just before his death Important retrospective exhibition in 1948 at Musée National d'Art Moderne

MATISSE, HENRI *(ma-teess')*
(French 1869-   )   PLATES 59-70
Painter, sculptor, draughtsman, graphic artist Born Le Cateau-Cambresis Early training for law 1889, entered Croisé's art school 1891-92, studied with Bouguereau 1892-97, pupil of Gustave Moreau with Rouault and Marquet Constant visitor at Louvre 1899, bought *Three Bathers* by Cézanne 1896-97, summers in Brittany Visited in Corsica and Southern France 1899, settled in Paris 1901-04, years of financial struggle Exhibited each spring at Salon des Indépendants Met Derain and Vlaminck 1903, first etchings, 1904, first one-man show, Vollard Gallery 1904, French Riviera, met Signac 1905, exhibited Salon d'Automne with Derain, Vlaminck, Rouault and others 1906 group was dubbed *Les Fauves* 1907, in Italy First lithographs 1905 Leo and the Michael Steins principal patrons until 1908, then Shchukin until 1914 1908, 1909, trips to Germany 1910, Munich and Islamic exhibition 1908-11, taught international group of artists, including Max Weber 1911-13, wintered in Tangiers 1908, first one-man show in U S. at Stieglitz' "291" Gallery 1912, exhibited Cologne, London and Armory Show, 1913 1914, portrait etchings and lithographs 1916, Nice, visited Renoir at Cagnes 1920-21, summers in Normandy 1921, Nice, where he remained until 1938 Resumed lithography 1930, travel to Tahiti 1931, large exhibition, Museum of Modern Art, N Y Commission for mural, *The Dance*, from late Dr Albert C Barnes, Merion, Pa Spent most of World War II at Nice and Vence 1937-44, creative period despite serious illness 1943-50, Vence Period 1948-50, decoration of Dominican Chapel of Vence 1945-51, retrospective exhibitions Paris, London, Brussels, Philadelphia, Lucerne Nice, Tokyo 1951, large retrospective exhibition Museum of Modern Art, N Y Lives in Nice

MERYON, CHARLES *(mer-ree-on')*
(French 1821-1868)   p 240
Graphic artist Son of English physician in Paris and a French dancer School at Passy Traveled to Marseilles, Nice, Genoa, Pisa, Livorno 1837, entered naval school, Brest 1839, voyage to Algiers and Levant On return studied with landscape painter at Toulon 1842, voyage to New Zealand 1846, resigned naval commission 1848, exhibited at Salon Abandoned painting due to color blindness Traveled to England, Normandy, and Bourges. 1851-52, second visit to Bourges, architecture of city fascinated him Copied old masters, especially the Dutch etcher, Zeeman 1852-54, published his Paris etchings. Admired by Victor Hugo Mental disease, said to be inherited from his mother, began to undermine his life and work 1858, entered an asylum at Charenton Recovered but was obliged to return, 1866 Died Charenton.

MEZA, GUILLERMO *(may'-za)*
(Mexican 1917-   )   PLATE 180
Painter and graphic artist Born Ixtapalapra Began painting at night art school for workers One of foremost artists of younger group in Mexico

MILLET, JEAN FRANCOIS
(French 1814-1875)   p 8
Painter, graphic artist Born near Cherbourg of peasant stock Encouraged to study painting, arrived in Paris in 1838 to study at the atelier of Paul Delaroche After Revolution of 1848 retired to Barbizon near Fontainebleau Best known for his painting of peasants With their emphasis on out-of-doors subjects, Millet and the artists of the Barbizon school were important forerunners of Impressionism

MIRÓ, JOAN *(mee-ro')*
(Spanish 1893-   )   PLATE 109, p 97
Painter, sculptor, graphic artist Born Montroig, Barcelona. Attended Academy, Barcelona Family insisted he enter business world, but quickly withdrew at 18 to study with architect Gali, Barcelona 1919, went to Paris 1920, participated in Dada demonstrations His art has become increasingly esoteric Designed sets for Ballet Russe Early work characterized by piquant humor 1941, exhibition Museum of Modern Art, N Y Lived at Majorca during World War II 1946, visited U S Has executed a mural for Terrace-Plaza Hotel, Cincinnati, and another for Graduate Center, Harvard University, Cambridge

MODIGLIANI, AMEDEO *(mo-deel-yah'-nee)*
(Italian 1884-1920)   PLATES 152-53, p 168
Painter, sculptor, draughtsman Born Leghorn At first preferred sculpture to painting Studied Academies Florence, Venice Visited Paris, 1906 Early drawings influenced by Toulouse-Lautrec and Steinlen Exhibition of Cézanne, 1909, and later the art of Brancusi were stimulating forces Exhibited Salon des Independants, 1908 Returned to Italy, 1909 Career in Paris began, 1910 Most important years, 1915-19. Influenced as well by Picasso and African Negro sculpture Aware of most advanced developments in art in Paris but consistently returned to Italian sources, especially the Sienese, Botticelli and the Mannerists of the 16th Century Premature death 1951, exhibition Museum of Modern Art, N Y

MONDRIAN, PIET *(mohn'-dree-ahn)*
(Dutch 1872-1944)   PLATE 147
Painter and draughtsman Born Pieter Cornelis Mondriaan, Amersfoort, Holland Studied Amsterdam Academy of Arts 1912, went to Paris where he felt brief influence from Cubism 1914, returned to Holland One of founders of *de Stijl* group Published articles on Neo-Plasticism in their magazines In Paris was made member of the Abstraction-Création group 1938, went to London 1940, established himself in N Y where he died 1945, exhibition Museum of Modern Art, N Y

MONET, CLAUDE *(mo-nay')*
(French 1840-1926)   PLATE 16
Painter Born Paris, son of a grocer Spent youth at Havre and taught by Boudin to paint in open air Moved to Paris, 1859 Worked at Swiss Academy where he met Pissarro 1860 at Havre met Jongkind 1862, entered studio of Gleyre, forming friendships with Renoir, Sisley and Bazille Together they studied nature at Fontainebleau First Salon exhibition, 1865 Visited Normandy Influenced by Courbet During war of 1870 visited England with Pissarro, admired painting of Turner 1872-78, resided at Argenteuil, a period of research into visual phenomena of light and atmosphere resulting in style which came to be known as Impressionism First one-man show, 1880 Traveled in Normandy, Brittany, England and Italy Lived from 1883 on in Giverny where he died

MOORE, HENRY
(English 1898-   )   PLATES 170-71
Sculptor and draughtsman Born Castleford, Yorkshire As boy impressed by carvings in Yorkshire churches Trained to be teacher 1917, joined army 1919, demobilized Attended Leeds College of Art where from books he first came to know African Negro and ancient sculpture 1921, attended Royal College of Art Spent much time in British Museum in Egyptian, archaic Greek, Etruscan and Sumerian galleries 1924, first showed interest in Pre-Columbian and Mexican sculpture At this time Moore became aware of import of Brancusi's sculpture 1925, won traveling scholarship, visited Paris, Rome, Florence, Venice and Ravenna In Italy profoundly influenced by old masters, but especially by 15th Century Florentine, Masaccio 1928, first one-man show, London Received commission for relief figure for façade of London Underground Railway at St James 1937, trip to Spain where he visited the prehistoric caves at Altamira 1939, World War II cut short his work in sculpture 1940, commissioned by War Artists Advisory Committee to draw underground-shelter scenes Served in Home Guard until end of War 1941, coal mine drawings for W A A C 1944, *Madonna and Child* for Church of St. Matthew, Northampton 1946, trip to U S Retrospective exhibition, Museum of Modern Art, N Y, same year

MORANDI, GIORGIO *(mo-rahn'-dee)*
(Italian 1890-   )   PLATES 159-60
Painter and graphic artist Born Bologna. Studied at Academy of Fine Arts, Bologna Early influence of Cézanne 1918-20, allied to *Scuola Metafisica* but worked independently Exhibited with *Novecento* group Received first prize at Venice Biennial Exposition, 1948. Considered in Italy foremost living Italian painter His paintings cover small range of subject matter, mostly still life, harmonious and sensitive in color Has remained in Bologna throughout his life

MUNCH, EDVARD *(moonk)*
(Norwegian 1863-1944)
PLATES 113-16, pp 125-26
Painter and graphic artist Born Engelhaug At 17 entered State School of Art and Handicraft, Oslo Influenced by two Norwegian realists, Krogh and Heyerdahl, and by writings of Ibsen and Zola. Earliest dated etchings, 1894 Began to break from realism towards strong expression in form and content Some influence from French Impressionism in 1880's 1883, began to exhibit with progressive group First one-man show in Norway, 1889 Same years received government stipend to study in Paris Influenced by French Impressionists, Seurat and Gauguin Exhibited in Berlin, 1892, under auspices of Union of Berlin Artists. Successful one-man show, Berlin,

1893 1892-1908, lived in Germany, spending most of 1896 and
1897 in Paris 1896, exhibited at Bing's L'Art Nouveau Gallery, Paris 1895, first began to exploit lithography, in color and
black and white German Expressionists influenced by his
woodcuts in particular 1908, entered a Copenhagen sanitarium Returned to Oslo in 1909, at time of large gift of his
paintings to National Gallery of Norway 1914, won compe-
tition for decoration of auditorium of University of Oslo
1912, had important position in Cologne Sonderbund Exhibition with Picasso, van Gogh, Cézanne Died Ekely, Norway
1950, retrospective exhibition, Institute of Contemporary Art,
Boston, Fogg Museum, Cambridge, and Museum of Modern
Art, N Y

NOLDE, EMIL *(nole'-deh)*
(German 1867-   )   PLATES 132, 134
Painter, graphic artist, sculptor Born Burkall, Schleswig
1884-86, studied in Flensburg. 1892-98, worked and taught in
St Gall, Munich, Paris, Copenhagen 1905, joined *Die Brucke*
in Dresden After 1909 lived in winter in Berlin and in summer
on farm in North Schleswig Exhibited with *Brucke* group
1906, 1907 His art became individual after alliance with
Brucke group and is notable for visionary, mystical quality
1913, visited Russian Siberia, China, Japan, and South Seas
One of foremost expressionists, he learned much from African
and Melanesian art His watercolors of unusual distinction

OROZCO, JOSÉ CLEMENTE *(o-roz'-co)*
(Mexican 1883-1949)   PLATE 175, p 195
Painter and graphic artist Born Zapotlán, Jalisco Lost left
arm and eyesight impaired in explosion Studied agriculture
and architectural drawing Mexico City Began painting, 1909
Series of illustrations, drawings, and paintings depicting war
scenes and life of revolutionary Mexico, 1910-17 1917-21,
worked in California as painter and enlarger of photographs
Frescoes in Casa de los Azulejos and Preparatoria, Mexico,
D F, and the Orizaba Industrial School, 1922-27 1927-32, in
U S Frescoes in Claremont, California, N Y City, and Han-
over, N H Europe, 1932 Returned to Mexico, 1934 Frescoes
in Palacio de Bellas Artes, Mexico, D F, the University, State
Palace and Orphanage, Guadalajara, Jalisco, Biblioteca
Publica, Jiquilpan, Michoacán 1952, retrospective exhibition,
Institute of Contemporary Art, Boston, and Fogg Museum,
Cambridge

PALMER, SAMUEL
(English 1805-81)   PLATES 166, 168
Painter, graphic artist Born Newington. Educated at home
Sold first oil painting at 14 John Linnell introduced him
to William Blake, whose influence was strong Drew from
antique in British Museum Went to live in Shoreham, Kent
1839-41, study and travel in Italy 1843, elected associate
of Old Society of Painters in Watercolor Gave up oil painting
from this time on 1848, moved from Marylebone to Kensing-
ton where he taught drawing 1861, moved to Reigate Admirer
of Claude and attentive student of old masters Illustrated
Milton's *L'Allegro* and *Il Penseroso*, Spenser, his own translation of Vergil's *Eclogues* Died Reigate

PICASSO, PABLO *(pee-cahs'-so)*
(Spanish 1881-   )
PLATES 86-90, 92-103, pp 2, 5, 93-96
Painter, sculptor, draughtsman, graphic artist, ceramist Born
Malaga, Spain, son of a drawing master 1896, went to Barce-
lona where attended Academy 1900, visited Paris, studied
Gauguin, van Gogh, Toulouse-Lautrec, Vuillard, Degas,
Renoir and the Impressionists Frequent visitor at Louvre
1901-04, Madrid, Barcelona and Paris. 1901, first met Max
Jacob Blue Period 1904, took residence in Paris His circle
widened to include poets, painters, intellectuals—Salmon,
Apollinaire, etc 1905, Circus Period. Leo and Gertrude Stein,
as well as Shchukin, became interested in his art Small
bronzes as well as about 16 drypoints and etchings appeared
1905-06, first Classic Period Began to show strong interest in
Iberian sculpture, African Negro sculpture and art of Cézanne
1907, painted *Les Demoiselles d'Avignon* 1908, bought large
Henri Rousseau painting Solidified his friendship with Braque,
with whom he created Cubism 1909-12, Analytical Cubism
Followed a combination of this form of Cubism with collage,
which led to Synthetic Cubism, 1912-21 1915, parallel with
Cubism appeared drawings in realistic style which reflect influence of Ingres Spent World War I years in Paris. 1917, trav-
eled to Rome, met Diaghilev, Stravinsky Designed costumes
and sets for Cocteau's ballet, *Parade* 1919-21, further ballet
designs. 1920 on, "Neo-Classic" Period begins 1921, *Three
Musicians* paintings appear in his advanced Cubist style 1925,
Surrealist period begins 1932, large retrospective exhibition,
Paris. Period of activity in sculpture begins. 1937, *Guernica*
painting, inspired by Spanish Civil War 1939, large exhibition,
Museum of Modern Art, N Y 1940-44, lived in Paris during
World War II Lives in Paris and Vallauris

PIPER, JOHN
(English 1903-   )   PLATE 169, p 183
Painter, illustrator, stage designer Born Epsom Attended
Epsom College Early interest in church architecture and
stained glass Clerk in father's office 1924, wrote and illustrated book of poems, *The Wind in the Trees* Contributed
woodcuts to *London Mercury* and *New Leader* Left family
business, 1928 Attended Richmond Art School, Royal College
of Art, and Slade School, 1930 Wrote for *Nation, New States-
man*, and *Listener* First important exhibition, Mansard Gallery, 1931 First one-man show, Zwemmer Gallery, London,
1933 Visited Paris 1933, met Hélion, Braque, Leger, Brancusi
Collaborated on *Axis*, a magazine of abstract art. Left London
for Henley-on-Thames Worked on "constructions" until 1935,
when he began his abstract painting Exhibition of collage,
London Gallery, 1938 Familiar with graphic processes of
lithography, wood engraving, etching, aquatint Published
Brighton Aquatints, 1939 1938 until World War II, extensive
travel in England and Wales studying churches and stained
glass Many works in watercolor During World War II made
series of oil paintings of the City Churches Designed sets and
costumes for ballet, *The Quest*, 1943. 1952, visited Italy.

PISANELLO, ANTONIO
(Italian c 1395-1455)   PLATE 121
Painter, draughtsman, medalist Born Pisa Active chiefly in
Northern Italy—Venice, Ferrara, Mantua, Milan, Pavia and
Verona 1431-32, Rome, 1448, Naples A follower of Gentile
da Fabriano, and strongly influenced by International Style of
Northern Europe. Died probably in Rome

PISSARRO, CAMILLE *(pees-sah-ro')*
(French 1830-1903)   PLATE 15
Painter, draughtsman, graphic artist Born St. Thomas, Virgin
Islands, son of French father and Creole mother Spent years
1842-47 in Paris as student. Returned to Antilles and met
Danish painter Melbye Traveled to Venezuela Returned to
Paris, 1855 Short periods in ateliers and in Swiss Academy
where he met Monet Felt influence of Delacroix, Courbet,
Corot and painted in open air Joined Impressionists Exhibited
at Salon des Refusés, 1863, and at official Salons, 1864-66
Moved to Pontoise, later resided Louveciennes 1870, trip to
England with Monet Moved to Eragny in 1884 1886-88, felt
influence of Seurat but later returned to earlier style. Died
Paris

POSADA, JOSÉ GUADALUPE *(po-sah'-da)*
(Mexican 1851-1913)   PLATE 174, p 195
Engraver, political caricaturist, illustrator Born Aguascalientes
of peasant stock. 1887, went to Mexico, D F, to work for publisher Vanegas Arroyo Illustrated periodicals *Argos, La
Patria, El Pasria, El Ahuizote*, and *El Hijo del Ahuizote*, all of
which were in opposition to Díaz regime Prolific output
mostly in political cartoons and popular life commentary His
cheap prints for the masses are often called "Posadas" after
him

PRENDERGAST, MAURICE BRAZIL
(American 1859-1924)   p 205
Painter Born St John's, Newfoundland Family moved to Boston two years later At 15 painted show cards as apprentice
1884, worked his way to Europe on cattle boat Spent three
years in Paris, studying at Academy Julian, and with Laurens
and Blanc 1889, returned to U S, settling in Winchester, Mass
1898-99, second trip to Europe, visited France, Italy 1901 on,
frequently visited N Y Same year won Bronze Medal for
Watercolor at Pan-American Exposition, Buffalo 1905, exhibited in Boston and N Y C 1910, visited Florence 1912, began
to summer in New Hampshire Spent two years in Boston before moving to Washington Square, N Y Member of *The
Eight* 1913, exhibited at Armory Show, N Y. Spent summers
on Massachusetts coast. Died N Y C

REDON, ODILON *(re-don')*
(French 1840-1916)   PLATES 47-51, p 38
Painter, draughtsman, graphic artist Born Bordeaux Began as
etcher Influenced by Delacroix, Corot and Bresdin From
1871 on worked in Paris 1875, began to use charcoal crayon
in drawing, a technique which he found stimulating. Lithography was suggested to him by Fantin-Latour Richness of his
lithographic crayon, in black and white chiaroscuro, evident
in his first portfolio, *Dans le Rêve*, 1879 Close contact with
Symbolist Movement Interest in science Sporadic works in
color lithography Author of about 200 etchings, lithographs
and numerous drawings First received public recognition in
America at the Armory Show, 1913.

RENOIR, PIERRE AUGUSTE *(ren-wahr')*
(French 1841-1919)   PLATES 21, 27
Painter, sculptor, draughtsman, graphic artist Born Limoges,
son of a tailor Early work as painter of porcelains. Began
study at Ecole des Beaux-Arts, 1862. Entered studio of Gleyre

255

where he met Monet, Sisley and Bazille. Joined them in painting trips to Fontainebleau From 1864 on, exhibited yearly at Salon. 1872, due to friendship with Monet, adopted Impressionist technique and painted in open air 1874, participated in first exhibition of Impressionists, but later returned to exhibiting at official Salons Early work shows influence of Delacroix Studied Ingres Visited Italy, 1881, where he studied art of Raphael and earlier Italian artists Began to detach himself from Impressionism 1892, period of travel in France and foreign countries Painted last years of his life with brush strapped to his paralyzed hand. 1906, moved to Cagnes where he died

RIVERA, DIEGO MARIA *(ree-vay'-ra)*
(Mexican 1886-   )   PLATE 176
Painter, draughtsman, illustrator Born mining district of Guanajuato Studied at San Carlos Academy, Mexico, D F Visited Spain, 1907 Traveled in France, Belgium, Holland, England Brief return to Mexico 1911-20, in Paris associated with Derain, Braque, Klee, Picasso, Gris, and studied Cézanne Visited Italy, 1920-21 Member of Syndicate of Painters and painted encaustic murals in Preparatoria, Mexico, D F Frescoes at Secretaría de Educación Pública, Chápingo, Cuernavaca 1927-28, in Moscow and U S S R 1927, Director of Escuela Central de Artes Plasticas, Mexico, D F Frescoes in San Francisco, Detroit, and N Y Replica of mural formerly in Rockefeller Center is in Palacio de Bellas Artes, Mexico, D F

RODIN, AUGUSTE *(ro-dan')*
(French 1840-1917)   PLATE 23
Sculptor, draughtsman Born Paris of humble parents Brought up in Beauvais At 14 began to study in drawing school of the Rue de l'Ecole de Medecine, Paris Attended Barye's zoological lectures 1864, *Man with Broken Nose* was rejected by Salon Worked in studio of Carrier-Belleuse and porcelain factory of Sèvres Influenced by Carpeaux Admired Daumier 1870-73, supported himself from small commissions from Brussels In Brussels probably learned to admire the Gothic 1875, trip to Italy, strong influence of Michelangelo 1877, exhibited at Salon Returned permanently to Paris Style increased in individuality Received important commissions but fame was as much due to impassioned critics as to admirers *Age of Bronze, St John the Baptist* and *Burghers of Calais* 1880's, mature style developed Died Paris His residence is now the Rodin Museum

ROUAULT, GEORGES *(roo-o')*
(French 1871-   )   PLATES 71-73, p 65
Painter, draughtsman, graphic artist Born Paris Grandfather, who loved works of Manet and Courbet, encouraged his artistic gifts At 14, apprenticed to stained glass artist Attended evening classes at Ecole des Arts Décoratifs Learned to restore Mediaeval stained glass Albert Besnard offered him large commission to make stained glass for Ecole des Beaux-Arts but he refused Pupil of Gustave Moreau for five years in whose studio he met Matisse 1895, Moreau advised Rouault to leave Ecole des Beaux-Arts 1898, Moreau died and Rouault named curator of Moreau museum Friend of Léon Bloy and of Huysmans with whom he often retired to monastery at Ligugé 1905, began to paint circus, prostitute and theatre subjects, judges 1910, Druet gave him first large exhibition 1916, Vollard became his principal dealer Success after World War I Period following war was rich in book illustration After 1924, seldom exhibited although in 1937 important group of his paintings and graphic works appeared at Salon des Indépendants. 1946, exhibited with Braque at Tate Gallery, London 1940, Institute of Contemporary Art, Boston, gave him a large exhibition which traveled to San Francisco and Washington. Lives in Paris. 1945 and 1953, retrospective exhibitions Museum of Modern Art, N Y

ROUSSEAU, HENRI *(le douanier)* *(roo-so')*
(French 1844-1910)   PLATES 76-77
Painter and poet. Born Laval 1862, trip to Mexico as musician in military band in service of Maximilian Returned to France, 1866, and became a lawyer's clerk. 1870, returned to military life 1885, retired by state with small pension Began career as self-taught painter. Received some guidance from Gérôme and Clement, academicians, who encouraged his naïve style Admired Bouguereau, Courtois and Courbet 1886, exhibited first important painting, *Carnival Evening*, at Salon des Indépendants Made many drawings from nature About 1890, taught drawing in municipal school Between 1886 and 1890 exhibited 20 works at Salon des Independants. Admired by Gauguin and Odilon Redon Constant visitor to Paris Zoo and Jardin des Plantes. 1892-97, continued to send pictures to Salon des Indépendants. 1894, his lithograph, *The Horrors of War*, was commissioned by de Gourmont for magazine *L'Image* Painted *Sleeping Gypsy*, 1897, which was later to influence Picasso, Braque and di Chirico 1906, met Delaunay, Vlaminck, Picasso, Apollinaire and others, who were attracted by his primitiv

256

ism and flawless technique. 1907, received first large commission from Madame Delaunay for *Snake Charmer* Promoted by Joseph Brummer, the dealer Friend of Max Weber, the American Admired by avant-garde group of Picasso and his friends Died in Paris hospital. 1942, exhibitions Museum of Modern Art, N Y, and Art Institute of Chicago

SARGENT, JOHN SINGER
(American 1856-1925)   p 202
Painter and draughtsman Born Florence, Italy, of American parents Studied at Academy of Fine Arts, Florence In Paris in 1874 was pupil of Carolus-Duran 1878, attracted for first time at Paris Salon Traveled in Spain and Morocco Lived most of later years in London Visited U S first time in 1888 Executed murals for Boston Public Library and Museum of Fine Arts Widely known as fashionable portraitist on canvas and in drawings, also brilliant watercolorist His rare lithographs translate style of his crayon drawings Died Chelsea (London)

SCHMIDT-ROTTLUFF, KARL *(shmit-rot'-looff)*
(German 1884-   )   PLATE 133
Painter and graphic artist Born Rottluff 1903-06 studied architecture at the Technical School, Dresden 1905, formed *Die Brücke* with Heckel and Kirchner The group, which was joined by Nolde, Pechstein and Otto Muller, dissolved 1913 1906, exhibited in first *Die Brücke* exhibition Admired van Gogh, Munch, primitive and barbaric art 1911, moved to Berlin Spent summers on Baltic 1923, traveled in Italy, 1925, Dalmatia, 1926, Paris 1930, taught at German Academy, Rome Lives Berlin where he teaches in his own art school One of most powerful of German Expressionists

SEGONZAC, ANDRE DUNOYER DE *(se-gon-zak')*
(French 1884-   )   PLATES 81-82
Painter, draughtsman, graphic artist Born Boussy-Saint-Antoine Attended Academy Saint-Cyr 1901, Ecole des Beaux-Arts, later studied with Laurens at Academy Julian and finally Academy of La Palette 1906, began to work alone Executed still-lifes with heavy impasto 1908, spent summer at Saint-Tropez in a villa rented from Signac Created his first landscapes During this period influenced by Impressionism but changed to even thicker impasto and dark tones 1914, served in infantry, later in camouflage, where he worked with other artists including Dufresne 1920-26, spent summers at Chaville Landscapes, nudes, still-lifes occupied him at this time 1922-24, period of nude figures in open air 1926, returned to Saint-Tropez and began to develop more fluid style which resulted in love for watercolor Winter and early spring themes constant in his work Active as a painter-engraver

SELIGMANN, KURT
(American 1900-   )   PLATE 110
Painter, stage designer, graphic artist Born Basel Studied in Basel, Geneva, Florence and Paris First one-man show, Paris, 1932 Has exhibited in America since 1939, most frequently at Durlacher Bros, N Y 1927-29, lived in Italy 1929-39, Paris 1939, settled in N Y Illustrator of books Designed sets and costumes for ballet, *Four Temperaments*, by Paul Hindemith Lives in N Y C

SEURAT, GEORGES PIERRE *(sur-rah')*
(French 1859-1891)   PLATES 2, 35-36, p 36
Painter and draughtsman Born Paris Pupil of Lehmann Disciple of Ingres at Ecole des Beaux-Arts Copyist of Ingres, Delacroix, Raphael and Holbein Developed scientific theory of divisionism in opposition to Impressionists After many sketches and studies, created his paintings in studio Became leader of Neo-Impressionists One of the most intellectual artists of century Died Paris.

SEVERINI, GINO *(se-ve-ree'nee)*
(Italian 1883-   )   PLATE 155
Painter and graphic artist Born Cortona 1901, studied painting in Rome, and about 1904 met Boccioni and Balla 1906, Paris, where he knew Modigliani, Max Jacob and others 1910-15, one of five members of original Futurist group with Boccioni, Carra, Russolo and Balla Influenced by Seurat's Neo-Impressionism. Became involved in Cubism and Neo-Classicism Gave up Futurism during World War I First exhibited in America at Alfred Stieglitz' "291" Gallery Lives in Paris

SHAHN, BEN
(American 1898-   )
PLATES 208-09, pp 209, 247
Painter and graphic artist Born Kaunas, Russia 1906, came to U S Worked as lithographer's apprentice while attending night school Brooklyn Studied at New York University and City College, N Y, where he majored in biology. Studied at National Academy of Design 1925-29, in Europe 1930, first

one-man show 1947, exhibition Museum of Modern Art, N Y Has worked in photography and made murals for large buildings in New Jersey One of most searing of commentators on American scene Lives at Roosevelt, N J

SHEELER, CHARLES
(American 1883-   )   PLATES 195, 197
Painter, draughtsman, photographer Born Philadelphia 1900-03, student at School of Industrial Art, Philadelphia 1903-06, student of William Chase, Pennsylvania Academy of Fine Arts 1904-05, traveled in England, Holland, Spain with Chase 1909, trip to Italy, Paris, and London 1910-19, lived in Philadelphia 1912, took up photography as means of livelihood 1913, exhibited at Armory Show 1915-17, exhibited with other Americans at Montross Gallery, N Y 1918, exhibition of photographs at Modern Gallery, N Y, same year, series of photographs of African Negro masks. 1919, moved to N Y 1920, collaborated on motion picture, *Mannahatta* Same year, one-man exhibition paintings and photography at de Zayas Gallery, N Y 1929, exhibited photographs at International Film and Photography Exhibition, Stuttgart 1931, one-man exhibition, Downtown Gallery, N Y 1939, Museum of Modern Art, N Y, exhibition paintings, drawings and photographs Lives in Irvington-on-Hudson, N Y

SICKERT, WALTER RICHARD
(English 1860-1942)   PLATE 167
Painter and etcher Born Munich, son of a painter and illustrator 1868, settled in England Studied at Slade School, London, and under Whistler Knew Degas, whose influence he felt 1886-88, exhibited at Royal Society of British Artists 1900-05, lived at Dieppe Settled in London Frequently visited Venice 1928, President, Royal Society of British artists 1934, Royal Academy, 1935, resigned 1941, exhibition of his work at National Gallery, London Died Bathampton, Bath 1947, *A Free House*, a selection of his comments on the arts, was published

SIQUEIROS, DAVID ALFARO (*see-kay'rawss*)
(Mexican 1898-   )   PLATE 178
Painter and graphic artist Born Chihuahua Studied Academy of Fine Arts (San Carlos) and original Open Air School of Painting, Santa Anita. 1913, joined Carranza s revolutionary army Visited Belgium, France, Italy and Spain 1919-22, fresco and encaustic murals in Preparatoria 1922, became leader of Syndicate of Painters Editor of *El Machete* 1924 on, devoted himself to Worker's Movement, traveling to congresses in Europe, South and North America. 1932, frescoes Los Angeles and Buenos Aires 1934, when in Mexico, attacked mural painting for its archaism and disputed in public with Rivera Lieut Col in Spanish Republican army until end Civil War, 1939 Painted duco mural in Sindicato de Electricistas, Mexico

SLOAN, JOHN
(American 1871-1951)   PLATE 185
Painter, draughtsman, graphic artist Born Lock Haven, Pa Reared Philadelphia At 16 supported his family Studied at Pennsylvania Academy of Fine Arts under Anshutz Staff artist on *Philadelphia Press* 1905, went to N Y Earned living as magazine illustrator Member of *The Eight* 1913, one of organizers of Armory Show 1914-31, taught at Art Students League President of same 1931-32. President of Society of Independent Artists since 1918 Lived in N Y and Santa Fe Died N Y Distinguished as etcher and painter of N.Y life

SPEICHER, EUGENE
(American 1883-   )   p. 238
Painter and draughtsman. Born Buffalo Attended Buffalo Fine Arts Academy 1906, received Albright Scholarship for study at Art Students League, N Y 1907, 1908 studied under Frank Vincent Dumond and William Chase. 1909, studied at evening class of Robert Henri, met Bellows and others Member of National Academy of Design, 1911 Extensive travel abroad in 1910 and 1926 Frequent prize winner, Speicher is represented in many American museums and has exhibited widely. Active in Woodstock, N Y, and New York City

STEINBERG, SAUL
(American 1914-   )   PLATE 200
Draughtsman, illustrator and mural painter Born Rumania Came to U S, 1942 Attended University of Milan, studying psychology, sociology, and architecture, which taught him precision of line Worked for Italian weeklies After enlistment in U S N R, went to China, India, Italy and North Africa In addition to well-known drawings for *The New Yorker*, spent brief period in movies. Expects before long to have exhibitions in London and South America. Recently tried hand at large wall decorations for business

STERNE, MAURICE
(American 1877-   )   PLATE 188
Painter, sculptor, draughtsman Born Latvia Came to America at 12 Studied at Cooper Union and National Academy of Design in New York, with Eakins Traveled in Europe Lived several years on island of Bali, Dutch East Indies, also Italy and Southwest, U S Lives in Mt. Kisco, N Y

SUTHERLAND, GRAHAM
(English 1903-   )   PLATES 172-73
Painter and draughtsman Born London Attended Epsom College Apprentice engineer, Midland Railway Works, Derby, 1918 1919-25, attended Goldsmith's School of Art, New Cross, where he began his first etchings. 1925, moved to London From 1927 until outbreak of World War II, taught etching at Chelsea School of Art 1935, began to teach composition and book illustration at Chelsea School Commissions for posters from Shell Co , Orient Line and London Transport Made designs for fabrics, papers and china Since 1937, lives Trottscliffe, near Maidstone Deeply admires Blake, Samuel Palmer and Picasso

TANGUY, YVES (*tong-ghee'*)
(American 1900-   )   PLATE 111
Painter and draughtsman Born Paris Began painting 1926. Became member of Surrealist group and exhibited with them and at Salon des Surindépendants Collaborated in various surrealist publications, and has signed all surrealist manifestoes since 1926 Left France 1939 for U S Little evolution in his art since early works Lives in Connecticut

TCHELITCHEW, PAVEL (*che'-lee-chef*)
(American 1898-   )   PLATES 202-03
Painter, draughtsman, stage designer Born Moscow. 1920, left Russia for Constantinople Lived in Balkans and Berlin until 1923 Received commissions to design scenery and costumes for opera, ballet and theatre. At this time, felt influence of machine-constructivism reflecting spread of abstract French and Dutch art into Germany 1923, moved to Paris Contact with Cubism Interest in amplified ovoid shapes Exhibited at Salon d'Automne and at galleries 1925, frequent studies of human head At this time was championed by Gertrude Stein in Paris and by Edith and Osbert Sitwell in England 1926, began to use dominant blue in his paintings and developed his multiple image technique Trip to Spain resulted in introduction of landscape into his work. 1928, designed sets for Diaghilev ballet, *Ode* 1931, exhibited at Balzac Gallery, N Y , and with Neo-Romantics (with whom sometimes grouped) at Wadsworth Atheneum, Hartford. 1934, series of tennis and bullfight pictures 1934, one-man show, Julien Levy Gallery 1936-38, *Phenomena*, one of his most publicized pictures 1940-42, *Cache Cache* (Hide and Seek), which is now in Museum of Modern Art, N Y. 1942, exhibition Museum of Modern Art, N Y. Has been identified with Surrealism and School of Paris, but considers himself independent of all these groups

TOULOUSE-LAUTREC-MONFA, HENRI MARIE RAYMOND DE (*too-looz-lo-trek'*)
(French 1864-1901) PLATES 25, 52-56, pp 38-39
Painter, draughtsman, graphic artist Born Albi, descendant of ancient aristocratic family 1878, at Céleyran, broke one leg and following year broke the other Because of these accidents the frail boy grew up a dwarf Began to draw as child and encouraged in school years by animalier, Princeteau 1882, entered studio of the academician, Léon Bonnat 1883, attended Atelier Cormon where he met van Gogh. 1884, set up studio at Montmartre. Knew many of Impressionists, also Gauguin, Seurat, Vuillard and Bonnard, but his idol always Degas. 1885, made first lithograph 1892, interest in lithography became serious and began to use as many as six or seven stones to create a color print At first influenced by Japanese woodcuts, but quickly developed own style 1889, exhibited Brussels with *Société des XX* 1894, visited Brussels where he knew and was somewhat influenced by *Art Nouveau* group 1899, physical breakdown Lived for three months in sanitarium near Paris Recovering, convalesced at seashore and traveled in Spain and Northern France, always working. Returned to Paris and his old life at cabarets, bars, nightclubs, and the circus and to ever more arduous artistic production. Died at his mother's castle of Malromé, Céleyran Created over 300 lithographs and many drawings and posters

VALLOTTON, FÉLIX-EDMOND (*val-lot-ton'*)
(Swiss 1865-1925)   PLATE 165
Painter and graphic artist Born Lausanne Early schooling at Lausanne. 1882, went to Paris and attended Academy Julian First Salon, 1885 To earn living, restored or copied old masters Contributed drawings to *Revue Blanche* of Thadée Natanson, also articles on art Knew Vuillard and Bonnard 1891-97, fascinated by art of black and white, and began making woodcuts almost exclusively although had previously experimented with drypoint, etching, and lithography Exhibited 1893, 1894, with Nabis, at Le Barc de Boutteville, and in 1906 was one of group including Bonnard, Vuillard, and Sérusier to receive

257

important exhibition at Bernheim-Jeune Wrote novels and dramas Large graphic oeuvre

VESPIGNANI, RENZO (*ves-peen-yah'-nee*)
(Italian 1924-   )   PLATE 161
Painter, draughtsman, graphic artist Born Rome Outstanding draughtsman and print maker One-man shows Rome, Milan, Stockholm, and N Y Lives in Rome

VILLON, JACQUES (GASTON DUCHAMP) (*vee-yon'*)
(French 1875-   )   PLATES 106-07, p 96
Painter and graphic artist Born Damville of Norman stock Whole family artists, brother and sister were painters and his brother, Raymond Duchamp-Villon, killed during World War I, was both sculptor and architect Brother also of Marcel Duchamp Early studies at Rouen 1895, went to study in Paris with Cormon and at Ecole des Beaux-Arts Made posters for cabarets and contributed to newspapers *Quartier Latin* and *Le Courrier français* with Steinlen. Willette, and Forain 1891, began to engrave, trained by his grandfather, Emile Nicolle and his friend the printer Delâtre who taught him color techniques Attached himself to Cubist group in 1911 and began to concentrate on painting rather than printmaking. Studio at Puteaux became one of Cubist centers and included Apollinaire, Cocteau, Léger, La Fresnaye, and others Inventor of the tag "La Section d'Or," 1913, and later a founder of the "Abstraction-Création" movement Mobilized 1914 1920-29 important period in graphic arts Reproduced paintings of Cézanne, Monet, Signac, Dufy, and Picasso Illustrated 35 plates for *Architectures* 1935, visited America Through Walter Pach, Villon's art introduced to U S After 1920 his art consisted of figure painting and still-life Later, his abstractions gave way to direct studies of nature, especially visible in landscapes made at Gascogne where he retreated in 1940 First prize at Carnegie International exhibition of paintings in Pittsburgh, 1950

VUILLARD, JEAN-EDOUARD (*vuee-yar'*)
(French 1867-1940)   pp 63-64
Painter and graphic artist Born Cuiseaux Attended Lycée Condorcet with lifelong friend, Roussel Spent two years at Ecole des Beaux-Arts Studied under Fleury and Bouguereau Attended also Academy Julian Met Maurice Denis, Bonnard, Vallotton, Sérusier Became attached to Nabis group but later retained aloof position in relation to their theories 1891, began to study lithography 1891-94, exhibited with Pont-Aven group Degas, Toulouse-Lautrec, Sérusier, Gauguin, and the

Japanese all influenced him Created many decorative panels for private houses, also lithographs of exquisite color harmonies 1903-04, exhibited at Vollards and Bernheim-Jeune One of founders of Salon d'Automne 1939, large retrospective exhibition at Musée des Arts Decoratifs Died La Baule Retrospective exhibition at Orangerie Museum, Paris, 1941-42 1946, retrospective exhibition at Palace of Fine Arts, Brussels

WEBER, MAX
(American 1881-   )   PLATE 189a, b
Painter, graphic artist, writer Born Byelostok, Russia 1891, came to America with parents Lived Brooklyn 1897-1900, studied Pratt Institute 1900-05, taught art at public schools, Lynchburg, Va 1905, Paris, studied at Academy Julian, Academy Colarossi and Academy de la Grande Chaumiere 1906-07, exhibited at Indépendants Salon, 1907, 1908, at Salon d'Automne Traveled in Spain, Low Countries, and Italy. 1908, student of Matisse, knew Picasso and became close friend of Henri Rousseau 1908, felt impact of Cézanne at the memorial exhibition, Paris Early work influenced by both Fauve and Cubist movements 1909, returned to N Y Studied primitive art and American Indian art in museums 1909, first one-man show at Stieglitz' "291" gallery 1920-21, taught at Art Students League, N Y. Has evolved personal style and is recognized as among foremost influential pioneers of modern art in America 1930, retrospective exhibition Museum of Modern Art, N Y 1949, Whitney Museum, N Y Lives in Great Neck, L I

WHISTLER, JAMES ABBOTT McNEILL
(American 1834-1903)   PLATE 182
Painter, graphic artist, writer Born Lowell, Mass Dismissed from West Point Was map engraver of U S Coastal and Geodetic Survey In 1855 went to Paris to study art Pupil of Gleyre, Paris. Influenced by Degas, Legros, Braquemond and Fantin-Latour Friend of many Impressionists, also of Toulouse-Lautrec Admired Japanese prints and Oriental art Long enjoyed reputation as greatest American etcher, producing some 400 plates Widely traveled in England and on Continent Died London

WYETH, ANDREW
(American 1917-   )   PLATE 207
Painter and draughtsman Born Chadd's Ford, Pa. Son and pupil of N C Wyeth, painter One-man shows Macbeth Gallery, N Y, 1937, 1939, 1941 etc. Lives in Chadd's Ford One of most competent and precise of contemporary American realists

MANET RAVEN LITHOGRAPH 1875

MANET CHARLES BAUDELAIRE ETCHING 1862

Bibliography

NOTE The two following lists do not attempt a comprehensive survey of the literature on the graphic arts of today A few general books on modern art, drawing and printmaking, mostly available in English, are listed first The selection of monographs that follows includes most of the artists whose work is reproduced and discussed in this book Detailed information about the various print techniques and processes appears in many of the books listed   P J S

Some Books on Modern Art, Drawing and Printmaking

Barr, Alfred H., Jr. · Cézanne, Gauguin, Seurat, van Gogh. N Y, Museum of Modern Art, 1929

Barr, Alfred H., Jr. · Cubism and abstract art N Y, Museum of Modern Art, 1936

Barr, Alfred H, Jr. · Fantastic art, Dada, Surrealism, 3rd ed. N Y, Museum of Modern Art, 1947

Barr, Alfred H., Jr. · Modern German painting and sculpture N Y, Museum of Modern Art, 1931

Barr, Alfred H., Jr. · Painting and sculpture in the Museum of Modern Art N Y, Museum of Modern Art, 1948

Barr, Alfred H, Jr. · What is modern painting? N Y, Museum of Modern Art, 1952

Baur, John I. H · Revolution and tradition in modern American art. Cambridge, Harvard Univ Press, 1951

Berger, Klaus · French master drawings of the nineteenth century. N Y, Harper, 1950

Bliss, Douglas P. · A history of wood-engraving N Y, Dutton, 1928

Bouchot-Saupique, Jacqueline · French drawings Loan exhibition, 1952-1953 N Y, Plantin Press, 1952

Cahill, Holger & Barr, Alfred H., Jr, eds. · Art in America. a complete survey N Y, Halcyon House, 1939

Cassou, Jean · Le dessin français au XXᵉ siècle Lausanne, Mermod, 1951

Cheney, Sheldon · The story of modern art N. Y, Viking, 1941

Clough, Rosa Trillo · Looking back at futurism New York, Cocce Press, 1942 Columbia Univ thesis

Craven, Thomas, ed · A treasury of American prints a selection of one hundred etchings and lithographs by the foremost living American artists N Y, Simon and Schuster, 1939

Friedlander, Walter · David to Delacroix. Cambridge, Harvard Univ Press, 1952

Goldwater, Robert & d'Harnoncourt, René · Modern art in your life N Y, Museum of Modern Art, 1949

Goldwater, Robert & Treves, Marco, eds. · Artists on art, from the XIV to the XX century, 2nd ed N Y, Pantheon, 1947

Grosser, Maurice · The painter's eye N Y, Rinehart, 1951

Hauser, Arnold · The social history of art London, Routledge, N Y, Knopf, 1951

Hayter, Stanley W · New ways of gravure N Y, Pantheon, 1949

Helm, MacKinley · Modern Mexican painters N Y, Harper, 1941

Hind, Arthur M. · A guide to the processes and schools of engraving London, British Museum, 1933

Hind, Arthur M · History of engraving and etching from the 15th century to the year 1914, 3rd ed London, Constable, 1927

Holman, Louis A. · The graphic processes intaglio, relief and planographic Boston, Goodspeed, 1929

Huyghe, René, ed. · Histoire de l'art contemporain la peinture Paris, Alcan, 1935

Ivins, William M · How prints look photographs with a commentary N Y, Metropolitan Museum, 1943

Ivins, William M. · Notes on prints N Y, Metropolitan Museum, 1930

Ivins, William M. · Prints and books informal papers Cambridge, Harvard Univ Press, 1926

Ivins, William M. · Prints and visual communication Cambridge, Harvard Univ Press, 1953

Johnson, Una E. · Ambroise Vollard N Y, Wittenborn, 1944

Johnson, Una E. · New expressions in fine print-making Brooklyn Museum Bulletin, vol 14, no 1, 1952

Kepes, Gyorgy · Language of vision Chicago, Theobald, 1944

Kuh, Katharine · Art has many faces the nature of art presented visually N Y, Harper, 1951

Lieberman, William S & Barr, Alfred H., Jr · The Abby Aldrich Rockefeller print room master prints from the museum collection Museum of Modern Art Bulletin, vol 16, no 4, 1949

Lucas, E. L. · The Harvard list of books on art Cambridge, Harvard Univ Press, 1951

Lumsden, Ernest S. · The art of etching Philadelphia, Lippincott, 1925

Mertn, Peter · Modern German art Harmondsworth, Penguin Books, 1938

Miller, Dorothy C. & Soby, James Thrall · Romantic painting in America N Y, Museum of Modern Art, 1943

Moholy-Nagy, László · Vision in motion Chicago, Theobald, 1947

259

Mongan, Agnes · Master drawings, selected from the museums and private collections of America Buffalo, Albright Art Gallery, 1934

Mongan, Agnes · One hundred master drawings Cambridge, Harvard Univ Press, 1949

Mongan, Agnes & Sachs, Paul J · Drawings in the Fogg Museum of Art 2nd ed Cambridge, Harvard Univ Press, 1946

Mongan, Elizabeth · Rosenwald collection Washington, National Gallery of Art, 1950

Mongan, Elizabeth · Selections from the Rosenwald Collection Washington, National Gallery of Art, 1943

Myers, Bernard S. · Modern art in the making N Y, McGraw-Hill, 1950

Pope, Arthur · The language of drawing and painting Cambridge, Harvard Univ Press, 1949

Popham, Arthur E · A handbook to the drawings and watercolours in the Department of Prints and Drawings London, British Museum, 1949

The print collector's quarterly. N Y, Keppel, 1911-50

Rathbun, Mary C. & Hayes, Bartlett H., Jr. · Layman's guide to modern art painting for a scientific age N Y, Oxford, 1949

Raynal, Maurice & others · History of modern painting 3 v Geneva, Skira, 1949-50

Read, Herbert · Art now, an introduction to the theory of modern painting and sculpture, rev ed London, Faber, 1948

Read, Herbert · The philosophy of modern art collected essays London, Faber & Faber, 1952

Reese, Albert · American prize prints of the 20th century N Y, American Artists Group, 1949.

Rewald, John · The history of impressionism N Y, Museum of Modern Art, 1946

Reynolds, Graham · Nineteenth century drawings, 1850-1900 London, Pleiades Books, 1949

Reynolds, Graham · Twentieth century drawings London, Pleiades Books, 1946

Robb, David M. · The Harper history of painting the occidental tradition N Y, Harper, 1951

Roger-Marx, Claude · French original engravings from Manet to the present time N Y, Hyperion, 1939

Ruhemann, H & Kemp, E M. · The artist at work Harmondsworth, Penguin Books, 1951

Sachs, Paul J · The pocket book of great drawings N Y, Pocket Books, 1951 (Pocket Book 765)

Schmeckebier, Laurence E · Modern Mexican art Minneapolis, Univ of Minnesota Press, 1939

Schniewind, Carl O. · Drawings, old and new Chicago, Art Institute, 1946

Sloane, Joseph C. · French painting between the past and the present 1848 to 1870 Princeton, N J, Princeton Univ. Press, 1951

Soby, James Thrall · Contemporary painters N Y, Museum of Modern Art, 1948

Soby, James Thrall & Barr, Alfred H., Jr. · Twentieth-century Italian art N Y, Museum of Modern Art, 1949

Sweeney, James Johnson · Plastic redirections in 20th century painting Chicago, Univ of Chicago, 1934

Upjohn, Everard M., Wingert, Paul S. & Gaston Mahler, Jane · History of world art N Y, Oxford Univ Press, 1949.

Venturi, Lionello · Impressionists and symbolists N Y, Scribner, 1950

Wechsler, Herman J · Lives of famous French painters, from Ingres to Picasso N Y, Pocket Books, 1952

Weitenkampf, Frank · How to appreciate prints, 4th ed N Y, Scribner, 1942

Wheeler, Monroe · Modern painters and sculptors as illustrators, rev ed N Y, Museum of Modern Art, 1947

Wheeler, Monroe, ed · Modern drawings N Y, Museum of Modern Art, 1944

Wight, Frederick · Milestones of American painting in our century N Y, Chanticleer, 1949

Wilenski, Reginald H · Modern French painters N Y, Harcourt, Brace, 1949

Zigrosser, Carl · The book of fine prints N Y, Crown, 1948

DAVID OATH OF THE HORATII OIL 1785 LOUVRE PARIS

Selected Monographs

Barlach · Jerrold Holmes 'Ernst Barlach' Parnassus, v 2, no 4, Apr 1930

Beckmann · Perry T Rathbone Max Beckmann St Louis, City Art Museum, 1948

Bellows · George W Bellows his lithographs N Y, Knopf, 1927

Bonnard · John Rewald Pierre Bonnard N Y, Museum of Modern Art, 1948

Braque Henry R Hope Georges Braque N Y, Museum of Modern Art, 1949

Calder · James Johnson Sweeney Alexander Calder, rev ed N Y, Museum of Modern Art, 1951

Cassatt · Adelyn D Breeskin The graphic work of Mary Cassatt N Y, Bittner, 1948

Cézanne · Gerstle Mack Paul Cézanne N Y, Knopf, 1935

Cezanne · Fritz Novotny Cézanne London, Oxford Univ Press (Phaidon ed), 1948

Cezanne · Meyer Schapiro Paul Cezanne N Y, Abrams, 1952

Chagall · James Johnson Sweeney Marc Chagall N Y, Museum of Modern Art, 1946

di Chirico · James Thrall Soby The early Chirico N Y, Dodd, Mead, 1941

Corot · Alfred H Barr, Jr Corot, Daumier N Y, Museum of Modern Art, 1930

Dali · James Thrall Soby Salvador Dali, rev ed N Y, Museum of Modern Art, 1946

Daumier · Alfred H Barr, Jr Corot, Daumier N Y, Museum of Modern Art, 1930

Daumier · Bernard Lemann Honoré Daumier 240 lithographs N Y, Reynal and Hitchcock, 1946.

David · David L Dowd Pageant-master of the republic Jacques Louis David and the French revolution Lincoln, Neb, Univ of Nebraska, 1948

Davis • James Johnson Sweeney *Stuart Davis* N Y, Museum of Modern Art, 1945

Degas • Paul A Lemoisne *Degas et son oeuvre* Paris, Brame et Hauke, 1947

Degas • Daniel C Rich *Degas* N Y, Abrams, 1951

Delacroix • Kurt Badt *Eugene Delacroix drawings* Oxford, Cassirer, 1946

Demuth Andrew C Ritchie *Charles Demuth* N Y, Museum of Modern Art, 1950

Eakins • Lloyd Goodrich *Thomas Eakins* N Y, Whitney Museum, 1933

Ensor • Libby Tannenbaum *James Ensor* N Y, Museum of Modern Art, 1951

Feininger • Dorothy C Miller, ed *Lyonel Feininger, Marsden Hartley* N Y, Museum of Modern Art, 1944

Gauguin • Paul Gauguin *Noa Noa* N Y, Brown, 1920

Gauguin • John Rewald *Gauguin* Paris, Hyperion, 1938

Géricault • Klaus Berger *Géricault drawings and watercolors* N Y, Bittner, 1946

van Gogh • Meyer Schapiro *Vincent van Gogh* N Y, Abrams, 1950

Goya • Aldous L Huxley *The complete etchings of Goya* N Y, Crown, 1943

Gris • Daniel Henry Kahnweiler *Juan Gris* N Y, Curt Valentin, 1947

Grosz • *Drawings* George Grosz, intro N Y, Bittner, 1944

Homer • Lloyd Goodrich *Winslow Homer* N Y, Whitney Museum, 1944

Hopper • Lloyd Goodrich *Edward Hopper* Harmondsworth, Penguin Books, 1949

Ingres • Lili Fröhlich-Bum *Ingres* London, Heinemann, 1926

Ingres • Walter Pach *Ingres* N Y, Harper, 1939

John John K M Rothenstein *Augustus John* London, Oxford Univ Press (Phaidon ed), 1944

Kandinsky • Wassily Kandinsky *Concerning the spiritual in art* N Y, Wittenborn, Schultz, 1947

Kirchner • Bernard Myers "Ernst Ludwig Kirchner and die Brucke" *Magazine of Art*, v.45, no 1, Jan 1952

Klee • Will Grohmann *The drawings of Paul Klee* N Y, Curt Valentin, 1944

Klee • Margaret Miller, ed *Paul Klee*, 2nd ed N Y, Museum of Modern Art, 1945

Klee • James Thrall Soby *The prints of Paul Klee*, 2nd ed N Y, Museum of Modern Art, 1947

Kokoschka • Edith Hoffmann *Kokoschka life and work* London, Faber, 1947

Kollwitz • Carl Zigrosser *Kaethe Kollwitz* N Y, Bittner, 1946

Leger • Katherine Kuh *Léger* Chicago, The Art Institute of Chicago, 1953

Maillol • John Rewald, ed *The woodcuts of Aristide Maillol* N Y, Pantheon, 1943

Maillol • Andrew C Ritchie *Aristide Maillol* Buffalo, Albright Art Gallery, 1945

Manet • Theodore Duret *Manet and the French impressionists* Philadelphia, Lippincott, 1910

Marin • MacKinley Helm *John Marin* Boston, Pellegrini and Cudahy, 1948

Matisse • Alfred H Barr, Jr *Matisse his art and his public* N Y., Museum of Modern Art, 1951

Matisse • William S Lieberman "Illustrations by Henri Matisse" *Magazine of Art*, vol 44, no 8, Dec 1951

Miró • Clement Greenberg *Joan Miró* N Y, Quandrangle Press, 1948.

Modigliani • James Thrall Soby *Modigliani* N Y, Museum of Modern Art, 1951

Mondrian • James Johnson Sweeney *Piet Mondrian* N Y, Museum of Modern Art, 1948

Moore • Herbert Read *Henry Moore sculpture and drawings* N Y, Curt Valentin, 1944

Moore • James Johnson Sweeney *Henry Moore* N Y, Museum of Modern Art, 1947

Munch • Frederick B Deknatel *Edvard Munch* N Y, Chanticleer, 1950

Picasso • Alfred H Barr, Jr *Picasso fifty years of his art* N Y, Museum of Modern Art, 1946

Picasso • William S Lieberman *Picasso his graphic art* N Y, *Museum of Modern Art Bulletin*, vol 19, no 2, 1952

Posada • Fernando Gamboa *Posada printmaker to the Mexican people* Chicago, The Art Institute of Chicago, 1944

Redon • William S Lieberman *Redon drawings and lithographs* N Y, *Museum of Modern Art Bulletin*, vol 19, no 2, 1952

Renoir • Walter Pach *Pierre Auguste Renoir* N Y, Abrams, 1950

Renoir • John Rewald *Renoir drawings* N Y, Bittner, 1946

Rivera • Bertram D Wolfe *Diego Rivera his life and times* N Y, Knopf, 1939

Rodin • Auguste Rodin *Art* N Y, Dodd, Mead, 1928

Rouault • William S Lieberman "Notes on Rouault as a printmaker" *Magazine of Art*, vol 47, no 4, April 1953

Rouault • James Thrall Soby *Georges Rouault paintings and prints*, 2nd ed N Y, Museum of Modern Art, 1947

Rousseau • Daniel C Rich *Henri Rousseau*, 2nd ed N Y, Museum of Modern Art, 1946

Segonzac • C Roger-Marx "Etched work of Dunoyer de Segonzac" *Print-Collector's Quarterly*, v 16, p 33-55, Jan 1929

Seurat John Rewald *Georges Seurat*, 2nd ed N Y, Wittenborn, Schultz, 1946

Seurat • Daniel C Rich *Seurat and the evolution of "La Grande Jatte* Chicago, Univ of Chicago Press, 1935

Shahn • Selden Rodman *Portrait of the artist as an American, Ben Shahn a biography with pictures* N Y, Harper, 1951

Shahn • James Thrall Soby *Ben Shahn* West Drayton, Penguin Books, 1947

Sheeler • Constance M Rourke *Charles Sheeler, artist in the American tradition* N Y, Harcourt, Brace, 1938

Sheeler • William Carlos Williams *Charles Sheeler* N Y, Museum of Modern Art, 1939

Sickert • Walter Sickert *A free house! Or, The artist as craftsman* London, Macmillan, 1947

Sloan • Guy P Du Bois *John Sloan* N Y, Whitney Museum, 1931

Steinberg • Saul Steinberg *The art of living* N Y, Harper, 1949

Sutherland • Robert Melville *Graham Sutherland* London, Ambassador Edit , 1950

Tchelitchew • Lincoln Kirstein, ed *Pavel Tchelitchew drawings* N Y, Bittner, 1947

Toulouse-Lautrec • Gerstle Mack *Toulouse-Lautrec* N Y, Knopf, 1938

Villon • William S Lieberman *Jacques Villon his graphic art* N Y, Museum of Modern Art, 1953

Vuillard • Andrew C Ritchie *Edouard Vuillard* N Y., Museum of Modern Art, 1954

Weber • Lloyd Goodrich *Max Weber* N Y, Whitney Museum, 1949

Whistler • Edward G Kennedy *The etched work of Whistler* N Y, Grolier Club, 1910